Revolution in Pakistan

A STUDY OF THE MARTIAL LAW ADMINISTRATION

D1514751

Revolution in Pakistan

A STUDY OF THE
MARTIAL LAW ADMINISTRATION

HERBERT FELDMAN

34777

London
OXFORD UNIVERSITY PRESS
LAHORE   KARACHI   DACCA
1967

ST. THOMAS AQUINAS COLLEGE LIBRARY

Oxford University Press, Ely House, London W.1

GLASGOW NEW YORK TORONTO MELBOURNE WELLINGTON
CAPE TOWN SALISBURY IBADAN NAIROBI LUSAKA ADDIS ABABA
BOMBAY CALCUTTA MADRAS KARACHI LAHORE DACCA
KUALA LUMPUR HONG KONG

© Oxford University Press, 1967

PRINTED AND BOUND IN ENGLAND BY
HAZELL WATSON AND VINEY LTD
AYLESBURY, BUCKS

FOREWORD

The hazards of writing contemporary history are too well known to call for emphasis here. The chronicler of his own times may be rebutted by events; he may be left high and dry by some quite unforeseeable change; he may be flatly contradicted by an election or a political *coup*, not to mention the passing annoyance of the blank, official *démenti*. His is the most vulnerable of situations for, upon the happening of any of these frustrations, he is denied even the comforting, unassailable refuge of the *long view*. His position is aggravated, furthermore, by many possibilities of giving offence and when, on top of all this, he writes with a cautious monitor whispering, at every sentence, to beware of inflicting injury on religious or national sensibilities, it is evident that the risks he runs are considerable.

That is not all. Whatever his rank in scholarship, and whether professional or amateur, his access to information is likely to be restricted since the current archives of governments are open to few and, usually, with a superimposed condition of secrecy even then. If the author has played some part in the events of which he writes, then the terms of his employment are likely to fetter the exercise of his knowledge, not to mention the possibility of prosecution if he commits some breach of a statute that enjoins total discretion.

That portion of the history of Pakistan with which this book deals comprises the forty-four months from October 1958 until June 1962, and is generally known as the 'Martial Law period', since the first presidential proclamation specifically states that 'until alternative arrangements are made, Pakistan will come under Martial Law'. General (as he then was) Ayub Khan's own proclamation simply stated that he judged it 'essential for national requirements to assume jurisdiction within the international boundaries of Pakistan'. All this seems clear enough although, for the purposes of these changes, no definition of the Martial Law under which Pakistan had come was ever attempted. No doubt, had it been necessary, the familiar authorities on constitutional law could have been invoked, but the question seems never to have arisen. In any case, it does not seem that from the chapters which follow, the reader will find difficulty in forming for himself a reasonably accurate idea of that kind of absolutism which Martial Law actually amounted to in Pakistan.

At the same time, it is important to mention that this period in Pakistan's history was closely associated with a revolutionary overthrow of the Constitution of 1956 and, notwithstanding that this overthrow was the work of men holding office under that Constitution, the marked tendency has always been to emphasize the revolutionary aspect of the régime and to minimize its military associations. All these matters are discussed later, in further detail, but it is necessary that the reader, when embarking upon a study of the subject, should have these considerations in mind.

Similarly, it is important for him to remember that the book is concerned with the Martial Law period and, if references are made to events which preceded that period, or which came after it, this has been done either to complete a story usefully, or to illustrate a situation or to assist the reader in forming a fair judgement on the measure of success or failure which policy achieved during the period. The connexion between the Martial Law régime and the Government which immediately followed was, manifestly, a close one and President Ayub Khan's post-Martial Law administration could scarcely avoid this. Consequently, some knowledge of post-Martial Law events serves usefully in understanding the Martial Law period itself.

I was living in Karachi when Martial Law was promulgated and, except for two visits to the United Kingdom, was resident in Pakistan throughout the whole period, travelling during that time both in East and West Pakistan, but more extensively in the latter. I had the opportunity of some acquaintance, as a private citizen, with the methods and operation of the Martial Law administration and, to some extent, that experience provides a background for certain suggestions or expressions of opinion on which I rely with confidence. Nevertheless, all assertions of fact have, to the fullest extent open to me, been related to published and authoritative sources.

For reasons already stated, no one should be surprised if these sources substantially comprise newspapers and official publications. They are, after all, the repository of *some* truth, even if not all of it, but of course, no author is expected to be so indolent as to limit his mining to such easily accessible lodes. The measure of my zeal in this regard will be apparent from the text, but on two important aspects some clarification is desirable.

For such rulings on Muslim personal law as have been referred to, use has been made (except where otherwise indicated) of Faiz B. Tyabji's *Muhammadan Law* (K. M. Tripathi, Bombay, third edition, 1940). On the subject of the traditions, Fazlul Karim's translation and commentary on the *Mishkat-ul-Masabih* (published by him, in Calcutta, in 1938 and 1939) have been consulted. I am aware that the branches of Islamic law with which Mr. Tyabji's book deals, as well as the manner of its treatment, form what is sometimes referred to as *Anglo-Muhammadan* law, a distinction often insisted upon by those who profess to study, or teach, or administer, a more pristine form of Islamic jurisprudence. There may be something material in this distinction, although whether the issues which find place in this volume are substantially affected, seems doubtful. Similarly, as to the use of the *Mishkat*, I am fully conscious that there exists an enormous literature on the subject of the traditions. This fact should not surprise when it is recalled that Imam Ahmed bin Hambal is credited with having narrated a million of them, while the great authority on the subject, Imam Bukhari, studied no less than six hundred thousand of which he selected 7,275 as authentic. The *Mishkat* has been selected, therefore, as giving a fair and valid view of the matters with which it deals, in the light of the traditions of Islam and its Prophet.

Inevitably, a considerable use (and, I believe, fair use) has been made of President Ayub Khan's speeches and interviews. These references have been taken (except where otherwise indicated) from the volumes published by the Government of Pakistan. Frequent reference was made inevitable, partly by reason of the strong association forged between President Ayub Khan and the *coup* of October 1958, and partly by reason of the prominence unfailingly given to his leadership. Certainly, it has not been my intention to saddle him with an undue share of responsibility for policies pursued and measures adopted, nor to indulge in the faintly malicious pastime of hoisting a speaker with his own petard.

It was, and is, very clear that among the group of generals responsible for the promulgation of Martial Law, President Ayub Khan stood out as a public speaker and as a platform personality. In these respects, only Lieutenant-General Azam Khan displayed any comparable ability. Lieutenant-General K. M. Sheikh showed no marked talent for oratory while Lieutenant-General W. A. Burki's pronouncements made no great impact. As for the civilian members of the Cabinet, it was in the nature of things that they should be unable to command a similar degree of public notice, whatever may have been the individual capacity for persuasive address. In short, President Ayub Khan was not only the principal spokesman for the Martial Law administration, he was also its ablest.

It is scarcely necessary to add that this is in no sense a law-book, notwithstanding reference to statutes and ordinances inserted partly as authority for what is stated and partly to guide the reader who wishes to examine further any particular point of interest. There has been some effort towards comprehensiveness which, I hope, will not be found tediously encyclopaedic. Voltaire may have been right when he said that if you want to bore the reader, tell him everything, but in a work of this nature, a fair measure of background material seems indispensable.

The book was completed before the elections of 1965. From the result of those elections some may deduce, among other things, a refutation of part, perhaps all, of the contents of this book. Be that as it may, there is nothing that I wish to change. For the sake of clarity, I should perhaps add that, in the interests of fairness, one or two footnotes have been expanded with reference to post-election happenings. The dates given will show where this has been done.

These remarks apart, the book must speak for itself and no amount of anticipatory apology or explanation can save or excuse its shortcomings. However, it needs to be said that if any source of offence can be traced in its pages—if, indeed, any injury has been done to those sensibilities spoken of earlier, it has been done unintentionally and without the least wish to wound.

A word of grateful thanks is due to officers of the Department of Information and of the Department of Films and Publications (both of the Government of Pakistan) for their willing help, rendered on numerous occasions. Thanks are likewise due to the staffs of *Dawn* and the *Morning News* (both published in Karachi) for the readiness to produce old files whenever asked for. All these courtesies were not only heart-warming, but of the utmost value.

Karachi, 1965   H. F.

354.54
F

CONTENTS

ABBREVIATIONS

The following abbreviations have been used in the notes:

CAD — Constituent Assembly Debates (pre-Martial Law Period).

D — *Dawn* newspaper, published in Karachi.

ES — *Economic Survey*, 1963, published by the Government of Pakistan.

MLO — Martial Law Order(s).

MLR — Martial Law Regulation(s).

MN — *Morning News*, Karachi edition.

O — *Outlook* weekly, Karachi (ceased publication).

TK — *The Times of Karachi* (ceased publication).

Like other Highlandmen, the Pathans of Pakistan will be found before long to be largely in control of the fortunes of their country.
Sir Olaf Caroe, *The Pathans*, London, 1957.

* * *

A new Constitution does not produce its full effect as long as all its subjects were reared under an old Constitution, as long as its subjects were trained by that old Constitution. It is not really tested till it comes to be worked by statesmen and among a people, neither of whom are guided by a different experience.
Walter Bagehot, quoted in D. E. Butler, *The Electoral System in Britain since 1918*, second edition, Oxford, 1963.

* * *

Sir Charles Napier was a simple-minded, pure-hearted and religious gentleman. All the faults of his government sprang from his placing undue confidence in those most near him, and thereby allowing himself to be guided in all matters pertaining to the civil government of the country.
Memoirs of Seth Naomal Hothchand, translated by his son and edited by Sir H. Evan M. James, Exeter, 1915: privately circulated.

* * *

Those fastidious fools who are afraid to dirty their hands, should keep out of politics.
Attributed to V. I. Lenin.

I

The Declaration of Martial Law

WRITING early in 1957, the late Professor Keith Callard, in his political study of Pakistan[1], concluded that 'if representative government collapses, it will be because its legs are not strong enough to sustain its own body . . . Pakistan, by its Constitution, is publicly committed to the operation of democratic institutions. It is too early to say whether those institutions are likely to mature.'[2]

Some eighteen months later, at 10.30 p.m. on 7 October 1958, Major-General Iskander Mirza, first President of the Islamic Republic of Pakistan, holding office under the Constitution to which Callard referred, issued a proclamation. Next morning, in banner headlines, the newspaper-reading public was informed that Martial Law had been declared, that the Central and Provincial Governments had been dismissed and the Central and Provincial Assemblies dissolved. Political parties were abolished and General (as he then was) Ayub Khan was appointed Supreme Commander of the Armed Forces of Pakistan and Chief Martial Law Administrator.[3]

In his 1,400-word statement, President Mirza explained that for two years he had been watching a ruthless struggle for power, corruption and shameful exploitation of the simple honest masses. This situation, according to him, had led to a dictatorship of the lowest order. He referred particularly to the continuing food crisis; to organized smuggling and black-marketing in the necessities of life; to the disgraceful episodes in the Provincial Assembly of East Pakistan. He considered the existing political parties were selfish, unscrupulous, and could not be relied upon to participate in fairly conducted elections. They did not, moreover, enjoy the confidence

---

[1] *Pakistan*, George Allen & Unwin Ltd., London, 1957, p. 329.
[2] The possibility of a breakdown of democracy in Pakistan had also been envisaged by Professor William Cantwell Smith. See his *Modern Islam in History*, Princeton University Press, 1957, chapter 5.
[3] The full text of the Proclamation is printed as Appendix I.

of the people. The existing constitution was, in his opinion, full of dangerous compromises, was unworkable, and threatened to bring about Pakistan's internal disintegration. He complained that he, personally, had been quite unjustly vilified as the author of Pakistan's misfortunes and as having encouraged 'palace' intrigues.

For all these reasons, and to avert the bloody revolution which those same politicans had threatened, the country must first be taken to sanity by a peaceful revolution and then a constitution would be devised more suited to the genius of the Muslim people. To save Pakistan from complete disruption, he had decided to place the country under Martial Law and to adopt those other measures he had stated.

Simultaneously with the issue of President Mirza's proclamation, General Ayub Khan issued a proclamation of his own which began: 'Whereas I adjudge it essential for national requirements to exercise jurisdiction within the international boundaries of Pakistan . . .' and proceeds to state that Martial Law Regulations and Orders would be published as soon as was conveniently possible and that Special Courts might be appointed. It is of some significance that General Ayub's statement makes no mention whatsoever of the delegation of power to him, by the President, nor is it anywhere said that he was issuing this declaration by virtue of any presidential appointment. However, in his message to the nation, broadcast on the evening of 8 October, General Ayub Khan made a reference to the President's proclamation abrogating the Constitution and appointing him Chief Martial Law Administrator.

Such, then, was the front-page news that greeted the citizens of Pakistan on the morning of Wednesday 8 October 1958, but, apart from the headlines and the verbatim statements of the President and the Chief Martial Law Administrator, there was little else to clarify this totally unexpected *coup*. One reason was, of course, that the Chief Martial Law Administrator had issued a directive that, until further orders, all newspapers should abstain from making any comment on the imposition of Martial Law and orders issued by the President.

The reader who was not, however, so stunned by this remarkable turn of events as to omit to turn the pages of his sheet, would discover, in the last columns, the detail of a Press Note, also dated 7 October, which, oddly enough, announced that the President 'has been pleased to make the following distribution of portfolios among Cabinet Ministers and Ministers of State'.[4] It proceeds to set out, in detail, the re-distribution of Ministries rendered necessary by the resignation of six representatives of the late H. S. Suhrawardy's party, the Awami League, which claimed that if they entered the Cabinet of Malik Firoz Khan Noon, the holding of general elections, scheduled for 15 February 1959, might be thwarted.

This announcement by the President's Secretariat is, of course, convincing evidence of the close concealment of the President's real intentions and of the fact that neither the Prime Minister, Malik Firoz Khan Noon, nor his Cabinet colleagues, nor, indeed, anyone active in current political affairs, had the least notion of what was in the wind. It is obvious, from the drastically effective manner in which the changes were made, that the *coup* had been planned with care and deliberation, as well as the utmost secrecy. There seems to be some evidence for the suggestion that a few people, outside the closed military circle, had been taken vaguely into confidence[5] in the sense that they had been approached, some time previously, on the question of accepting Cabinet office should there be ministerial changes, but they had been warned to keep counsel and they did.

And so the citizen proceeding to his work on the morning of 8 October, doubtless startled and in some measure, perhaps, disturbed by the news, could only remark the quietly unobtrusive appearance, on the streets, of armed and helmeted infantry and the occupation of certain buildings, to be established as military headquarters from which the military administration was to be achieved. It was perfectly obvious that the military take-over had been achieved without fuss[6] but, at the same time, it was very soon made evident that the declaration of Martial Law and the abrogation of the Constitution had not been idly undertaken. That, at least, was the impression firmly given. Still, the most that could be observed that day was the country's unruffled tranquillity and, otherwise, the citizen's ignorance of what awaited him under the new dispensation.

[4] *D*, 8 October 1958.
[5] See, for example, *The Times of India*, Bombay, 31 December 1958.
[6] See, for example, the *Daily Telegraph*, London, 13 October 1958 and onward.

General Ayub's broadcast, that evening, did not add much to his slender knowledge. This address was couched in terms with which he was already quite familiar. It was, in the main, a reiterated attack on venal and irresponsible politicians, smugglers, and black-marketeers. There was an unequivocal promise of a return to democracy 'but of a type that people can understand and work'. It was proposed to use civilian agencies to the maximum, but Martial Law Regulations would be introduced to tighten the law on malingering and inefficiency among officials, bribery, corruption, hoarding, smuggling and other types of anti-social activity. General Ayub made it clear that the Army had entered the political arena with reluctance and he said that he had previously refused several offers made to him by the late Mr. Ghulam Mohamed, formerly Governor-General of Pakistan, 'to take over the country'. Finally, he gave it as his opinion that only by hard work and maximum effort on the part of everyone could the country be restored to its rightful place among the nations of the world.

On the following day, 9 October, the nature of things to come was made very much more apparent with the publication of the first batch of Martial Law Regulations.[7] There were twenty-nine of them of which the first three dealt with the division of the country into three Martial Law Zones,[8] the constitution of Special and Summary Military Courts, scales and types of punishment these Courts could impose, and a partial definition of the interesting word *recalcitrant*. Regulation No. 4 imposed a military pre-censorship on any matter touching Martial Law which it was intended to publish, in Pakistan, by radio, printing-press, or telegraph. The remaining Regulations dealt with offences such as hoarding, smuggling, molestation of women, abduction, child-lifting, disobedience to Martial Law, false evidence, injury to public property, and so on. In nine instances, the maximum punishment was death. In two other instances (Regulations 6 and 7) the delinquent was to suffer death *and no less punishment*.[9]

The two offences singled out for the sole punishment of death were those of assisting '*the*[10] recalcitrants' or joining them, but the word recalcitrant was not fully defined. Regulation No. 3 stated

---

[7] This first group of Martial Law Regulations is contained in Appendix III.

[8] Karachi, Federal Area; West Pakistan excluding Karachi Federal Area; and East Pakistan.

[9] Author's italics.   [10] Author's italics.

that this word included any external enemy of Pakistan, mutineers, rebels or rioters, so that the unfortunate impression was left that anybody, at any time, might be labelled a recalcitrant with lamentable consequences indeed for those who might recently have been assisting or collaborating with him. The fact that the word was used in Regulations 6 and 7 with the definite, rather than the indefinite, article, raised a supposition that there must be some recalcitrants around somewhere, but nobody could quite make out who these were. It is now a matter of history that no specific accusation of any person, to this effect, was ever made and no one was ever charged with being such. No trial, conviction, or punishment under Regulations 6 and 7 ever took place and there can be no doubt that these two Regulations were minatory in purpose and completely successful. The fact is that after Martial Law was promulgated not a single voice, defending lost liberty, was heard. No one raised a hand; not a barricade was mounted. No one lost his life; not a drop of blood was shed;[11] and the Constitution, to which Callard had made reference, quietly expired, quite possibly unlamented, but certainly without a published word of obsequy from even its most devoted admirers.

On 10 October General Ayub held his first Press conference and replied, in a genial, re-assuring manner, to widely ranging questions on legal and constitutional points, intended reforms, the inevitable conundrums to do with India, Kashmir, Indus waters, Afghanistan and even a question about his namesake, Mr. Mohamed Ayub Khuhro, a former Defence Minister who had, that day, been arrested on a charge of black-marketing.

The publication of Martial Law Regulations, with their references to hoarding and black-marketing, were already having their effect and, where it was discovered that there was a reluctance to enter into the spirit of the times, police and others were on duty to remind merchants and shopkeepers of the necessity for compliance. Within ninety-six hours of the initiation of these great changes, the citizens of Pakistan were beginning to experience some very tangible consequences. Already, it was estimated that the prices of consumer goods had fallen by twenty-five per cent.[12]

[11] In 1963, the Leader of the Opposition in the National Assembly, Sardar Bahadur Khan, declared that physical violence had been resorted to during the Martial Law period. The instances mentioned by him were not impressive and do not seem to have been substantiated. *MN*, 29 June 1963.

[12] *D*, 11 October 1958.

and there were substantial reductions in the retail cost of textiles, medicines, watches, cooking spices, *ghee*,[13] and eggs, not only in Karachi, but throughout the country. Trade associations had started to come forward offering revised, fixed prices for the goods sold by their members and lists showing the new prices were advertised in the daily newspapers for public guidance.[14] In the ensuing days, the public was to witness an avalanche of falling prices touching almost every commodity in daily use, and many luxuries besides.

By 14 October the prices of foodstuffs such as milk, vegetables, sweetmeats, as well as *biri* leaves (for making a locally used type of cheap cigarette) and even laundry and hair-cutting charges, had been fixed in Karachi, Lahore, and other important centres. It was reckoned that the retail prices of imported manufactured goods had already fallen by forty to sixty per cent and the streets of the major cities were thronged, from morning to evening, with people who, for the first time in years, were able to buy cloth, crockery, glassware and, indeed, practically everything on the shelves at prices they could afford. Goods appeared from stockrooms as if by magic and vanished just as quickly in the possession of an intoxicated shopping public.

It was reported that, in Lahore, on a single morning, *ghee* to the value of Rs.90,000[15] was purchased by the public immediately following the announcement of the new prices, and such were the dimensions of the shopping spree, as it was called, that very soon an appeal had to be made urging people not to overbuy. Yet it was difficult to restrain the enthusiasm and even more difficult to attach blame. For years, the public had been ruthlessly mulcted by artifically contrived shortages, by a totally corrupt civil administration of rationed goods and by every business manipulation that avarice could suggest. There was scarcely anything that could be purchased except at prices so grossly inflated as to amount to complete denial apart from the really prosperous. That the buying craze seized everyone with even a little money in his pocket was not surprising, but the economic consequences were disturbing

---

[13] Clarified butter used as a cooking medium. It is comparatively expensive and its adulteration is common. People also use hydrogenated cottonseed oil, usually called *vanaspati*.

[14] See, for example, *D*, 18 October 1958, where 105 grocery items are listed showing voluntarily-fixed controlled prices.

[15] £6,750 or US$18,900.

and, by 17 October, it became necessary to institute a system of rationing and other discouragements.

The difficulty was, and the President himself underlined the point, that it was not necessarily the retail shopkeeper who had been getting the benefit of high prices. They, themselves, had usually to pay exorbitantly for their stocks and the inflated profits really went to those (often in high places, or the friends of those in high places) to whom import licences or manufacturing facilities had been granted. The summary reduction of prices and the total absorption of stocks caused loss and hardship, particularly among smaller shopkeepers who, to stay in business, had acquired those stocks at black-market rates. But what was to be done and how to discriminate? At least, it could be argued that if a shopkeeper was being compelled to sell cheaper, he was also buying his own daily needs in similar circumstances and perhaps the best that can be said is that, on the whole, rough justice was probably done. And, after all, the last of the matter had not yet been heard.

Meanwhile, military and police parties were carrying out raids on suspect hoards. Bhit, Shamspir, and Baba Islands, for long notorious as lairs of Karachi smugglers, were raided and contraband goods to the value of Rs.200,000[16] were recovered. On 15 October it was reported that 10,000 bags of grain, other foodstuffs, bales of cloth, and imported luxury goods, to the value of Rs.835,000[17] had been seized in Karachi, part having been found concealed in the mangrove swamps. In Kohat, and other centres in West Pakistan, dealers in grain and other essential supplies were arrested for hoarding and further Regulations were issued requiring declaration of all stocks in excess of a defined minimum. On 26 October it was reported that in Panjgur (a small town in the Makran District of West Pakistan) hoarded cloth to the value of Rs.529 lakhs[18] had been declared to the authorities. This is a very high figure indeed and seems open to doubt but, at the same time, it had long been common knowledge that large quantities of consumer goods were entering West Pakistan illegally through Iran, Afghanistan, and along the Makran coast of the Arabian Sea.

The problem of smuggling was not, it must be added, simply one of smuggling *in*. In East Pakistan, particularly, it was very much a question of smuggling *out*, namely, to India, where certain

---

[16] £15,000 or US$42,000.   [17] £62,625 or US$175,350.
[18] £3,967,500 or US$11,109,000.

categories of imported goods were just as scarce as in Pakistan. Calcutta, with its heavy population and vast wealth exercised magnetic influence on such commodities and the innumerable waterways on both sides of the border facilitated such illegal despatch. The problem offered here was considerable and the measure of success in solving it was indicated by the rise in the Calcutta price of those very articles.

Some very impressive figures have been published to show the vast quantities of foodstuffs and imported consumer goods brought to light in consequence of the Regulations that dealt with hoarding.[19] These stocks were declared by merchants and traders in compliance with those Regulations and are distinct from stocks which were detected by the Martial Law authorities in their cleaning-up activities. It is not at all certain that declared stocks had been either illicitly acquired or were not being disposed of in the ordinary way of trade, apart from the question of inflated and exorbitant prices. The official statements on the subject tended to be disingenuous, as is not unusual with much that emanates from 'information services' and it is unfortunate that official propagandists have still not learnt that when one begins by stating too much, one often ends by being credited with too little.

On 18 October came the first important announcement concerning specific reforms which the new administration proposed to introduce. A Land Reforms Commission, under the Chairmanship of the Governor of West Pakistan, was promised and, thirteen days later, orders were issued accordingly. To this important matter we shall return in a later chapter.

At a lower level of reforming zeal, Martial Law Regulations were issued with the object of inducing and teaching a greater sense of civic responsibility, a general regard for cleanliness, hygiene, and civic well-being. In the Karachi Federal Area, for instance, urinating in public places was made punishable by one year's rigorous imprisonment. Persons guilty of molesting women were liable to five years' rigorous imprisonment; begging was prohibited on pain of six months in jail and a whipping; throwing refuse on the streets was made punishable. The general impulse towards a better sense of social obligation was reflected in similar Regulations issued throughout the country.

[19] See, for example, *Administration under Martial Law*, Pakistan Publications, Karachi, no date, p. 15, under the heading *Hoarded Stocks Declared*.

The offices of the abolished political parties were sealed and orders were issued by the Finance Ministry instructing banks to treat their cash balances as frozen.[20] It was announced that the Civil Service (Prevention of Corruption) Rules were to be given rigid effect and, for this purpose, the staff of the Special Police Establishment was to be increased. By 12 October the veteran leader, Khan Abdul Ghaffar Khan, an old stalwart in the cause of freedom from foreign rule, as well as G. M. Syed, a Sind politican and former Congress sympathizer, were both taken into detention on security grounds. Likewise, Maulana Bhashani, an East Pakistan leader of leftist sympathies, was detained under the Security of Pakistan Act.

In East Pakistan there were, at this time, other arrests very much more sensational in character. Former Central Government Ministers, Hamidul Huq Choudhury and Abul Mansur Ahmed, along with two other members of the dismissed National Assembly, Abdul Khaleque and Sheikh Mujibur Rahman, were arrested on charges under the East Pakistan Anti-Corruption Act of 1957 and Ordinance LXXII of 1958. With them were arrested several senior East Pakistan civil servants, including the Industrial Development Commissioner and *ex officio* Secretary of Commerce Industries and Labour Department of the Government of East Pakistan.[21].

By 15 October, in Karachi and elsewhere, Information Receiving Centres were set up at Martial Law Headquarters whose purpose was to collect information about such undesirable activities as espionage, subversion, smuggling, hoarding, profiteering, illegal dealing in currency, and so on. The public was invited to co-operate by giving to the administration whatever information it possessed about persons involved in these anti-social occupations, either by telephone, personal visit, or in writing.[22] It is evident that anonymous communications were not desired, but it is equally evident that a good deal of anonymous material was received which was not necessarily ignored.

It cannot be disputed that, in this, there is a distinctly unpalatable aspect. The intentions of the administration were doubtless in the public interest, but it is certain that malicious attempts were made to utilize this machinery as a means of paying off old scores

[20] *TK*, 12 October 1958.   [21] *D*, 13 October 1958.
[22] Failure to communicate knowledge of any breach of MLR or MLO was made an offence. MLR 56.

or of satisfying some personal grudge. No doubt, the authorities were aware of the risk and did their best not to become the unwitting instrument of private revenge, but the difficulties, especially for Army officers, working in a new and quite unfamiliar milieu, are obvious. This raises, in a way, the entire question of the attitude of the Armed Forces, the police, and the civil administration in the discharge of the new duties that had been placed on them. It is fair to say, looking at the subject in retrospect, that the attitude was, on the whole, impartial. Clearly, the intention of the administration was to be reasonable and just, but also determined. It was, furthermore, a period of some excitement in which certain groups of people were entrusted with unusual powers and unusual responsibilities. This is a situation in which individual personality, integrity, and circumstance count for a great deal and although there seem to have been cases of harshness, of peremptory attitude, and even the causing of unnecessary distress, the instances were not numerous. It was very evident that the officers of the Armed Forces wished, and had probably been so instructed, to give a good example of courtesy tempered with firmness, but whether the police were quite so amenable to these considerations is perhaps less certain. When General Ayub claimed, as he did in an interview with foreign correspondents,[23] that the Martial Law régime was benign and intended to help the civil power to clear up the existing mess, he did not overstate or misrepresent the position. The civilian administration had been brought into association, from the start, by making the Secretary-General, Mr. Aziz Ahmed, a Deputy Chief Martial Law Administrator[24] and by forming an Advisory Council composed of the permanent civil service heads of the Central Government Ministries, to advise the President and the Chief Martial Law Administrator. Within a few weeks, the appearance of soldiers on the streets was diminishing and General Ayub could justly claim that, in a sense, the Army was 'pulling out.'[25]

Moreover, no time was lost in adapting the existing and familiar machinery of the law and government to the new situation. A

---

[23] *D*, 20 October 1958.

[24] He relinquished the appointment on 30 October 1958. MLO No. 11.

[25] On 10 and 11 November 1958 troops on Martial Law duties were withdrawn and all Military Courts wound up. Special Military Courts to deal with Martial Law offences were constituted instead.

presidential Order[26] was promptly issued which stated that, henceforward, the Islamic Republic of Pakistan would be known as 'Pakistan'. It stated that, although the Constitution of 23 March 1956 had been abrogated, the country would, as nearly as possible, be governed in accordance with its provisions. This meant that, excluding the arrangements for a representative National Assembly and the powers to be exercised by the President, those parts of the 1956 Constitution which dealt with national administration, would continue to apply for all practical purposes. The courts of law were to function as before and were to be bound by the law declared by the Supreme Court which, along with the High Courts, continued to have power to issue the well-known prerogative writs.[27] The vital exception was that no Court had power to call into question the fact of declaration of Martial Law, or the acts of the Martial Law authorities and no prerogative writ would lie against the administration.

Three weeks later, the claims of the new régime were to receive their legal sanction. In a Supreme Court judgement, delivered by the Chief Justice of Pakistan on 27 October,[28] it was observed that a victorious revolution or successful *coup d'état* was an internationally recognized method of changing a constitution. As to what had come in place of the old constitution, the citizen already knew —a military executive wielding absolute legislative power and utilizing, as far as was possible, the administrative machinery which the citizen knew and understood. It is, of course, improbable that even if the Supreme Court's entire Bench had risen as one man in protest and opposition, it would have made the slightest difference to the changes that had taken place and, in any case, it seems that the Chief Justice was speaking *obiter*.

The fact was that all the immediate objectives had been secured with complete and striking success, including total acceptance— welcoming or grudging, it did not matter much so long as people did not make nuisances of themselves—of the fact of change. The correspondent of the *Daily Telegraph* might remark: 'How far and how long the hundreds of political figures of West and East Pakistan, the late Central and Provincial Ministers, party chiefs and members of the vast party machines will acquiesce peacefully

---

[26] Laws (Continuance in Force) Order, 1958.

[27] *Habeas corpus, mandamus, quo warranto*, and *certiorari*.

[28] *Pakistan* v. *Dosso*. Full judgement reported in *D*, 28 October 1958.

as it all now is remains to be seen.'[29] In fact, nothing remained. The members of the dismissed Central and Provincial Assemblies dispersed quietly to their homes. Out of them, not less than thirty-four were holding office as Ministers, either in the Central Government, or in the Provincial Governments of East and West Pakistan. They vacated their official bungalows, yielded up their official transport, personal staff and revolver-carrying bodyguards, with which each of them was provided. Unceremoniously flung out of office, stripped of power, they now supinely awaited, not without anxiety, the outcome of the severe animadversions that had been pronounced and those who were abroad at the time, deemed it wiser not to hasten their return.

Very swiftly there had appeared that meaner tribute of the ready sycophant for whom, it seems, the exercise of power by others is irresistibly seductive. Within a day or two of the proclamation, the tide of adulation for the new régime began to rise. Whether this was founded so much upon a truly unalloyed esteem as upon the anxiety to be counted among those who had rushed eagerly to its support is, perhaps, uncertain, but it was most observable and rarely has the principle of expedience in mundane affairs been so widely followed and rarely with equal haste. The following passage is typical of what was, within a very short time, being published.

UPP adds: A large number of women at Nazimabad and Drigh Road bus stations felt grateful when military officers on duty off-loaded male passengers from two buses and put on all waiting ladies to take them to their destinations yesterday.[30] In Nazimabad, school-children warmly clapped hands for the army men when military authorities gave them accommodation on a whole bus, etc., etc.

It is fair to say that the tendency of the Government was to discourage the grosser forms of flattery and the use, for instance, of Ministers' names to adorn schools, hospitals, etc., was not permitted. At any rate, not without prior sanction.[31]

Meanwhile, at top level, much more important matters were on the move. On 25 October it was reported that President Mirza

---

[29] London, 13 October 1958.

[30] What the male passengers felt is not stated.

[31] Much later it was ruled that the naming of places and institutions, while Ministers held office, was not permitted. *D*, 17 February 1962.

had constituted a twelve-man Cabinet to replace the Advisory Council. The proposed Cabinet consisted of the following:

General Ayub Khan (Prime Minister)
Lieutenant-General Azam Khan (Rehabilitation)
Lieutenant-General W. A. Burki (Health and Social Welfare)
Lieutenant-General K. M. Sheikh (Interior)
Mr. Abul Kasem Khan (Industries and Works)
Mr. Habibur Rahman (Education and Information)
Mr. Manzur Qadir (Foreign Affairs)
Moulvi Mohamed Ibrahim (Law)
Mr. F. M. Khan (Communications)
Mr. M. Shoaib (Finance)
Mr. Zulfikar Ali Bhutto (Commerce)
Mr. Hafizur Rahman (Agriculture and Food)

Of these, four could be said to represent East Pakistan: Mr. Abul Kasem Khan, a businessman; Moulvi Mohamed Ibrahim, Vice-Chancellor of Dacca University; Mr. Hafizur Rahman, a former civil servant; and Mr. Habibur Rahman, at that time Pakistan's Ambassador in Brussels. Mr. Manzur Qadir came from Lahore where he was a well-known practising lawyer. Mr. Zulfikar Ali Bhutto, a very much younger man, a lawyer by profession and among whose intellectual attainments was that of having been a Lecturer in Law at the English University of Southampton, came from the Sindhi-speaking community. Mr. F. M. Khan and Mr. M. Shoaib had previously belonged to the public services. It was evident that the four soldier-members constituted the hard core, the others having been brought in for their administrative ability, specialist knowledge and, except in the case of Mr. Abul Kasem Khan and Mr. Habibur Rahman, the fact that they had had negligible contact with the country's political past.

Nine members of the new Cabinet, including General Ayub Khan, were sworn-in on the morning of 27 October, but that very same night occurred the last memorable event of a certainly memorable month. General Ayub's three military colleagues went to President Mirza, at 10 p.m. to inform him, on behalf of General Ayub, that it was now considered he had been 'too much associated with politicians responsible for bringing about the state of affairs in the country'. Hearing this, President Mirza showed himself 'very gracious and said that if it was in the interest of the country that he resign, he was prepared to do so.'[32]

On 28 October, therefore, the country became aware that President Mirza had relinquished his high office in favour of General Ayub and was proceeding, temporarily, with his wife, to Quetta. The office of Prime Minister was, at the same time, abolished and General Ayub Khan became President with a Cabinet comprising the Ministers already named. In a message to the nation, the outgoing President said he had come to the conclusion that any semblance of dual control was likely to hamper performance of the great task, and that an unfortunate impression existed that General Ayub and he might not always act in unison. He had therefore decided to step aside and hand over all powers to General Ayub Khan.[33]

Of course, it did not escape notice that whereas, on the morning of 27 October, General Ayub and his Cabinet colleagues were prepared to serve under President Iskander Mirza, some twelve hours later it was discovered that Mirza had too many undesirable past political associations, and, simultaneously, Mirza had himself come to realize the undesirability of any semblance of dual control, as well as the existence of an unfortunate impression as to the relationship between General Ayub and himself. Questions about all this soon became audible and Miss Fatima Jinnah who, since her distinguished brother's death had, up to this time, participated but little in Pakistan's affairs, grimly observed that the people were happy over Mirza's exit.[34]

The summary nature of Mirza's departure could hardly be disguised and he proceeded, soon after, to the United Kingdom.[35] The reasons given by himself, and by General Ayub Khan, were doubtless accurate as far as they went, but it was clear enough that the whole story had not been told. In an interview with foreign correspondents, on 30 October, the new President said: 'Certain things came to my knowledge. I would not like to say what.'[36] These things, whatever they may be, have never since been disclosed and the only other piece of published information, bearing on Mirza's character as a public figure, came later in a statement given by one Kasim Bhatti, appearing before a Special Military

[32] D, 31 October 1958.   [33] TK, 28 October 1958.   [34] D, 28 October 1958.

[35] It is fair to both sides to mention that the pensions due to him in respect of past service were assured.

[36] D, 31 October 1958.

Court on charges of withholding information about smugglers and for being in possession of smuggled gold.[37]

In this statement, Bhatti alleged, for what it is worth, that when Mirza was Minister of the Interior, he was introduced to the Deputy Inspector-General of Police, in the Anti-Smuggling Department. This officer claimed to be Mirza's trusted assistant and right-hand man and said that if he, Bhatti, wanted to survive, he would be well-advised to live under the benign patronage of this eminent person and, of course, meet his needs in terms of money.

In the same statement, Bhatti implicated a former Governor-General, the late Ghulam Mohamed, as well as Malik Firoz Khan Noon, Prime Minister when Martial Law was declared. According to himself, Bhatti had been specifically encouraged in his smuggling activities, but was obliged to pay large sums of money and make expensive gifts to the many police officers and other officials whom he named. The fact is that if Bhatti's statement was intended to convey the impression of a simple boatman, grossly exploited and much wronged, so as to bring tears to his judges' eyes, he did not do too badly.

But with this sort of unsupported testimony, given by a man who shows himself to be an accomplice, very little can be done. There is nothing in his statement that justifies serious consideration and the only pertinent questions that remain are: Is it correct that Mirza was too closely associated with the old, discredited politicians? What was the true relationship between General Ayub Khan and himself?

Major-General Iskander Ali Mirza had spent most of his life in the service, having been trained at Sandhurst and subsequently entering the Indian Army from which he transferred, while still a young officer, to the Political Service. In this capacity, he spent a number of years in the North West Frontier administration. After the creation of Pakistan, he became a senior civilian official of the Ministry of Defence and, in 1954, was its administrative head. Consequent upon the troubles in East Pakistan, in that year, he was appointed Governor of that Province and it is really at this point that his entry into public life began. He acquired the reputation of being a 'strong man', but whether he really possessed the kind of steel that gives a truly invincible adherence to purpose, or

[37] *D*, 23 May 1959.

whether people were deceived by a bluff, forthright way of saying things, is not so easily decided.

However, this was the man to whom fell the opportunity of becoming the first President of Pakistan and it is certain that, in that capacity, he participated frequently, and used his influence often, in the ebb and flow of political activity. To be sure, the course of that activity was always strenuous and frequently alarming. Within a few weeks of the creation of the Republic, in 1956, there were recurrent crises, usually with the Provincial Governments, but sometimes at the Centre, and the necessity for giving the new Constitution a smooth passage and a fair chance did nothing to abate the general zeal for the crudest political machinations.

The question of motive here is undeniably important. If Mirza did intervene unnecessarily in political affairs, it does not of necessity follow that he did so in the promotion of his own interests. At any rate, it seems probable that he did, at times, act in the interests of people he wished, or thought it useful, to support. It seems likely that among these was the Prime Minister, Mr. Mohamed Ali Choudhury, a man of considerable ability whose personal integrity has never been questioned. His health, in those days, was not always good and it may be he felt the need of the President's active interest,[38] which does not mean that even this altruism on Mirza's part was everywhere welcome. The Muslim League stalwarts—indeed, all who had been active in pre-partition politics and had made their contribution to the independence movement and the emergence of Pakistan—were resentful of men like the late Ghulam Mohamed, Iskander Mirza, Mohamed Ali Choudhury, who had served under the British and, reaching considerable seniority in service, acquired an ascendancy in Pakistan which enabled them to rise to the highest offices in the State. It cannot be disputed that a specific antagonism grew up between these two groups and the feeling which inspired it still persists. Thus, Mian Jaffer Shah, speaking in the Constituent Assembly on 24 August 1955, said: 'A few ex-servicemen have conspired together to rule the country according to their whims. They abused politicians and condemned them.'[39] Here, 'ex-servicemen' does not mean ex-soldiers, but persons formerly in

[38] See, however, note 42 on page 17.
[39] Quoted in Feldman, *A Constitution for Pakistan*, Oxford University Press, Karachi, 1955, p. 101.

the civil and armed services. It was partly for this reason that Mirza constantly found himself at odds with the Muslim League and, with good reason, suspected their desire to be rid of him. Similarly, it cannot be doubted that the creation of the Republican Party by Dr. Khan Sahib, whose name was anathema in Muslim League circles and who was, at that time, Chief Minister of the Province of West Pakistan, was a direct consequence of Iskander Mirza's interest, with the collaboration of the Provincial Governor, Mr. Mushtaq Ahmed Gurmani. The immediate purpose was to retain Dr. Khan Sahib and thwart the efforts of the Muslim League to remove him. In his book another Mr. Mushtaq Ahmed wrote: 'Dr. Khan Sahib . . . had the Provincial Government under his control. Of that Government he was the undisputed master not by dint of following which he did not possess, but because he had been put there by the powers that be.'[40] If, among those powers, the author did not include President Iskander Mirza, it would indeed be interesting to know whom he did include.

Mirza became sensitive to criticism based on his unwarranted intervention in political affairs for, in his Pakistan Day Message of August 1957, he said, doubtless with unconscious irony: 'As your President, I am sworn to implement and defend the Constitution and I wish to make it perfectly clear that I shall do so without any other consideration.'[41] Later, in his statement of 7 October 1958, when he referred to the unjust accusation of 'palace intrigue', he advanced the explanation that he had laboured to bring about coalition after coalition, hoping it would stabilize the administration and that the affairs of the nation would be run in the interests of the masses. But it could not be denied that a Republic having been formed, with himself as its first President, there were elections to be faced. No doubt, much of what he was doing had this prospect well in mind. In playing an inherently risky game, he had made enemies for himself, and Miss Jinnah's published observation on his departure was not made for nothing.

In his study of democratic institutions in Pakistan,[42] Dr. G. W.

[40] *Government and Politics in Pakistan*, Pakistan Publishing House, Karachi, 1959, p. 167.
[41] *MN*, 14 August 1957.
[42] *Democracy in Pakistan*, Green Book House, Dacca, 1963, *passim*. Dr. G. W. Choudhury quotes Mr. Mohamed Ali Choudhury as having repudiated Iskander Mirza completely and stated that Iskander Mirza was solely concerned to remain as President and even aspired to kingship!

Choudhury makes no bones about asserting Iskander Mirza's desire to perpetuate his own succession and his interference in politics, on behalf of 'vested interests', to keep Dr. Khan Sahib in office. The Report of the Constitution Commission, instituted in 1960 by President Ayub, also takes the view that one of the reasons for the breakdown of the 1956 Constitution was interference by Heads of State and it can scarcely be doubted that Iskander Mirza, among others, was meant.

So much, then, for the first question. Now arises the matter of the relationship between the two men who, in October 1958, abolished the 1956 Constitution and, for better or for worse, set Pakistan upon a fresh path. They were, of course, no strangers to one another. By birth and ancestry President Ayub Khan belongs to the North West Frontier where Iskander Mirza had served for many years. This acquaintance continued, after the creation of Pakistan, for Mirza became the permanent civil service head of the Ministry of Defence and had witnessed Ayub Khan's advancement to the command of the Pakistan Army—the first Pakistani to hold that high appointment. They had been associated in the political changes instituted by Ghulam Mohamed and were both in London when those changes were discussed. For a time they had been colleagues in the last Cabinet of the late Mohamed Ali (of Bogra) to which subject we shall later return. General Ayub Khan had also accompanied Iskander Mirza when the latter, as President, had undertaken journeys in the Middle East.

To what extent and at what stage they had come to know each other's mind concerning the events of October 1958 is purely a matter of speculation although, as far back as 1954, Iskander Mirza had been talking publicly of 'controlled democracy'.[43] At any rate, so far as the October *coup* is concerned, it is clear enough that the matter was broached between them some time before 7 October and that, secondly, the decision to impose Martial Law and sweep away existing institutions was taken at the Army's insistence and initiative. It has never been denied—rather, it has been affirmed—that had Mirza refused his collaboration, the Army would have acted alone. To this extent, it may therefore be said that Mirza was helpless in the matter although all the indications are that the proposal was congenial to him. But it is of some importance to note that the Army had, for some time, been

[43] See Feldman, op. cit., p. 66.

watching the deteriorating situation in the country, as was made manifest in General Ayub's broadcast of 8 October. The newspapers of 10 October show, just as clearly, that the President had acted on General Ayub's initiative which, from the outset, and always thereafter, evidently lay with him.

That the duumvirate was sometimes an uneasy one and that there was a sense of rivalry became first indicated when President Mirza stated, in an interview with foreign correspondents, that Martial Law would be retained for the shortest possible time and, thereafter, the nation's affairs would be managed by a National Council of some twelve to fifteen persons.[44] At the same time, a body of competent men of international repute, would be assembled to prepare a satisfactory constitution for the country. Next day, however, there appeared a statement from General Ayub to the effect that there would be no premature lifting of Martial Law until the 'allround mess was cleared up' and again, on 20 October, it was reported that General Ayub had said: 'The President and I discuss and make policy. My job is to see it executed.' There could be no doubt, here, as to with whom the balance of power lay.

But if this was the sum total of things and if, on this basis, General Ayub and his military colleagues had, by the evening of 27 October, reached the simple conclusion that it was desirable and necessary that he should emerge as the sole policy-maker and executive, Mirza could have been retained as what is sometimes called 'a constitutional head of state'. Evidently, no such option was extended to him or, if it was, it was refused. This leads to the supposition that an adequate explanation can only be sought in those things which came to General Ayub's knowledge and of which he did not wish to speak. Since the new President did not wish to reveal them, it may seem unfair to hazard guesses, but it remains a matter of public interest about which history will continue curious, even although the moment for disclosure may not yet have come.

Excluding the possibility of some personal blemish in character (which seems remote and, even if it existed, must have been known before, let us say, midday on 27 October 1958), the only explanation that suggests itself is that even while Mirza was preparing to induct his new Cabinet, he was preparing also for a trial of

[44] *D*, 16 October 1958.

strength. There are grounds for thinking that he was already regretting the loss of his position as Supreme Commander of the Armed Forces which, under the Constitution just swept away, was vested in him by virtue of Article 40 and it seems to have been at his instance that Lieutenant-General Musa was made Commander-in-Chief of the Army and promoted to the rank of full general, although General Ayub Khan continued to be Supreme Commander.[45]

Of course, what is suggested here presupposes a regrettable duplicity of conduct for which, however, there was a recent precedent that could not be ignored. On the morning of 7 October, while he was yet preparing to announce a *coup* that night, he was occupying himself with distributing portfolios to Malik Firoz Khan Noon and his new Ministers, the people in fact who, a few hours later, were to be dismissed peremptorily to their homes. He had acted, then, with deliberation and foreknowledge and, what is more, with success. It seems improbable that, faced with similar prospects on a second occasion, he would develop qualms.

But how, and in what manner, Iskander Mirza proposed to measure himself against generals who undoubtedly commanded the respect and confidence of their troops, it is impossible to imagine. A man whose years were spent in the old Political Service and, later, as a civil administrator in the Defence Ministry, is scarcely in a position to capture any exceptional or powerful regard or loyalty, either with the general public or with the Armed Forces. He was, neither more nor less, another career man, most of whose life had been spent in the service of the British in which, it may be added, there was nothing dishonourable to either side. But, *ipso facto*, he did not belong to the group of men who had spent their years, and had risked much, for the creation of an independent Pakistan. He was, notwithstanding the impressive rank of Major-General, a regular soldier *manqué* and, despite an oft-mentioned attachment to the soldierly life, he was mainly a civil servant for whom, later in his career, it is not unfair to say that the cards had fallen well and, let it also be said, he played them for a time with skill. But to suppose that he possessed such resources, either of personality or in the allegiance of others, as would make possible for him the final arbitrament of force, was a grossly false assessment and, if it be true that he nourished any

45 *The Times of India*, Bombay, 31 December 1958.

such intention, it meant that his judgement was failing. He was bound to lose, and he did lose.

However all that may be, on 27 October General Ayub Khan became the undisputed leader of the country. From this time is claimed the true commencement of the new era and, ever since, its anniversary has been celebrated on that day. Still, by this time, a pattern had been formed and many assurances—some replete with interest and others with disquiet, depending on the point of view —had been given. What the nation now awaited was their implementation.

II

Circumstances Preceding the 1958 Coup

BEFORE we can usefully trace the course of events following President Ayub Khan's assumption of power, we should first consider briefly whether the substance of Iskander Mirza's proclamation finds reasonable support in the facts, for it must be remembered that although, by 28 October, Mirza had been disavowed, his pronouncement of 7 October had not. The further aspect, touching upon the Army's interest in, and relationship with, political events in Pakistan, of which President Ayub had spoken in his broadcast of 8 October, will be discussed in the next chapter.

In his declaration Mirza had made several points, of which perhaps the most important was the assertion that the existing Constitution was unworkable and full of compromises dangerous to the integrity of Pakistan. In passing, it may be said that he was Governor-General of Pakistan when this Constitution was drafted, under the Prime Ministership of Mr. Mohamed Ali Choudhury, and although it is to the latter that credit for this piece of work is usually given, it is improbable that Iskander Mirza was unaware of, or indifferent to, the shape that the 1956 Constitution was taking.

However, to continue with his proclamation: he spoke of the selfishness of politicians, their ruthless thirst for power, lack of patriotism, and general misconduct. In particular, he specified certain recent happenings in the East Pakistan Provincial Assembly. He mentioned the spread of social evils, the misfortunes that had overtaken the helpless masses, and the generally deplorable situation into which the country had fallen, along with the politicians' own talk of the prospect of 'bloody revolution'.

Now, history is not without earlier instances of *coups d'état* justified by reference to the misdeeds of the overturned régime and with lamentation for the unhappy plight from which the nation was being rescued. Mirza, in following this formula, could assert two things as evidence of his sincerity. It is on record that he had long preserved doubts as to the practicability, in Pakistan, of parliamentary government on the British model. We have already referred to his *Daily Telegraph* interview, some six years before, when he used the expression 'controlled democracy', and thereby caused some eyebrows to lift. At that time, there were implausible official attempts to explain this away[1], but no one really doubted what Mirza meant, least of all the man himself. The second point lies in Callard's carefully phrased feat of prescience and his conclusion that, by 1957 at any rate, Pakistan had not yet established a working democracy, notwithstanding which he felt that democracy was what the people wanted. Yet, and this too is worthy of notice, he added that these same people also admire an act of strength and rally to support the man who has acted.[2]

It is evident that Callard was impressed, as all must be, by the immense difficulty which preceded and attended the passage of the Constitution through the Assembly in 1956. The nine years that had already passed, were chequered indeed in their political history, culminating in Ghulam Mohamed's summary dismissal of Khwaja Nazimuddin, in 1953 and, in 1954, his proclamation of a state of emergency out of which evolved a new Constituent Assembly of eighty members, charged with the duty of preparing a Constitution for the nation. These eighty people have been defined as comprising 'men of great wealth and affluence as well as belonging to the humblest strata of society; men with high educational qualifications as well as semi-literates . . .'.[3] The last mentioned description may sound harsh, although it does not follow that an uneducated man is necessarily foolish or incompetent. Possibly, the author had in mind that one of Pakistan's misfortunes, from the day of its creation, has been the undue participation, in public affairs, by people to whom the management of the parish pump could not safely be entrusted.

When Mirza spoke of 'bloody revolution', he was simply quoting from the opening speech, made on behalf of the Opposition, when the 1956 Constitution Bill came before the House. This cheerful assurance, given by the Honourable Member, was founded upon

---

[1] Feldman, op. cit., p. 66.
[2] Callard, op. cit., p. 326 and *passim*. Callard contains much information on the history of those times. See also Feldman, op. cit.
[3] Mushtaq Ahmed, op. cit., p. 115.

a line of argument not fully clear, but it certainly provided a key in which subsequent debate was mostly pitched.[4] The proceedings were not only contentious but obstructive in the extreme. The Official Report contains page after page of sustained nonsense for which, however, the Opposition was by no means alone responsible and which, it must also be said, was not confined to debates on the Constitution Bill. All the Assembly proceedings contain, in full measure, those puerile and vulgar elements which are inseparable from political discussion everywhere.

The closing of the debate, and the final approval of the Bill, were marked with scenes of considerable bitterness. On the last day, 29 February 1956, the late H. S. Suhrawardy appealed to the Government coalition to agree to a round-table conference to discuss the issues still in dispute. The appeal was ignored and the opposition parties left the House. In this unhappy atmosphere the Constitution was adopted.

Despite this unpromising background, the question remains whether the Constitution was, in itself, unworkable. It is not a point which can be proved with mathematical certainty. One can only read the signs of the times and watch the straws in the wind. Those principally concerned with its production—for instance, Mr. Mohamed Ali Choudhury—afterwards held that the 1956 Constitution never had a chance and that thirty months were not long enough in which to test its potentialities. In his subsequent examination of the subject, Dr. G. W. Choudhury seems to conclude there was no inherent flaw and the tendency of the Report of the Constitution Commission, set up later by President Ayub Khan, is clearly towards the view that the trouble lay with the men rather than with the measures.[5]

Even here there is a profound cleavage of opinion for while men like Mirza thrust all the odium upon the 'politicians', the politicians claimed that it was men like Ghulam Mohamed and Iskander Mirza who had flouted all recognized parliamentary practice and had played ducks and drakes with all established convention. Much of this opinion is, of course, *ex post facto*, but it is worth noticing that Callard also takes the view that a high price was paid, in terms of the parliamentary system, for Ghulam Mohamed's

---

[4] CAD, 16 January 1956, p. 1814.
[5] G. W. Choudhury, op. cit., chapter 5.

coup of 1953 which, he says, undermined the basis of Cabinet Government in the country.[6]

It was none the less true that the politicians, comprising the wealthy landlords, the lawyers, and the journalists who, between them, dominated the Central and Provincial Assemblies, formed no very commendable group of people.[7] The example of Cincinnatus, while not unknown among them, was by and large exceptional. The fluid and mercurial nature of politics in those days had to be experienced to be believed. Parties came and went; loyalties changed, burgeoned, and vanished overnight. The National Assembly of June 1955 counted among its eighty members, seven distinct parties and six independents. The same National Assembly, in December 1957, counted ten distinct parties and nine independents. To be sure, the appearance of four new parties was principally due to the break-up of East Pakistan's United Front, but, with or without this, the position was sufficiently complex.

Everyone knows that political activity has no purpose unless it be the acquisition of power and, sometimes, the spoils that may go with it. Certainly, not everyone is concerned with spoils, and, in some countries, they do not amount to much. The point here is that when one group of people, in politics, accuses another group of seeking power or being hungry for it, they are accusing themselves at the same time. There is only the unstated assumption that 'we' want it for the good of the country, whereas 'they' want it for the good of themselves. In Pakistan, in those days, there was unending badinage of this sort, but it was mostly a case of the pot calling the kettle black. The wealthy landlords were concerned to retain both land and wealth. The rising class of industrialists and bankers was not prominently represented (Mushtaq Ahmed counts only seven in a National Assembly of eighty)[7] but, armed with their cheque books, there was plenty they could do in the lobbies, without having to go to the trouble of becoming members of the House. The lawyers were interested in what the first Earl of Birkenhead once called 'the glittering prizes'. In addition, there

---

[6] Callard, op. cit., p. 137.

[7] Mushtaq Ahmed, op. cit., p. 115. He indicates the following break-down from a total of eighty members in the National Assembly: twenty-eight landlords, twenty-three lawyers and fourteen retired officials. All the landlords came from West Pakistan, twenty of the lawyers came from East Pakistan. A similar composition was doubtless reflected in the Provincial Assemblies.

was the entourage, attached by blood or by party affiliation, whose claims were usually pressed with much insistence and could scarcely be refused.

The degree to which people are susceptible to the temptations and persuasions too often associated with high office and political position depends on many factors, and one of the most important is the prevailing standard of public morality. In Pakistan, as in India and elsewhere, this standard had, in the middle of the twentieth century, been much depleted by a combination of unfortunate circumstances.

The entry of Japan into World War II, had made the Indo-Pakistan sub-continent a truly active participant and the moral and economic impact was enormous. Military, naval, and air force installations were multiplied overnight; numerous airfields had to be constructed. The arrival of more troops from abroad—British and American—was itself a great inflationary influence. The subsidiary camps, cantonments, training centres, protective works—even the operation of a scorched-earth policy—all brought forth a torrent of public spending. There promptly ensued a fierce scramble for contracts and profits, with an equally prompt effect on the integrity of the public services, whose own standards of ability and character had already been lowered by the recruitment of temporary officials needed solely to meet the exigencies of the hour.

The rapid deterioration of those days is well borne out by evidence which is sometimes grim. The Report[8] of the Commission which inquired into the Bengal Famine of 1943 refers to the contribution made by greed and corruption which 'was widespread'. The Commission flatly stated that enormous profits were made out of the calamity in which the deaths were estimated, by the Commission, to amount to some 1,500,000 persons. It was estimated that the illicit gain made out of the famine was in the order of Rs.1,500,000,000, or 1,000 rupees profit on each person that died.[9]

In another Inquiry, presided over by the late Sir Archibald Rowlands, into the administration of Bengal, it was stated[10]: 'So

---

[8] Government of India, New Delhi, 1945.
[9] Jawaharlal Nehru, *The Discovery of India*, The Signet Press, Calcutta, 1946, pp. 606–7 f.n.
[10] Quoted in Nehru, op. cit., p. 600.

widespread has corruption become and so defeatist the attitude towards it that we think the most drastic steps should be taken to stamp out the evil which has corrupted the public service and public morals.' Revealing, also, as evidence of the temper of those days, is the Report of the Committee set up by the Government of India, in 1946, to investigate problems relating to the disposal of surplus military stores.[11] The Committee referred to the fact that corruption was generally rife and made special mention of the undesirability of members of legislatures and of persons occupying positions prominent in public life, negotiating for the purchase of surplus goods, or acting as brokers or agents for purchasers, which is an interesting reflection on the subsidiary occupations of pre-partition India's elected representatives.

Corruption, jobbery, and five-per-centing did not, of course, constitute phenomena introduced into the sub-continent, for the first time, by World War II. There were lengthy and quite well-established traditions, but not, perhaps, on the scale provoked by the war. And, unhappily, before the least respite was possible, before any better example or wiser counsel could prevail, there came the turmoil of partition and the emergence of two new and independent nations, each with its own particular attitude.

The consequences were various. Among other things, virtually all jobs in the public service—high, medium, and low—were doubled. In both countries, also, the premature retirement of many British officials created immediate vacancies and opportunities for accelerated promotion. It did not always follow that suitably qualified men were available to fill this plethora of jobs. Thirdly, the migration from India to Pakistan, and vice versa, created a vacuum in property ownership which human nature rushed to fill.[12] It is scarcely necessary to elaborate the detail of so many opportunities for illegal gratification, peculation, dispossession, favouritism, nepotism, and even violence, in the guise of legal action. The wonder is not that public morality suffered, but that any sense of it survived.

Such were the cancers attacking the nation's moral well-being,

[11] Government of India, New Delhi, February 1947.

[12] The irregular, unfair, and illegal re-distribution of property abandoned by migrant Hindus and Sikhs, at the time of partition, grew into a gigantic scandal. An inquiry, conducted by a retired British judge, Sir Thomas Ellis, was instituted by the Pakistan Government, but under various political pressures, the scope of the inquiry was so curtailed as to make it useless.

and they produced a fever of acquisition that defied all attempts at healing. Inevitably, it was discovered that this is a disease which, if not cured, grows progressively worse. Gerrymandering and such-like traffic can never be contained at the stage of simple bribery, manipulation, buying and selling. The physical manifestations must sooner or later appear; the ultimate resource of exasperated losers.

This is the explanation for the incidents in the East Pakistan Provincial Assembly, in September 1956, to which Iskander Mirza referred. An account is recorded in the *Dacca Gazette*[13] containing the Report of the Commission, consisting of a High Court judge, to inquire into the affair. The revealing and lamentable contents throw light on the sordid condition of representative politics in the country.

The story is a complicated one, based mainly upon the contest in the East Pakistan Assembly between the Krishak Sramik Party and its associates on the one hand, and the Awami Muslim League[14] on the other. It is a tale of desperate party manoeuvre to secure office and retain a majority. So bitterly was this struggle conducted that, within a short time, after the inception of the 1956 Republican Constitution, representative government in East Pakistan had to be suspended by the President, exercising his constitutional powers. In the two years that followed the Republic's commencement, the East Pakistan budget could be passed, only by means of those constitutional provisions which enabled the Central Government to authenticate it. There was, furthermore, abuse of office by the Speaker of the Provincial Assembly, and his Deputy was considered unfair and unreliable.

In this prolonged struggle for ultimate influence at the Centre, not a weapon went unused. Every vote in the Provincial Assembly counted and every kind of persuasion, blandishment, and pressure was employed to ensure them. Mr. Abu Hossain Sarkar's Government included not less than forty Ministers, Deputy Ministers, Parliamentary and Political Secretaries.[15] Lucrative patronage was extended wherever it was acceptable and likely to produce results,

[13] Registered No. DA–1, dated 9 May 1959.
[14] Later re-designated the Awami League. It was led by the late Mr. H. S. Suhrawardy.
[15] A recognized method of retaining a majority. Malik Firoz Khan Noon, Prime Minister of Pakistan from December 1957 to October 1958, tried to increase his Cabinet to twenty-six out of a total membership of eighty in the

but other methods were not excluded. A permanent civil servant, Syed Mahbubur Rahman, who was at that time Secretary to the East Pakistan Assembly, testified how he was conducted to the Speaker's Room and threatened, the object being that he should influence his wife, a member of the Assembly, to revert back to her former party affiliations and he stated that, night after night, these menaces continued.[16]

The events were leading up to a crisis and, in no atmosphere of secrecy, the possibility of an invasion of the House by ruffians and the forcible ejection of the Speaker, was discussed. It appears that on the morning of 20 September 1958, the Speaker sent a telegram to the President stating that he had been threatened with personal violence and that on the previous evening one of his relations was assaulted. He said, also, that members of the House were being intimidated or forcibly taken out of Dacca.

In this state of alarm, the East Pakistan Provincial Assembly met. It is not necessary to narrate, in detail, the disgraceful scenes that followed. The Speaker was assaulted and compelled to leave the Chair, but, in doing so, somehow intimated that the House stood adjourned. Later, it appears, he was discovered taking refuge in a tin shed. On 21 and 22 September there was an agreed truce, and the House met again on the 23rd, with the Deputy Speaker in the Chair. But the truce, it seems, was only to regain breath and re-deploy forces. There was a fresh enactment of violence and the Deputy Speaker was injured amid pandemonium and the hurling of chairs, tables, lamps, microphones, and whatever people could lay hands on. The police were called and about thirty members were forcibly removed. Some days later, the Deputy Speaker died and it is generally stated that his injuries were the cause of death. About this there may be doubt since he was already an ailing man, but it could not be denied that his death was accelerated by the violence inflicted.

These deplorable happenings made their mark upon the conscience of the nation which fully understood what impact they would have outside the country. It is obvious, too, that this affair helped to sharpen the resolve of those who were observing

National Assembly. See Mushtaq Ahmed, op. cit., pp. 199 and 200. It could be argued, of course, that if a Cabinet of twenty-six was too many, a National Assembly of eighty was not enough.

[16] *Dacca Gazette*, op. cit., p. 609.

the steady decline and were forming a determination to do something about it, for who could say to what this violence was leading?

Although there was not quite the same element of desperation in the proceedings of the West Pakistan Provincial Assembly,[17] its members could not altogether be acquitted of malpractice. The usual party manipulations, made possible and effective by the customary rewards and favours, were practised without restraint; and the fact that both Mr. Mushtaq Ahmed Gurmani and the late Dr. Khan Sahib remained in office, as Governor and Chief Minister respectively, from 1955 to 1957, could only be attributed to the flexible attitude that prevailed and to the President's covert support.[18] There were, furthermore, accusations of wholesale changes among provincial civil servants and police officers based solely on political motives.[19] It was at the instance of the Republican Party, essentially a West Pakistan organization, that Suhrawardy was compelled to prune the scope of the Ellis Inquiry into evacuee property scandals. In short, when General Ayub Khan referred to politicians' 'free-for-all type of fighting in which no holds were barred', he did not have to point further than the West Pakistan Provincial Assembly Building in Lahore.

Nor, in the matter of stability, was the situation very much better at the Centre. In the space of thirty months, following the proclamation of the Republic, there were no less than four different Prime Ministers. Mohamed Ali Choudhury, who piloted the Constitution Bill through the Constituent Assembly, was deserted by his party and compelled to resign six months later. He was followed by H. S. Suhrawardy who lasted some thirteen months and resigned after he lost the support of the Republican Party which he had done so much to accommodate. The question, at that time, turned on the administrative consolidation of West Pakistan, usually termed 'One Unit', which interested persons desired to see broken up with a reversion to the old system of smaller Provinces within West Pakistan. His successor, I. I. Chundrigar, an old Muslim League veteran, who had also played a prominent part in the formation of the Constitution of 1956, lasted two months. He resigned on the question of whether, for

---

[17] Charges of manhandling and forcible removal were made. *D*, 21 May 1956.
[18] Choudhury, op. cit., p. 122.   [19] *D*, 17 and 20 May 1956.
[20] Broadcast to the nation 8 October 1958.

the purposes of political representation, the country should be treated as one, irrespective of religion, or whether each religious community should have its own representatives in the legislatures. Lastly came Malik Firoz Khan Noon, for many years a well-known figure, and representative of the Punjab landlords.

Of course, a Central Assembly, comprising a membership of eighty, divided into nine parties and nine independents, with no single party able to wield an absolute majority, could scarcely ensure stable administration. However, it should also be explained that although the post-constitution National Assembly consisted, broadly speaking, of the same eighty persons who had framed it, the Constitution actually provided for a single-chamber Parliament comprising three hundred members, divided equally between East and West Pakistan. These members were to be elected by a system of adult franchise and, for the purpose of preparing electoral rolls and organizing both central and provincial elections, an Election Commission was provided and was, in fact, appointed.

Unfortunately, none of this was fruitful. Inside and outside the House, controversy raged on the question of whether the electorate should be divided according to religion or not. On this point, there was a clear and irreconcilable difference of opinion as between East and West Pakistan. Since most of the minority religious communities live in East Pakistan, that Province was totally unwilling to give way. Eventually the compromise suggested by Suhrawardy was adopted. In West Pakistan, the electorate would be divided on a religious basis; in East Pakistan, there would be no such division. It was a quite remarkable triumph that he was able to secure this measure of agreement on so delicate an issue and it enabled the work of the Election Commission to go forward. As a result, 15 February 1959 was appointed as the last date by which general elections were to be held throughout the country and, by the time that Martial Law was declared, in October 1958, a good deal of the necessary work of preparation had been completed.[21]

It did not, of course, pass unnoticed that the *coup* took place only four months before the elections were due to be held and the

---

[21] Up to this time, there had been no general elections in Pakistan. There had only been provincial elections.

point deserves consideration.[22] It is particularly relevant to consider the weight that could have been attached to this circumstance by those responsible for sweeping away the first Republic. It seems fair to say that, among them, the only man whose position could have been adversely affected was Iskander Mirza himself for, unless he could ensure the unchallengeable return to power of his political friends at the forthcoming elections, his prospects of continuing as President were, to say the least, doubtful. During the disturbed times of 1954 in East Pakistan, Iskander Mirza became Governor, administering the Province under what was known as Section 92A. In effect, this meant that he governed with the assistance of the civil administration, but with no ministers or representative legislature. As we have seen, he acquired the reputation of being a 'strong' administrator, a term that one can interpret as one likes, but it is certain that his application of 'strength' did nothing to increase the number of his friends in East Pakistan. Further, as we have already seen, he was not universally popular in West Pakistan's political circles. The prospect of ensuring his continuance as President of Pakistan, after the elections now clearly in sight, was not unduly promising and therefore, when the intentions of General Ayub Khan and his military colleagues first became known to him, they could not have been unwelcome. Unfortunately, his judgement in other respects proved to be less sound.

The position of General Ayub Khan was not the same. He became Commander-in-Chief of the Pakistan Army in 1951, the appointment being for a term of five years. In 1956, the appointment was renewed for a further period of five years so that, in October 1958, only half of the second term had expired. In the normal course of events, therefore, he could look forward in 1961 either to a fresh renewal,[23] or, what was perhaps more likely, to retirement with—if he desired it—the prospect of an interesting appointment, at home or abroad, of comparable rank and status. Thus, in the face of elections, as such, he had nothing to lose as Commander-in-Chief.

[22] Hence, perhaps, the reference to 'fairly conducted elections' in President Mirza's proclamation.

[23] The age of President Ayub Khan does not seem to have been officially disclosed. That would, of course, have affected the prospect of a third term as Commander-in-Chief. In *D*, 31 October 1958, there is a note which says: 'He is 51.' In *Who's Who*, 1964, no date of birth is given.

While, therefore, it is reasonable to consider the effect of the comparative proximity of general elections upon the judgement of those most closely concerned, not too much can be deduced from it. In any case, tradition in Pakistan being what it was, the idea of revolutionary change could never have taken hold in the absence of specific and compelling *raisons d'être*. Where government is reasonably sound and the people reasonably prosperous, revolution is not possible for the reason that no one has cause to think about it. The tolerance with which the new régime was received, both in Pakistan and abroad, is itself evidence that the nation's affairs had fallen into gross decline which could only be arrested by swift and decisive action. Of course, there follows afterwards the pragmatic test of what the new administration actually achieves—something which must be reserved for later pages.

At any rate, the principal thesis of the declarations of 7 and 8 October was the failure of the Constitution and of the men who had to work it. On whether or not the Constitution was workable, it is difficult, in the absence of the general elections, to express a decided opinion. Technically, it seems to have been a feasible structure, a republic based on parliamentary traditions consistent with ideas with which Pakistan was familiar and about which it had heard much. The political thinking of its intellectuals, lawyers, and politically active people was certainly on these lines and it stands to reason that an evolved constitution must, and will, be conformable to the shape of such thinking. As we have seen, the tendency of Pakistani observers is towards the view that the 1956 Constitution was not inherently defective and that the fault lay mainly with the people most intimately concerned to work it.

No doubt, any study of the active politics of those times and, perhaps less important, the debates of the National Assembly, will lead to the decided conviction that the members had done their best to discourage all hope of orderly government within the constitutional framework. And, it must be remembered, the experience of the preceding eleven years did not lead to any strong belief that representative politics in Pakistan could be either efficient, clean, or constructive. It is obvious that no one viewed the future with confidence and that, perhaps, is why the concensus of world opinion, as reflected in reports that followed the

Martial Law declaration, indicated no hostility to the new dispensation, but rather an aspect of relief.

There were, of course, in Iskander Mirza's not too well drafted statement, subsidiary themes not very deeply elaborated. He complained that the foreign policy of the country, even the country itself, had been traduced by some Pakistanis in an injurious manner which, in some cases, amounted to 'high treason'. He referred to people 'screaming' for war with India 'knowing full well that they will be nowhere near the firing line', a piece of sarcasm directed, it seems, at his former colleague, Mohamed Ali Choudhury, who had been making some injudicious and sabre-rattling speeches on Indo-Pakistan relations. He mentioned, as a specific instance of the impossibility of conducting a fair franchise, the recent Karachi Municipal Corporation election in which only twenty per cent of the electorate exercised the vote and, of the votes cast, half were found to be bogus. Of those social evils associated with corruption, black-marketing, and hoarding, he made brief mention, but then the public did not need to be told much. They already knew, as did the officers and men of the Armed Forces.

III

Position of the Armed Forces in Relation to Politics

I F the officers and men of the Armed Forces had reason to know, from personal experience, of the social evils to which the Proclamation referred, their knowledge was not limited to these deplorable matters. Therefore in assessing the role of the Armed Forces in the *coup* of 1958, it is necessary to look more closely at preceding events which had afforded them an insight into the state of the country's political affairs.

In January 1951 General Ayub Khan became Commander-in-Chief of the Pakistan Army and, on the occasion of that promotion, he issued a statement to the troops under his command in which, among other things, he advised them to 'keep out of politics', although he added that they could and should take an intelligent interest in national affairs. The whole tenor of that statement was, in fact, consistent with the duty of an Army Commander in a country where political affairs are tranquil, well-ordered, and from which the Armed Forces strictly abstain.[1]

With this in mind, his broadcast of 8 October 1958 shows itself very much more forceful. He then said: 'Ever since the inception of Pakistan, we, in the Armed Forces, saw very clearly the internal problems facing the country and the external dangers to which it was exposed . . . We solemnly decided to build a true National Army free from politics . . . We kept severely aloof . . .'

No one who had any contact with the Armed Forces of Pakistan can doubt that both officers and men did desire to remain aloof and any suggestion that political considerations might sway them simply aroused denial and the thought of it, dismay. Of course, as well as being officers and men, they were also citizens entitled to exercise a vote and interest themselves, to that extent, in the country's affairs. But other things were becoming only too ap-

---

[1] The statement is contained, verbatim, in *D*, 23 January 1951.

parent, and they needed no instruction from indignant and troubled wives about the rising cost of food and clothing, the expense of educating children, and the scarcity of simple necessities. As has often provoked anger and resentment at other times and in other places, they experienced the common spectacle of sleek men driving, or being driven, in large and shiny motor-cars and not being quite able to say where the money came from. And, as for what was going on in the councils of the nation, they could read the newspapers as well as the next man.

Much closer to the point, in some respects, is the fact that during the eleven years preceding Martial Law, the Armed Forces had, on more than one occasion, been brought, willy-nilly, into active contact with the disturbed and unruly state of things. Some knowledge of those instances is very relevant now, not to show that there was any continuous thread which culminated in the October *coup*—I do not believe that there was—but to show their ultimate consequences. It cannot now be questioned that the deeper importance of those instances lies in their impression on the military mind, an impression which matured slowly and surely into a belief that in Pakistan, parliamentary democracy was not working well; that the civilian administration was defective; that the poor were suffering; that rich men were becoming richer by the power of their purses; that the situation of the country was deteriorating and must, unless there were a change, continue to do so.

It is necessary to understand clearly that we are concerned now only with the unsought, unwished-for participation of the Armed Forces, in certain internal happenings. We are not concerned with the part they took in the organization of partition, the escorting of migrants, and the keeping of order during those difficult days. Similarly, the question of Kashmir hostilities is not now under discussion. Finally, we are not concerned with those other occasions, both in East and West Pakistan, when riotous mobs were quelled solely by police action, even to the extent of opening fire, sometimes with fatal consequences. In the preservation of internal order, the functions of the police and the military are totally distinct and the Armed Forces could play no part unless and until the civil power requested aid. It is for this reason that military participation is described as being unsought by the Armed Forces. At the same time, it cannot be overlooked that even when the troops were not called upon in times of civil disturbance, they fully appreciated these events and, perhaps, knowing a good deal more than ever appeared in the newspapers, were even then drawing their own conclusions.

The first manifestion of military interest in politics was peculiar, highly irregular, and by no means representative of military ideas and military thinking. It is an event which has largely disappeared from people's consciousness and it has long ceased to have any importance. Still, to keep the record complete, it needs brief mention here. This affair, known as the Rawalpindi Conspiracy Case, occurred early in 1951 and because, after the conspiracy was unmasked, the facts were kept shrouded in secrecy from the start, not a great deal is known. It was confined to a small group of serving officers and a few civilians, led by a major-general. Indications gleaned from the foreign Press, for what they are worth, point to a plan to overthrow the then existing Government of which the late Liaquat Ali Khan was Prime Minister.[1] The Prime Minister's own statement to the Constituent Assembly was vague as to what precisely happened, or was intended to happen, and he withheld detail on grounds of security.

Fourteen people were convicted in this case by a tribunal especially set up by statute for the purpose.[2] The trials, held in camera, took place at Hyderabad[3] in circumstances of great secrecy and everyone concerned, including counsel for the defence, was under oath not to reveal what was stated during the proceedings. The conspirators were sentenced to varying terms of imprisonment, but in 1955 those still in jail were quietly released after a fair measure of agitation relating to the constitutional validity of the special statute under which the trials were held and the accused convicted.[4] From such scraps of information as are here and there

---

[1] See, for example, *The Times*, London, 9 April 1951.

[2] The Rawalpindi Conspiracy (Special Tribunal) Act, 1951, and the Rawalpindi Conspiracy (Special Tribunal) (Amendment) Act, 1952.

[3] In West Pakistan.

[4] The circumstances are complicated and peculiar. As a result of the constitutional *cause-célèbre* (*Federation of Pakistan* v. *Maulvi Tamizuddin Khan* (P.L.D. 1955 Federal Court 240) the constitutional validity of certain statutes enacted prior to Maulvi Tamizuddin Khan's case, was called into question. Among these were included the Acts referred to in note 2 above. The terms of this Special Tribunal legislation were not such as to encourage confidence. The law of evidence was specially altered to suit the occasion and, without this alteration, it is probable that no conviction would have been secured. There

available, the correct conclusion probably is that the Prime Minister gave undue significance to an affair which, it seems, was amateurish and unreal. The people concerned seem to have been leftist in sympathy although not necessarily in class background. They may have been much concerned with what they thought to be a failure of Liaquat Ali Khan's Kashmir policy and their object was, apparently, to overthrow the existing Government and set up a kind of dictatorship, backed by the Army. Whatever it was, the conspirators were not, as far as can be judged, very efficient at conspiring, and it is perhaps just as well—if only by reason of this demonstration of incompetence—that they failed in their purpose.

The nation's first experience of the direct and constitutional use of troops to deal with civil commotion occurred in January 1953, in Karachi. During that month, student discontent backed, so it was claimed by the authorities, by foreign encouragement and support, degenerated into extensive violence. As happens on such occasions, hooligans and vagabonds, avid for plunder, joined in. Shops were looted and liquor shops smashed up. The premises of three dealers in arms and ammunition were broken into and a considerable quantity of fire-arms and ammunition stolen. The police, despite resort to rifle-fire, in which about ten people were killed, could not control the situation. A curfew was imposed, troops were called upon and deployed in the city.

Three months later, a very much more serious situation developed in Lahore based, ostensibly, on a growing antagonism towards a sect known as 'Ahmediyas' or 'Qadianis' or 'Mirzais'. This group, which has its origins in the Punjab and can now be traced in many parts of the world, although Islamic in its mode of worship and prayer, preserves a separate identity, and there are Muslims who do not admit that its members come within the fold of Islam. We are not now concerned with that controversy which was then being used as a covert means of whipping up opposition to Khwaja Nazimuddin's administration at the Centre and, in general, to create a highly-charged political atmosphere.[5]

were other equally objectionable features. After Maulvi Tamizuddin Khan's case, this Special Tribunal legislation came under very heavy criticism and was described as being against 'all the universally accepted principles of justice and equity . . .' See *D*, 10 August 1955.

[5] The story is told in Feldman, op. cit., p. 37.

Eventually the Government was compelled to act, and certain leaders of the anti-Ahmediya movement were arrested at the end of February. News of these arrests became known immediately, and almost at once trouble broke out in several Punjab cities. In Lahore, parties of men roamed the streets, forcing shopkeepers to close and intimidating others who tried to hold out. Violence developed so rapidly and in so alarming a manner during the ensuing days, that the situation passed out of police control. Members of the Ahmediya community were attacked, their property destroyed, and some lives lost. Police officers, trying to do their duty in the face of very heavy odds, were likewise butchered. The telephone system, the railways, and electrical distribution equipment were damaged and by 6 March it seemed as if Lahore might fall totally into the hands of the mob, and the Army's assistance was requested.

Martial Law was declared, military courts were set up, and the city was placed under military administration which was retained until May. Violence was firmly put down, although not without resistance on the part of the trouble-makers, and many leaders were arrested. These men, including well-known and influential figures like Maulana Maudoodi, head of the Jamaat-i-Islami, were tried before military courts and sentenced to death. However (and it is interesting to note this), no death sentence was ever carried out and the Governor-General commuted them to imprisonment for life. Having served comparatively brief periods in jail, these men were released after, in the case of Maulana Maudoodi, well-organized and determined agitation.

In the following year, trouble shifted to East Pakistan. The facts and circumstances were different, but the underlying pattern was the same, namely, the employment of divided sentiment to create a situation which would produce political advantages for interested people. In this case, the ends to be served sprang from differences between the Central Government and the East Pakistan Provincial administration led by the late A. K. M. Fazlul Haq. In the month of May violence broke out in the Adamjee Jute Mill, at Narayangunj, some four miles from Dacca. This mill, one of the biggest in the East, has two thousand looms and employs a vast army of workers. Rioting apparently occurred between Bengali workers and those who had migrated from Bihar, but, whatever its cause, the determination and the pattern show it was no sudden, unpremediated flare-up.

The loss of life, including women and children, ran into hundreds and was accompanied by appalling barbarities. The situation passed beyond police control and military assistance was called for. It was this trouble that triggered the situation, already mentioned, by which Iskander Mirza became Governor of East Pakistan, by which Section 92A was imposed, and by which, among other things, the East Pakistan Rifles, a provincial militia, were placed under the operational control of the Army.

It has already been said that these happenings in the two Provinces formed no deliberately contrived *catena*, a fact which did nothing, of course, to weaken their impact on the public mind. For, in those dreary days, it was beginning to look as if this fierce and, at the same time, unilluminating political conflict, terminating usually in civil bloodshed, was acquiring an aspect of reckless, not to say irresponsible, desperation. Pakistan was stumbling from one political crisis to the next, unable to frame its constitution, unable to rescue its fast-deteriorating economy, and unable to disembarrass itself of a Constituent Assembly which had been in office for seven years, producing nothing but profitless party squabble. Well might the Chief Justice later say: 'There is, however, one obvious lacuna in the Indian Independence Act which is otherwise a masterpiece of draughtsmanship—it contains no express provision as to what was to happen if the Constituent Assembly did not or was unable to make a constitution, or resigned *en bloc*, or converted itself into a perpetual legislature.[6]

Thus it came about that, in October 1954, the then Governor-General, Ghulam Mohamed, declared a state of emergency throughout the country, dismissed the Constituent Assembly and invited the Prime Minister (the late Mr. Mohamed Ali of Bogra) to reform his Cabinet. In this new Administration General Ayub Khan came in as Minister of Defence, and no doubt it is to this circumstance that we can trace Ghulam Mohamed's suggestions, mentioned in the broadcast of 8 October 1958, that General Ayub Khan should 'take over the country'. There are reasons to suppose that Ghulam Mohamed did make such proposals. The idea would

[6] *Federation of Pakistan and Ors.* v. *Maulvi Tamizuddin Khan* (P.L.D. Federal Court 280).

be conformable to his determined, authoritarian character and to his easily exhausted fund of patience. With this we need not now trouble, but it seems that Ghulam Mohamed pursued his ideas with characteristic determination and actually committed his proposals to paper. He persevered to the extent that General Ayub Khan, accompanied by General Musa, found it necessary not only to dissuade Ghulam Mohamed from these intentions, but to warn him that if he persisted in them, he ran the risk of being arrested. Hearing this, the late Governor-General, according to General Ayub Khan, was considerably frightened.[7]

Beyond reflecting upon the feverish state of politics in Pakistan, it does not seem that any of this is tremendously important, but it is important that the proposals were categorically declined. Indeed, on behalf of the new Government, it was made clear that, in spite of General Ayub Khan's Cabinet appointment, there was no intention of involving the Army in politics.[8] A few months later, when a new Constituent Assembly was elected, General Ayub Khan did not put forward his name and he left the Cabinet.

From all accounts available, it seems clear that Ghulam Mohamed's plan to dismiss the Constituent Assembly once and for all and to start again, was worked out with General Ayub's prior knowledge.[9] It is, moreover, probable that without the assurance of the Army's support, Ghulam Mohamed might have hesitated. The presence of General Ayub in the Cabinet was intimation enough that this was no time for nonsense. But, for our present purpose, the true importance lies in the closeness of this brief period of contact between politics at Cabinet level and the Army High Command. Callard in 1957, three years later, wrote: 'The civil service and the Army have shown no desire to back any potential dictator.'[10] This was undoubtedly true, but ideas sometimes form and converge subconsciously, and who knows what impressions were registering themselves in the mind of General Ayub Khan during those few months of 1954 and 1955 when, as Minister of Defence, he was attending Cabinet meetings?

Even so, in 1955, this period of association came to an end.

[7] See President Ayub Khan's statement in London. *D*, 4 May 1960.
[8] The *Daily Telegraph*, London, 12 November 1954.
[9] Callard, op. cit., p. 40.   [10] ibid., p. 328.

General Ayub Khan relinquished Cabinet office and continued as Commander-in-Chief. The new Constituent Assembly was formed and proceeded with the agonized manoeuvres that produced the Constitution of 1956. Except for one curious incident which preceded the Martial Law declaration by only a day or so, the Army was not called upon again until the final breakdown.

This incident, which does not fit exactly into the pattern we are now discussing, but which throws its own light on the general state of affairs, was an attempt by the Khan of Kalat to break away from the Federation of Pakistan. Along with the three other States of Kharan, Mekran, and Lasbela, he had acceded in March 1948, after these matters had been discussed at a *durbar*, held at Sibi, in the preceding month, at which Quaid-i-Azam Mohamed Ali Jinnah was himself present. There is some ground for thinking there was reluctance on the part of these States to accede—they were among the last to do so—and that they were influenced in this by the Khan of Kalat.

At all events, Instruments of Accession were executed and accepted and, three years later, the four States were brought together into a Baluchistan States Union of which the Khan of Kalat became the Khan-i-Azam.[11] As time passed, however, he showed himself increasingly dissatisfied and evidence accumulated that he was seeking to promote and foster a sense of local patriotism, separatist in tendency. He complained that in the Sibi negotiations of 1948 he had been misled and placed under unfair pressures.

In September 1958 he was invited to Karachi to discuss with the President the reasons for his discontent, but the invitation was declined. Instead, in his own territory, the Khan lowered the Pakistan flag, raised his personal standard, and offered armed defiance. Once again, it was necessary to have recourse to the services of the Army. A brief action ensued, the Khan surrendered and was hurried away to confinement elsewhere.

What could have persuaded this ruler to challenge the obviously superior strength of the Pakistan Government has never adequately been explained, and the breach has since been healed.[12] It is at least

[11] The Khan of Kalat is, in fact, of Brahui stock.
[12] In November 1962 all differences were composed and the Khan was restored to his former status and powers.

possible that, as things stood in Pakistan in those days, he was tempted into the belief that the time had come when he might successfully take the risk. So far as the Pakistan Army was concerned, the incident could only serve as fresh proof of a grievously disrupted nation and of crumbling authority throughout the land.

IV

Economic Reforms

IN the two preceding chapters, we have glanced at the circumstances which can be said to have brought about that degree of exasperation which precipitated the events of ctober 1958. We are in a position now to resume the thread of thac narrative which began in the first chapter.

Upon the departure of Iskander Mirza, there was no longer room for uncertainty as to with whom power and the last word lay, nor as to the retention of Martial Law for whatever period was deemed necessary to fulfil the aims and purposes of the new régime. With the new President and his three military colleagues forming the kernel of the administration, there was no imminent risk of further change at the top and, for better or for worse, the citizen knew exactly where he stood.

He knew that he was expected to collaborate unstintingly with a government confessedly authoritarian, claiming to derive its sanction from the necessities of a desperate situation and promising, unequivocally, to justify itself by a resolute purification of public life, by a programme of indispensable reforms, and by the adoption of a fresh constitution which would adequately and appropriately satisfy the citizen's right to speak and participate in his country's affairs. He had already seen evidence that the attack on national problems would be searching and broad-based, embracing not only the arrest and punishment of individuals, but also the framing and application of new policies on several fronts. It also seemed evident that the initial tendency was to put prior emphasis on economic subjects[1] and, following this line of approach, it is to these that we should look first.

Since 1952 Pakistan's economy had stumbled through recurrent crises springing, fundamentally, from an inability to solve the agrarian problem; from a chronic shortage of foreign exchange; from a widely ranging economic imbalance, and from a constant

[1] See the President's statement made on 28 October 1958.

inflationary tendency that was, seemingly, beyond control notwithstanding a generally high order of financial administrators. It need scarcely be added that the situation was aggravated by selfish manipulations, both industrial and commercial, and largely associated with politics and politicians; the illegal retention of foreign exchange earnings abroad and falsified tax returns.[2] With these primary and secondary factors appeared all the subsidiary consequences—high prices, black-marketing, smuggling, hoarding, trafficking in import licences, permits, and similar sources of privileged profit. In addition, there was the foisting of imitation and spurious goods upon a helpless public, with special reference to the odious crime of food adulteration.

I have already mentioned that within a few days of the declaration of Martial Law, the public enjoyed a somewhat anarchic measure of relief by *ad hoc* reductions in the prices of consumer goods and this was so eagerly grasped that almost at once it became necessary to impose restraint by a rough and ready system of rationing. In a broadcast speech made on 1 November, the President announced the introduction of Martial Law Regulations[3] to control the prices of certain categories of imported goods, goods manufactured in Pakistan, and imported foodgrains. Control of locally produced foodstuffs was left to the provincial or other local authorities, to be imposed as they thought fit in the light of the local situation.

The range of commodities brought within Martial Law control directly revealed those avenues through which the man-in-the-street had been subjected to the heaviest economic pressures. Cloth, foodgrains, cooking media, sugar, construction materials (steel and cement), cigarettes, tea, school textbooks, spices, typewriters, machinery spare parts, crockery, glassware—these necessary articles, in constant use or consumption, along with others, were regulated as to price, and the margin which the retailer could claim for himself was also fixed. There was no attempt, however, at fixing the price of everything for, the President said, it was the firm belief of his Government that traders themselves would only charge fair prices. This measure of confidence may sound naive, but it was not without foundation for in those days manufacturers

---

[2] The excessive cost of national defence was also an important factor, but this did not lie within the nation's sole control.
[3] MLR No. 42.

and dealers were only too anxious to display their bona fides. Indeed, notices were exhibited everywhere to the effect that if, by some unhappy inadvertence, the prices charged turned out to be incorrect (i.e. in excess of the limits envisaged by the Martial Law Regulations) the customer was particularly requested to bring it to the notice of the shopkeeper immediately, when all would be put right to the satisfaction of everyone. Those days, when traders were leaning over backwards in order that it should not even appear that they were charging too much, constituted a noteworthy and refreshing change.

Perhaps they should not be jeered at for this. Martial Law Regulations were often drafted in a hurry and not always with absolute felicity.[4] Furthermore, the President's statement contained a note of grim humour. He said that Martial Law Regulations would not be applied retrospectively. 'I want to give them a categorical assurance that Martial Law Regulations will apply only to offences, if any, committed after Martial Law comes into force. For earlier offences, the laws then prevailing would naturally be applicable.' It was doubtless a comfort to many to be told that the long arm of Martial Law would not reach into the past, but under its impulse the parallel system, administered by the civil courts, might operate a good deal more effectively than had hitherto been the case. The continual news of arrest for infractions of the law dealing with price control, hoarding, and similar offences, doubtless justified these apprehensions.

At the same time a ban was placed on the buying and selling of import licences,[5] and industrial importers of specified goods were required to declare their stocks to the authorities. On the assumption that the method specified in Martial Law Regulation No. 42, for the control of prices of imported goods, would be effective, there could be little room for profit in irregular dealing in import licences and it was forbidden. Underlying this prohibition was the attitude of the new administration which was adverse to the practice of trafficking in licences and permits, usually bad in itself, and,

---

[4] MLR No. 42, as re-drafted, contained a provision which read: 'Spare parts . . . shall not be sold at a price higher than the manufacturers' listed retail price or *seventy-five per cent of the landed cost* whichever is lower.' [Author's italics.]

[5] *Gazette of Pakistan (Extraordinary)*, 3 November 1958, revised by *Gazette of Pakistan (Extraordinary)*, 17 February 1959, so as to exclude from these restrictions import licences granted under the Export Bonus Scheme.

in any case, closely associated in the public mind with political corruption. A man received a licence to import this, or a permit to do that, argued the people, as a reward for political attachment, not because he was established in this business or that industry, or even because he wanted to be. The privilege was simply farmed for cash, as was the intention, and as always the consumer paid in the long run. It was not suggested that genuine commercial men and industrialists did not receive a share of what was going, but whether they did and in what proportion is not now the point. The objection was to the use of these things as political spoils and even as political weapons which was unfair, injurious to the economy and, of course, a great spur to corruption.

Nevertheless, the facts of economic life in Pakistan could not be disguised. There was a shortage of foreign exchange[6] and, consequently, a shortage of many things the country needed and could not produce for itself. In such circumstances, human nature being what it is, there is always someone prepared to pay a little more for something he needs, or thinks he needs, but which is not readily available. In times of scarcity the menace of the black market is always present, and countries claiming to be better organized than Pakistan have not escaped it.

It was against this background that, in January 1959, a decision was taken to introduce an Export Bonus Scheme which, in brief stated that an exporter of Pakistani produce would receive a voucher entitling him to an import licence equivalent in value to a certain percentage of the total value of the goods exported. The range of products to which the scheme applied, and the percentages allowable, could be, and from time to time were, varied. By this Scheme, the Government expected to apply stimulus to the export trade and, at the same time, prevent surreptitious markets in imported goods. The vouchers were freely marketable, even at a premium, and these premia have since ranged from between eighty to one hundred and seventy per cent of the face value of the

---

[6] In the period 1949–63 the lowest level at which the State Bank of Pakistan's gold, dollar, and sterling reserves have stood was in September 1954, when they amounted to 5,606 lakhs of rupees (£42,045,000 or US$117,726,000). In September 1958, the figure was 7,262 lakhs (£54,465,000 or US$152,502,000). The average for the whole period of fourteen years is in the order of 10,000 lakhs (£75,000,000 or US$210,000,000). See the Report on Currency and Finance, 1962–63, State Bank of Pakistan, p. 222.

voucher. The Scheme operated through existing banking institutions and its mechanics were simple and speedy.

The merits of the Export Bonus Scheme have been, and doubtless will continue long to be, much debated. Its advantages were the obvious and prompt stimulus to export trade and to those forms of raw material production and industry upon which that trade was substantially based. By facilitating the range of goods that could be imported, there was a tendency towards eliminating black markets as such, although so long as bonus vouchers were selling at a premium, prices could not come down. Moreover, the Government could effectively control those prices by the simple expedient of extending or narrowing the operation of the Scheme by varying, as it willed, the range of products to which it applied (both for export and import) and the percentages to be earned in terms of bonus vouchers. The range of importable goods and/or the percentage to be earned were the two factors that influenced the premium at which the bonus vouchers could be disposed of and which influenced the number of importers who could enter the bonus voucher market. This was immediately reflected in the prices which a consumer had to pay and applied with particular force to luxury items and imported preserved foodstuffs.

The objections to the Scheme were that it constituted a tacit admission of a decline in the true value of the Pakistani rupee. Secondly, the benefit of improved export trade did not reach everyone alike since the poor could not afford to pay the high prices at which goods, imported under the Scheme, were marketable in the country and, in any case, the poor were not interested in luxury goods and preserved foodstuffs. Thirdly, essential stores, which were required by agriculture and industry and imported under this Scheme, had necessarily to be purchased at high prices and this constituted an additional burden in terms of production cost. Fourthly, irrespective of whether goods were imported under normal commercial or industrial licences (for which no premium was charged or could be paid) or under bonus voucher licences, everything tended to be priced as if it had been imported under the bonus voucher Scheme.[7]

The force of these objections cannot be disputed, but on balance

[7] The current phrase was: 'Everything is on bonus vouchers.' An attempt was made to correct this in the 1964 Budget. See the Finance Minister's Budget speech dated 12 June 1964.

the Scheme has evidently justified itself because the alternatives would have been far more injurious, even to the poorer classes. The Export Bonus Scheme must be seen for what it is—an expedient adopted to overcome the problems which arise when a country is an inadequate producer. It is obvious that if Pakistan were producing wealth, either in raw materials or in manufactured goods, or in both, sufficient for its reasonable needs, recourse to such measures would not be necessary. The Export Bonus Scheme was one of the earliest and most important economic measures instituted by the new administration and was, in all probability, the most effective answer to the only two questions that needed answering: What is the least troublesome expedient and, very much more important, how should the circumstances that render such expedients necessary be overcome?

Meanwhile, at a somewhat lower level of endeavour, strenuous cleaning-up measures designed to combat smuggling and unearth economic irregularities continued, sometimes with remarkable results. In October, the Karachi offices of twenty-two wool exporters were sealed, pending investigation into alleged foreign exchange offences. In Lahore, the account books of ten prominent firms,[8] along with documents seized from the houses of the proprietors, were taken into custody for the purpose of inquiring into alleged black-marketing, profiteering, and smuggling. In November, no less than Rs.60 lakhs worth of contraband gold was dredged, in one operation, from the seabed in Karachi.[9] Just how the authorities came suddenly to know the gold was lying there and just how they knew where to dredge are interesting topics. The indications are that not only was the 'social vermin'[10] dashing for cover, but that it was squealing at the same time. It is not difficult to imagine just how many secret understandings and sworn promises were shattered in those unexpected days.

Simultaneous with the measures of price control, Martial Law Regulations[11] were issued with the object of gathering in taxes on undisclosed income and foreign exchange balances irregularly held abroad. Under these new regulations it was made possible for

[8] The proprietorship of five of them was, in fact, in one set of hands.
[9] *D*, 4 November 1958. The value equals £450,000 or US$1,260,000.
[10] General Ayub Khan's broadcast, 8 October 1958. Altogether two tons' weight of smuggled gold was recovered at this time.
[11] MLR 43, 44, and 45 *Gazette of Pakistan* (*Extraordinary*) 4 November 1958. See also Central Board of Revenue Instructions dated 20 December 1958.

anyone who, for the income year 1953–54 and any subsequent years, had filed returns which he had reason to believe were incorrect (a euphemism for understated income) could, before 31 December 1958, file revised returns showing his true income and no questions would be asked. He could even, if he wished, go back before the income year 1953–54 and, if he was one of those blithe optimists who had never filed a return of income at all, this was the opportunity to rectify that omission.

To guard against revised returns which might be termed 'halfhearted', Martial Law Regulation No. 44 prescribed penalities for making false returns under various existing taxation acts, for failure to produce accounting records, and for non-payment of taxes within a specified time.

Having complied with all these invitations, the delinquent could then compound with the Government by paying, at the same time, a sum equal to thirty-one per cent of the total excess disclosed. If payment was not made promptly, but within thirty days of disclosure, the compounded rate would be thirty-three per cent. It was made very clear that no extension of time would be granted, and Regulation No. 44 was, by itself, earnest of the Government's intentions.

Martial Law Regulation No. 45 enabled the owner of foreign exchange irregularly held abroad to surrender these balances without the risk of punishment, receiving in return Pakistani rupees at the official rate of exchange. Nor did he have to pay tax on the amounts surrendered, provided all this was done by 1 December 1958. Here, too, there was a promise of no further inquiries so long as there was prompt and full compliance.

These regulations were received by the business community with sentiments of doubt and hesitation. Certain questions came naturally to mind. Would the Government keep its promise not to look behind the revised returns? Would the Government keep its promise not to reopen these matters at some future date? What was the assurance that, having once disclosed these illegally retained earnings and paid the tax, there would not be further exactions on some other ground? After all, it was of the essence of the new administration that it could make whatever laws it thought necessary in the national interest, with no one to question or argue. In the case of some business groups the sums were very large indeed and might give rise to all sorts of probing questions. It was one thing to have the Martial Law authorities coming round of their own volition to impound books and papers for examination and inquiry. It was quite another to step forward, like artless school-boys, and confess to having understated income for the purpose of evading tax. Businessmen do not, on the whole, believe in the protective virtues of innocence, but that, of course, may be because they do not have any.

At all events, with nothing actually stated, it became evident that the attitude towards these Regulations, particularly that relating to taxation, was mixed and in business circles much private and anxious discussion was going on, principally with reference to disclosure of income and hidden wealth; so much so, indeed, that the possibility of a failure of these Regulations could not be ignored and a failure would have been particularly damaging for two important reasons. It would defeat the prior purpose which was to gather up illicitly held and much needed foreign exchange; to recover taxes on earnings which had not been disclosed; and to bring back into circulation very large sums earned in various reprehensible ways and retained in cash variously hidden. Secondly, and of much more importance, failure would damage the moral ascendancy which the new administration had so effectively secured.[12]

Thus it was that early in December four officials of leading commercial organizations were arrested and lodged in Karachi jail. It appeared that the authorities had come into possession of evidence that these men,[13] along with other commercial and industrial people, were conspiring to defeat the purposes of the Government by means of false returns of undisclosed income, by false statements as to foreign exchange balances held abroad, and by persuading indigenous industry to adopt a 'go-slow' policy with the object of forcing the Government to give way on its system of price control.[14] They were arrested under Martial Law Regulations Nos. 20, 43, and 45, but no charges were preferred against

---

[12] See *The Times of India*, Bombay, 2 January 1959. This newspaper's reporting on Pakistan is not always free of bias.

[13] They were: M. A. Rangoonwala, Chairman, Federation of Chambers of Commerce and Industry; J. S. Lobo, Secretary, Karachi Chamber of Commerce and Industry; Ahmed A. Karim; A. K. Sumar, Secretary, Pakistan Merchants' Association.

[14] *MN*, 16 December 1958. A. K. Sumar was arrested about a week after the others.

them, nor did they ever stand trial and the evidence, said to be in the Government's possession, was never made public. Some weeks after the closing date by which the revised returns were to be submitted, they were released by what was described as 'a gesture of goodwill'.

It was all very arbitrary although, in other times and at other places, it may be supposed they might have fared a good deal worse. There are grounds for thinking that some highly injudicious correspondence had been going on, among commercial and trade associations, discussing the attitude to be adopted towards these somewhat alarming Regulations which called peremptorily for disclosure of excess income and foreign exchange balances. As could have been foreseen by people far less shrewd than these commercial gentlemen, copies of the correspondence immediately found their way into official hands. Whatever may have been the true purpose of their clumsy proceedings, they certainly provided the authorities with an instrument for reminding the business community that no nonsense would be tolerated and, as a result, none was attempted, so far as is known.

The Government collected a sum of Rs.24 crores[15] by way of taxes on excess income, and hidden wealth which amounted to Rs.134 crores.[16] These sums may not seem large by comparison with the sums that circulate in more prosperous countries, but in the context of Pakistan's economy they were significant. At that time, the total money supply was in the order of Rs.500 crores[17] of which about Rs.350 crores represented the note circulation. Thus if, as was probable, a substantial part of the illegally retained wealth was concealed in the form of currency notes, this by itself was injurious, involving an artificial contraction in money supply which the authorities could not run the risk of attempting to correct by the issue of further notes.

Thus not only did a substantial sum of money accrue to the public treasury, but the release of hidden currency provided a welcome easing of pressure. It was good on several grounds that this illicitly accumulated wealth should come to light, even if its owners were fortunate in the facility with which they escaped the consequences of past misconduct. As we shall shortly see, they

[15] £18,000,000 or US$50,400,000.
[16] £100,500,000 or US$281,400,000.
[17] £375,000,000 or US$1,050,000,000.

were fortunate, too, in the future consequences, but it was undoubtedly better for the country as a whole that the shady business should be swept away with the hope that it would not recur, or, if this were unduly optimistic, at least not in the same magnitude. The national reserves were augmented by a sum of Rs.44,000,000[18] in the form of surrendered foreign exchange, and the Finance Minister was right in saying that none of these swift and necessary financial disciplines would have been possible without Martial Law.[19].

It should also be added that the promises given by the Government have been reasonably well honoured. There has been a tendency on the part of the Income Tax Department to ask taxpayers if any declaration was made under these Regulations, but it cannot be said that even this comparatively harmless piece of curiosity has been pressed to any serious disadvantage or embarrassment.

Such, then, were the immediate results. The ultimate consequences were more significant and enduring. They endure to this day and, so far as can be foreseen, will continue to do so. This concealed wealth, now effectively bleached so that it need no longer be kept in secret hoards of 'black' money, was in the hands of a comparatively small number of business people and even then, was by no means evenly divided. In a few cases, the individual sums involved were enormous and, although details have not been published, it seems possible that among a dozen or so of the biggest cases possibly Rs.100 crores[20] were concentrated out of which 31 crores were paid as compounded tax. Thus a very small group of business families had at their disposal large sums of freely usable money, henceforward to be treated as capital, with which they could confidently enter new markets and fresh business.

In Pakistan, as in India, banking, industry, and commerce have tended to be monopolized by certain communities of people and it was naturally into the hands of the same people that these

[18] £3,300,000 or US$9,240,000. This figure was given by the Finance Minister, see *D*, 22 April 1962. An official publication, *Two Years*, issued by the Department of Films and Publications, Government of Pakistan, 1961, gives a figure of Rs.82.2 crores which is nearly double.

[19] *D*, 22 April 1962.

[20] £75,000,000 or US$210,000,000. This suggestion is founded upon hearsay and some general knowledge of the kind of wealth that is in the hands of a few business families in Pakistan.

windfalls—if they can be so described—promptly fell. It is for this very reason that the oligarchy of wealth in Pakistan has become stronger and more firmly entrenched so that, today, banking (excluding the foreign banks), insurance, industry, and a very large part of the country's commercial activity are the near monopoly of a restricted group.[21] It is evident, from repeated official statements, that the Government became aware of this development and many assurances were given that the smaller man would not be crushed, that steps would be taken to prevent the growth of cartels,[22] and that other communities within the nation would not be denied the opportunity of economic advancement.

On these assurances only two comments are possible. Firstly, the Government has allowed every encouragement to leading capitalists with the very clear object of stimulating and hastening the growth of local banking, insurance, shipowning, and industry. Considering the initial hesitation with which capitalists, both large and small, undertook such investments, it is not surprising that the Government is unwilling to blight this change of heart. From all that we have so far seen, it may well be that these men, at any rate the more prosperous among them, may not, *ex hypothesi*, be among the most scrupulous but, in their own way, they are certainly among the most vigorous and able, and their wealth and ability have been harnessed to promote activity, particularly in those fields of economic endeavour where Pakistan has been lagging.

Secondly, while official assurances concerning the future of the smaller man in commerce and industry may be sincere, the question whether they can be made meaningful is something quite separate. All experience shows that the gravitational attraction of money in mass brings constant accretions to the great financial monoliths and leads to the elimination or absorption of smaller businesses. It is true that measures such as the formation of a National Investment Trust make it possible for the middle-class investor to associate himself with capitalist enterprise and, in Pakistan, this method has been adopted. But such institutions are,

[21] On this subject, see article entitled 'The Development of Entrepreneurship in Pakistan' by Dr. Gustav F. Papanek, Chamber of Commerce and Industry, *Karachi Trade Journal*, June–July 1964.

[22] *D*, 8 August 1963. See also Finance Minister's Budget speech in *D*, 15 June 1965, but the approach to the problem has so far borne the marks of extreme caution.

themselves, simply an extension of the financial grasp wielded by the principal capitalists and much more important are the undoubted signs of a managerial revolution overtaking industry in Pakistan. Direct personal control is diminishing simply because one man and his family possess neither the time nor the knowledge to manage and administer a number of large and diverse enterprises. This circumstance provides fresh and remunerative opportunities for the educated middle-class.[23]

The main purpose of this chapter was to discuss those measures which the new administration adopted to assist the poor and regularize an unbalanced and strained financial situation. But, as part of its first year's work, it proceeded to set up commissions to investigate Pakistan's commercial maritime affairs, the textile industry, the jute industry, and company law. It also published the objectives of the Second Five Year Plan. To these matters we shall in due course proceed. Meanwhile, a more proximate reform must be considered.

[23] For the appearance, in Pakistan, of the 'organization-man', see Papanek, op. cit.

V

Land Reforms and Agriculture

THE appointment of a Land Reforms Commission[1] was one of the very earliest measures adopted by the new administration. It was an indication, not only of the importance attached to the necessity for agrarian reform, but also of the impact of agriculture on the national economy. Just as noteworthy was the speed with which the recommendations of the Commission were implemented.

In January 1959 the Commission completed its labours, submitting a Report which was unanimous except in one particular. This dealt with an important point relating to the maximum area of land which it should be permissible for an individual to retain and own. Two members took the view that, on this issue, the recommendations of the Commission were unduly liberal. However, the majority opinion prevailed and four days after the Report was submitted, the President's Cabinet issued orders to give effect to the measures proposed.

In its terms of reference, the Commission was asked 'to consider problems relating to the ownership and tenancy of agricultural land and to recommend measures for ensuring better production and social justice as well as security of tenure for those engaged in cultivation'. Although it was not made specifically clear at the time of appointment, the work of the Commission related solely to those problems as they existed in West Pakistan and there is nothing in the Commission's Report which touches on the eastern Province at all.

The reasons for this are solid enough. Circumstances relating to land tenure in each of the Provinces were entirely distinct, springing from the fact that Bengal had been under British administration from the time of Lord Clive, some two hundred years before. During the Governor-Generalship of Lord Cornwallis, just before the close of the eighteenth century, the revenue terms on which

[1] On 31 October 1958.

land was settled in the hands of Bengal landlords were fixed, once and for all, by what was called the 'Permanent Settlement'. This gave rise to a situation vastly different from that prevailing in West Pakistan whose territories did not come under British rule until the middle of the nineteenth century and no permanent settlement had ever been attempted there.

Furthermore, the East Pakistan Provincial Government had, some years earlier, instituted its own reform of land tenure in the Province by the East Bengal Estate Acquisition and Tenancy Act of 1950. The principal object of this Act was to extinguish by payment of compensation, all the subinfeudations and rent-receiving interests that had come into existence over the years between the actual cultivator and the landlords with whom the Permanent Settlement had first been effected. These intermediary interests were the inevitable result of a permanent revenue settlement and the decline in the value of money over a period of two centuries and they had created immense complications. The Act also provided a ceiling on holdings in certain circumstances and allowed for the acquisition, by the State, of certain categories of non-retainable lands. In 1956, the East Pakistan Government acquired all intermediary rights, but otherwise the implementation of the Act was very slow and in December 1958 the new administration appointed a Land Revenue Commission to analyse the difficulties, and its Report was submitted in July 1959. It was evident that a great deal of administrative work was needed in order to bring the land revenue records up to date and so achieve, throughout the Province, uniform application of the Act and the recommendations of the Land Revenue Commission. But, so far as any kind of land reform in East Pakistan is concerned, the essence of the matter lies in the fantastic pressure of population on the soil, which exceeds 900 persons per square mile.

However, President Ayub Khan's land reforms concerned only the Province of West Pakistan and they provided that no individual could own more than 500 acres of irrigated land, or 1,000 acres of non-irrigated land plus, where necessary, any additional area as might be necessary to give the equivalent of 36,000 produce index units.[2] In addition, he could also retain 150 acres of

[2] A method of assessing the productivity or value of land whose fertility naturally varied in different parts of the Province. The Land Reforms Commission produced a schedule giving produce indices for each type of soil in each land revenue assessment circle.

orchard land and, in certain circumstances, could also make gifts of land to members of his family and to female dependents, but the total of these gifts could not exceed the equivalent of 18,000 produce index units. In effect, a single individual, along with members of his family, could retain a maximum area of about 900 acres of irrigated land, the precise area depending on the produce index value of the soil. Land in excess was to be surrendered to the Government in return for compensation in the shape of the Government of Pakistan redeemable bonds bearing interest at four per cent. The actual amount of compensation paid was also dependent upon the produce index value of the soil calculated on the published scales.

Land held by way of *jagir* (signifying land whose income was granted by the State to some beneficiary called a *jagirdar*) or on which the land revenue was assigned to some beneficiary, was to be resumed by the Government without compensation.[3] To the limitation on holdings, there were exceptions in favour of recognized stud farms, educational institutions, and certain types of charitable trust or land whose income was wholly devoted to religious, educational, or charitable purposes.[4]

The Commission's proposals included recommendations for the further protection of tenants, the enhancement of their security of tenure, the abolition of intermediary interests, and the compulsory consolidation of fragmented holdings.[5] With these principal measures of reform, there were subsidiary proposals to take care of consequential effects upon such matters as certain types of family trust, alienation, impartibility and so on. The Report also touched on the old and vexed question of occupancy tenants—a category that could not be evicted from their land and yet did not own it—but legislation already existed by which occupancy tenants could become full owners of the soil and therefore the Martial Law Regulations which gave legal force to the recommendations made no reference to this subject.

[3] An exception was made in favour of *jagirdars* having *mukkadhami* rights. The amount involved was trifling.

[4] The Roman Catholic Diocese of Lahore was permitted to retain about 700 acres of land with an income of Rs.3 lakhs (£22,500 or US$63,000). The Ahmadiya Anjuman-i-Ishaat-i-Islam was permitted to retain 3,200 acres with an income of approximately Rs.7 lakhs (£52,500 or US$147,000). *D*, 25 June 1959.

[5] The law on the subject was later tightened by the West Pakistan Consolidation of Holdings Ordinance, 1960.

No time was lost in publishing these Regulations[6] and a notification appeared early in February 1959. By means of Press statements, a broadcast explanation by the Governor of West Pakistan, and a further address, in June 1959, by the Central Government Minister of Commerce,[7] the public was made more familiar with the new administration's purpose and intentions. The Regulation provided for a West Pakistan Land Commission, consisting of the Governor of the Province and five others whom he was to appoint, and their task was to see the reforms put into effect. As a result, some 2,547,000 acres were surrendered by 902 landowners[8] (of whom 147 were *jagirdars* and therefore not strictly the owners of the soil) involving an amount of Rs.75,000,000[9] by way of compensation in four per cent redeemable bonds.

No doubt original public anticipations considerably exceeded these figures. According to Mushtaq Ahmed,[10] it was estimated that 7,500,000 acres would become available for redistribution and the number of landlords surrendering land was freely spoken of as being in the order of 5,000. However, the figures, as we have seen, were very much less and, of the land actually resumed under the Reforms, rather less than half had been redistributed by March 1964[11] so that, all things considered, it cannot be said that the West Pakistan land reforms achieved anything astronomical. Bearing in mind that the total cultivable area in the Province is estimated to be in the order of 46,000,000 acres, of which perhaps 35,000,000 are sown at any one time, the area of surrendered land was approximately five per cent of the total cultivable area. If we assume redistribution on the basis of a subsistence holding of 12·5 acres,[12] then, out of a total agricultural labour force of 7,500,000, 204,000 agriculturalists who were landless before could be re-settled with a holding of their own afterwards. But, as it happens, redistribution was not undertaken on that basis. The resumed land was first offered for sale to the tenants cultivating it at the time of surrender and then, if they did not wish to buy, to other desiring

[6] MLR No. 64 (later amended) *Gazette of Pakistan (Extraordinary)*, 3 March 1959.
[7] Mr. Zulfikar Ali Bhutto. He, with other members of the Bhutto family, surrendered considerable areas in the former Sind Province.
[8] *ES*, p. 33. The proportions of irrigated and non-irrigated land are not stated.
[9] £5,625,000 or US$15,750,000.   [10] Mushtaq Ahmed, op. cit., p. 218.
[11] *ES*, p. 33.   [12] MLR No. 64 I (11).

purchasers. The sale-money, realized by instalments, was to be utilized for the redemption of the compensation bonds. For these reasons, therefore, it is difficult to trace whether the landless peasantry has received any conspicuous benefit by the change.

In West Pakistan, the average farm is some ten acres in extent[13] so that the 755 proprietory landowners, retaining, in some cases, as much as 900 acres of irrigated and orchard land, were still considerable magnates for along with their landed income they enjoyed interest on their compensation bonds. (Doubtless, retention of their former broad acres would have been preferred.) Still, by the same token, their influence was considerably weakened. The average area surrendered by each of these landowners according to the figures given in the *Economic Survey* already quoted, was in the order of 2,500 acres, but the individual cases varied greatly. The Nawab of Hoti was understood to have surrendered some 8,000 acres and Colonel Amir Khan, a former minister in the West Pakistan Provincial Government, surrendered about 13,500 acres. In the Multan District, three members of the Daultana family surrendered about 16,000 acres, but the total area given up in that District by some thirty-seven landlords, was estimated to be 40,500 acres. In Hazara District, 154 landlords surrendered 68,000 acres (after distributing 21,000 acres to female dependents as permitted by the reforms).[14] Thus, from the political point of view, it seems that within this small band of surrendering landlords and *jagirdars* there was a tiny nucleus of very large proprietors who could, and did, exercise immense influence in the Province and who could, and probably did, determine to a large extent who should enter the National and Provincial Assemblies so far as concerned the rural areas of West Pakistan. The political implications were weighty and, although by no means extinguished as a class, the great landed magnates no longer represented the same vast and sometimes inert agglomeration of power.

In its Report, the Commission was careful to say that it had not been asked to suggest measures whose purpose was the breaking-up of oligarchy rooted in large estates, but it admitted that its proposals, if adopted, would tend towards that result.[15] No one, after all, had ever doubted that in the long run the old,

[13] *ES*, p. 29.   [14] *D*, 25 June 1959.
[15] Land Commission Report, p. 19.

landed interests in West Pakistan had been able to control the Provincial Assembly and exert immense influence in the national chamber. We have already noticed that out of eighty seats in the National Assembly, no less than twenty-eight were occupied by West Pakistan's landlords or their representatives. To these people, Callard's observation was particularly relevant.[16] He wrote: 'In Pakistan, politics is made up of a large number of leading persons who, with their political dependents, form loose agreements to achieve power and maintain it. Those who lack fixed ideas but who control legislatures, money or influence have tended to prosper in political life.' It was precisely this kind of influence that the great landlords were able to exercise and it was commonly understood and agreed that all of them 'controlled' seats in the provincial legislature, that is to say, by virtue of influence among the tenantry and agricultural workers, a landlord could ensure his own election (if he desired it) and that of his nominee in those districts where he owned substantial property.

Under the reforms, alienations of land made after 7 October 1958 were deemed ineffective. Attempts at forestalling the recommendations of the Commission were, to this extent therefore, nullified, but it is probable that some time before the Commission was appointed, and certainly before the crucial date of 7 October, a number of landowners had effected some redistribution of their property inside the family. Indeed, the Report of the Commission explicitly recognized this[17] and even suggested the reasons which, apart from an intelligent anticipation of reforms leading to a limitation on land-holdings, had also to do with avoidance of taxation.

Such an intelligent anticipation should not have caused surprise. The possibility of a limitation on land-holdings was, after all, no new thing. It had been talked about often enough by reformers, even if in the abstract, and, as far back as 1949, the Muslim League had set up its own Inquiry Committee and had suggested measures a good deal more strenuous than those of the 1958 Commission.[18] There had, furthermore, been sporadic attempts by provincial legislatures before the administrative consolidation of West Pakistan, but those measures were palliative rather than

[16] Callard, op. cit., p. 67.   [17] Land Commission Report, p. 36.
[18] See also views on land reforms expressed in the *Report on the First Five Year Plan*, Government of Pakistan, Karachi, 1958, p. 318.

penetrating and no marked change was ever experienced. It was, indeed, for the somewhat insecure reason that certain owners had made these anticipatory gifts of land within their families, that others were permitted, by the recommendations of the Reforms Commission (albeit with one dissenting voice among its members), to do so to an extent of the equivalent of 12,000 produce index units or about 165 acres.

Granting the principle of private ownership in land, it would be wrong to assume that agrarian reform is primarily, or even mainly, a matter of taking from the rich to give to the poor. This, doubtless, was the most spectacular aspect of the subject, but the problems of tenancy and the ultimate political outcome were equally important. Moreover, in the last analysis, any type of reform would lose most of its meaning if it did not lead to greater efficiency in the industry and to the greater production of of food and cash crops. To this point I shall return.

From the point of view of the new administration, the fact that land *was* being taken from the great landed magnates and was being made available to its cultivators and to others was itself important, since it lent much support to the claim that the interests of the impoverished tenants and landless cultivators were at last receiving the attention they had so long merited. These changes, whatever the limitations on their scope, were formidable proof of the authority that the new administration wielded. It is unthinkable that within a space of three months any previous government, even that of Liaquat Ali Khan, could have accomplished the surrender, virtually without argument, of 2,500,000 acres in return for four per cent bonds, redeemable by instalments. Here was evidence indeed of the new determination and of the strength which sustained the Martial Law government, and by it the political hegemony of the great Pakistan landowners, exercised for so many years, was rudely shaken, although not broken up.

It is true that their influence was curtailed and not destroyed.[19] Apart from the fact that most of them belong to family groups which, between them, still form substantial proprietors, long-standing attachments do not dissolve instantly and those of the

---

[19] It is noteworthy that, in his speech at Lyallpur on 12 October 1959, President Ayub Khan referred to '*rationalization* of big land holdings'. (Author's italics). Again, in London five years later he said: 'We did not want punitive land reforms . . .' *D*, 9 July 1964.

old, landed families, who still wished to take part in national affairs, continued to have favourable prospects when the time should come. In a country whose principal business is agriculture, it is perhaps well that this should be so. At the same time, it is in the long run no disadvantage to the land-owning class that, as time passes, its prospects in political life should depend more and more upon usefulness, ability, and force of character, and less and less upon the mere power to put unseen, but none the less tangible, pressures upon a subservient tenantry. The banking and industrial dynasts, whose influence has been enlarged for reasons already mentioned, are now beginning to enter politics and unless the traditional leaders of the rural masses undergo a change of heart, we may fully expect to witness that same nineteenth-century process by which the landed aristocracy of the United Kingdom was swept into political impotence by the rising *bourgeoisie* of the banking, industrial, and commercial classes.

The reforms, as I have said, did not end with the redistribution of land and, had they done so, they would have been far from sufficient. The protection given to tenants and the promotion of the interests of the actual cultivator were just as important. This becomes very much clearer when we remember that of the total farm area in West Pakistan, fifty-one per cent is tenant-operated and, of that area, nearly nine-tenths is cultivated on a share-cropping basis.[20] The whole tendency of the reforms is, therefore, directed to the material advantage of the small farmer, the tenant-farmer, and the agricultural worker who possess a mere fragment of land. The social consequences of these changes are likely, as time proceeds, to make themselves more tangibly felt, especially with the spread of education in rural areas.

However, as I have indicated, if land reform—any kind of land reform—means anything at all in Pakistan, the ultimate test must lie in the contribution that reform makes in terms of actual production. Agriculture is still, and for long promises to be, Pakistan's principal industry and occupation. It accounts for fifty-four per cent of the national income. It provides seventy-four per cent of the population with employment and it produces seventy-six per cent of the country's foreign exchange earnings.[21] Notwithstanding this impressive role, agriculture obstinately fails to accomplish its prior task which, in a country with limited commercial and

[20] *ES*, p. 33.   [21] ibid., p. 16.

industrial capacity to pay for imported food, is to feed the nation. In order to maintain an average daily ration of slightly less than fifteen ounces of foodgrains *per capita*, Pakistan has been obliged, during the sixteen years ending in 1963, to import no less than 10,650,000 tons of foodgrains, against which must be allowed the earnings from the export of 1,330,000 tons of superior qualities of rice.[22] Further, this ration of fifteen ounces includes the production of barley, maize, *bajra*, and *jowar*[23], somewhat coarse eating.

It has long been recognized that this recurrent necessity for importing foodgrains constitutes a millstone round the neck of the national economy and although the Second Five Year Plan (1960–65) has as a prior objective production by the nation of its own foodgrain requirements, it is by no means certain that under this, or any plan, this objective can be achieved. In recent years, good rice harvests have provided overall figures for foodgrains grown within the country, which are reassuring, but the wheat deficiency is considerable.[24] It appears that nothing less than an annual production of some 5,000,000 tons of wheat would suffice to keep the nation secure against the necessity for importing, and annual production is nearly a million tons below that figure. These calculations are, it should be understood, approximations based on population and consumption statistics, but even if not precisely accurate, their tendency is reliable enough and they accurately demonstrate the pattern. Things have changed sadly since the day when, before World War I, Karachi was one of Asia's principal centres in the wheat export trade.

There are various causes of difficulty. One springs from the stagnant or even declining crop-yields, which are among the lowest in the world.[25] In West Pakistan, where the need for wheat is greatest, salinity and water-logging are turning considerable wheat areas into derelict, uncultivable waste. One of the earlier measures towards a solution of this grave problem was the establishment in 1960 of the Salinity Control Project. In April of the following year, President Ayub Khan called for a 'master-plan' to be ready by 15 May 1961, and the plan was, in fact, submitted on or about that

[22] ibid. Table 9. It does not appear that the imports stated in this Table include outright gifts of foodgrain from donor countries.

[23] Forms of millet.

[24] The total imports of wheat in the year 1964 were estimated to be 1,600,000 tons. *D*, 28 August 1964.

[25] *Second Five Year Plan*. Government of Pakistan, Karachi, 1960, p. 127.

date. But the scope of the entire subject is best revealed by the Revelle Report, a study of salinity and water-logging in West Pakistan, carried out by Dr. Roger Revelle and his colleagues at the expense of the United States of America. The Report and its recommendations disclose the extent to which land has been lost to the country and the expense involved in reclaiming it. The solution proposed in the Revelle Report envisages an expense of 2·3 billion dollars over a period of twenty-five years, rehabilitating 1,000,000 acres of lost land yearly.[26] Nothing illustrates better than these figures the nature of the problem and the grievous losses it involves.

In both wings of the country, cultivators are still attached to old and not always desirable methods and to wean them from practices hallowed by antiquity, if not by anything else, is a tedious and often unrewarding business. There is still a resistance to the idea of abandoning age-old-methods and the adoption of better techniques. To be sure, the fact that a method is new does not prove it is better, but the uncritical rejection of something simply because it involves the necessity of understanding and trying, is disastrous.[27] In West Pakistan, the agricultural census indicates that not more than six per cent of farmers use chemical fertilizers.[28] In East Pakistan, the corresponding figure is four per cent.[29] In both Provinces, plant has been erected for the production of fertilizers, using local reserves of natural gas as the basic raw material. So far, however, it has been difficult to overcome the farmer's reluctance or ignorance and, notwithstanding the importance of these locally produced chemical fertilizers, the bulk of the production appears so far to have been exported. However, indications are that this contradictory situation will not be permitted to continue and that farmers in Pakistan will be much more actively encouraged to use fertilizers produced inside the country.

When all things have been considered, the principal obstacle to self-sufficiency in foodgrains lies in the inability to produce food with the same facility as the mouths to consume it are produced. It seems as if the benefit of each succeeding irrigation and land development project is offset by a corresponding rise in population

[26] *D*, 18 August 1964.

[27] Uncritical acceptance can be equally damaging. The almost reckless utilization in the West of chemical applications such as pesticides to the soil, is by no means above criticism.

[28] *ES*, p. 30.   [29] ibid., p. 31.

and any Malthusian philosopher who stands in need of material to sustain his theories will find that Pakistan is as good a place as any in which to seek it. The rate at which the population is increasing, as disclosed by the Census of 1961, came as a surprise to forecasting statisticians.[30] It is possible that the factor of annual increase (2·16 per cent as against 2 per cent for the whole of Asia) has been slightly over-assessed by reason of inadvertent duplication and similar errors in enumeration. On the other hand, it has been suggested with some force that there has been under-enumeration. It remains true, however, that every anticipation proved to be substantially less than what is very evidently the case.[31]

It would be wrong, however, to give the impression that the new Government stood inactive and helplessly by. In the first year of its existence, a Food and Agriculture Commission was set up to investigate the state of the industry, and in 1960 an agricultural census was taken in collaboration with the United Nations' world-wide agricultural census programme. The Credit Inquiry Commission gave special emphasis to the question of agricultural credit, and in 1960 an agricultural crash programme was launched in some districts with the object of introducing, testing, and applying new agricultural practices and techniques. The object was stated to be the achievement of methods that would enable the country to be self-sufficient in food within two years.[32] A brave but forlorn hope!

It seems true that the most decisive contribution to the advancement of agriculture, at any rate in West Pakistan, was the Treaty signed on 19 September 1960 by President Ayub Khan and the late Pandit Jawaharlal Nehru, to resolve, once and for all, the problem of the Indus Basin and its invaluable waters. Ever since partition, this vexing and crucial problem had remained unsolved. It was a striking achievement that a decision was taken, a treaty signed, and the vast work of re-organizing West Pakistan's vital system of irrigation put in hand, one step following the other with-

[30] The First Five Year Plan assumed an increase factor of 1·4 per cent per annum compound. The Second Five Year Plan assumed a factor of 1·6 per cent, rising to 1·8 per cent.

[31] Census of Pakistan, 1961, Bulletin No. 2, p. 4.

[32] D, 5 April 1960. The fluctuating and not entirely satisfactory situation is discussed in an evaluation of the progress made in the first three years of the Second Five Year Plan, entitled *Mid-Plan Review*, published by the Government of Pakistan and dated May 1964.

out delay. Unfortunately, this major act, lacking as it did the Robin Hood touch, failed to seize the public imagination in quite the same way as did the land reforms.[33]

In retrospect, the regrettable probability is that the impetus given to national affairs by the new administration had, and continues to have, the least impact on agriculture. The Second Five Year Plan stated: 'Until agricultural productivity is vastly increased, general economic growth will be stunted.' There is, unhappily, no compelling reason to suppose that success is in sight, much less secure. The land reforms with which this chapter is primarily concerned, being one of the new administration's immediate and most widely publicized measures, have made no significant contribution that can be traced. The reforms were undoubtedly a courageous, if admittedly limited, attempt at grasping a refractory nettle, but the country's agricultural industry, with or without reforms, continues to be a root cause of Pakistan's economic predicament.

[33] The terms of the Treaty have not been published and it is understood the document is treated in Pakistan as classified, i.e. not to be made publicly available. Although I consider that the Government was right in resolving this long-outstanding dispute, I am aware of a substantial body of professional opinion in Pakistan which does not approve its terms. President Ayub Khan said: '. . . whereas there is no cause for rejoicing . . . we have been able to get the best that was possible'. Broadcast to the nation on 4 September 1960.

ST. THOMAS AQUINAS COLLEGE LIBRARY

VI

Reform in Public Life and in the Public Services

IN Chapter II I suggested that part of Pakistan's inheritance was a deeply ingrained system of corruption and jobbery in public life as well as in the public services and that the acceptance of bribes, as well as other kinds of misconduct and abuse of office, had become a feature of the public administration.[1] Even if the tales that circulated were often much exaggerated, there was no doubt in the mind of the people that corruption was widespread. References to it, in Assembly debates, in newspapers, in speeches, and in hortatory appeals by leading public men were so numerous that any specific reference would be invidious and merely superfluous. It was not for nothing that a promise to change all this figured largely in the new Government's programme.

Of course, there had long existed laws and regulations on the subject. Civil servants and other categories of public officials had their own Conduct Rules which, not surprisingly, were stringent in their disapproval of bribery and corruption. At various times, as these practices seemed to flourish in spite of Conduct Rules, attempts were made to tighten the law and to keep a closer watch on the rising prosperity of individuals. In Pakistan, the Special Police Establishment was organized to deal specifically with corruption. Public officials were required to give statements of their possessions and might at any time be asked to explain the wealth they appeared to own. It must be admitted that none of this seemed to work very effectively. It was distinctly noticeable that, prior to Martial Law, the number of Class I civil officials charged with corrupt practice (not to speak of conviction) was so small as not to warrant consideration. The only conclusion could be that either this, the most senior category of government servant, was virtually incorrupt or that there was something wrong with the law

[1] As used in this Chapter, the word 'corruption' specifically means the exaction of money or money's worth. It does not include sexual vice or traitorous conduct.

and administration on the subject. Public opinion favoured the latter view.

For those in public office (as distinct from public service), ministers of the Central and Provincial Governments, there existed only the general law and the conventions of public life. More specific legislation was not deemed necessary because, after all, these men were supposed to be chosen for their ability to present an example of moral rectitude and, it is fair to say that, as with government officials, most of them justified these expectations. Such being the legal position with respect to men in public office, it was (in Pakistan at any rate) an innovation when in 1949 a law was introduced, generally referred to as 'PRODA',[2] whose purpose was to make it possible after judicial inquiry to debar from public life, for a period not exceeding ten years, persons found guilty of misconduct while holding office.

It was a simple form of impeachment but Callard[3] referred to its operation as 'highly abnormal' and it was, indeed, an unusual piece of legislation. Although passed on 6 January 1949, it was made retrospective to 15 August 1947, the day on which Pakistan began its life. The definition of 'misconduct' included such vague terms as 'favouritism, nepotism, *wilful*[4] maladministration . . .' By the Rules made under the Act, an application, signed by not less than five persons, could be addressed to the Governor-General or to the Governor of a Province[5] requesting him to refer a case against the person named in the application to the appropriate tribunal. The application was required to state the avowed facts and, as evidence of good faith, the applicants were required to deposit Rs.5,000. It is scarcely necessary to elaborate the questionable potentialities of all this. Any five persons, with Rs.5,000 between them, could put any minister or ex-minister into a very uncomfortable situation, and Callard points out that at one time every minister except one, in the former Provincial Government of Sind, was the object of inquiries under PRODA.[6]

Still, beyond creating a precedent of which use was afterwards to be made, that is of no great importance now. There is little

[2] Public and Representative Offices (Disqualification) Act. It applied to Ministers, Deputy Ministers, and Parliamentary Secretaries in the Central and Provincial Governments.

[3] op. cit., p. 81.   [4] Author's italics.

[5] In those days there were, in effect, five Provinces.

[6] Callard, op. cit., p. 103.

doubt that PRODA had its origin in politics. It was used as a
political weapon and it succumbed to political considerations. In
September 1954 the Act was repealed, one of the moves in the
struggle between the then Governor-General, Ghulam Mohamed,
and the Constituent Assembly. But like most events in history,
PRODA did not disappear without trace. It left a remembered
pattern which was utilized by the new régime when it turned its
attention to the politicians who had been ousted in October 1958.

But, before we go on to consider what measures were adopted
by the Martial Law authorities in their efforts to cleanse public
life and the public services, it has to be said that in their tren-
chant animadversions they did a little less than justice to government servants, in one important respect. My remarks here do not,
I think, apply to those who had occupied public office. Such men
are, or should be, judged by a different and perhaps higher standard of conduct although in Pakistan, by October 1958, it is
probable the nation had long ceased to credit most of its political
leaders with any such aspirations. However, the particular omission on the part of President Ayub's administration which I now
have in mind was the failure to do anything about corrupt practice
in banking, industry, and trade for, whatever might be the shortcomings of government officers, they did not exercise a monopoly
and there was no reason to suppose that men in private employment were necessarily models of integrity.

I do not now, of course, mean the reprehensible practice of
offering bribes to government servants. That is only the other side
of the coin as its affects the public service. I am speaking of corrupt practice within financial, industrial, and commercial institutions—the requiring of bribes and gifts by officials of such
institutions as, for instance, purchase officers who have the control of contracts for the supply of materials; bank managers who
give credit facilities and take a share in the profits; company
officials who expect rewards for granting agencies and other
forms of profitable franchise. There is absolutely no difference
between this and corruption in the public service, and the consequences are just as harmful. But it does not appear that any of these
corrupt practices received the attention of the new administration
which scarcely seems just, even if no direct intervention was
possible. Presumably, however, it is never too late to take notice.

The action which the new Government did take was directed,

first, towards public servants, not because their moral stature was markedly inferior to that of the departed politicians—there is a good case for suggesting that the reverse might be true—but because there were more of them, because they were closer to, and had more dealings with, the public. Moreover, instruments for disciplining government officials were close at hand whereas, in the case of delinquent politicians, the instruments had to be devised. And, of course, the politicians *had* departed, while the government officials were still performing their duties.

I do not now propose to enter into any precise analysis of what bribery and corruption are. It is unfortunate that so little has been written on the subject of these evils, which form one of the mainsprings of human action in this not very commendable world. Pakistan may have suffered acutely from corruption, but Pakistan does not stand alone in this respect.[7] It is an insidious disease, difficult to trace in its early stages, difficult to check, and difficult to eradicate. By its nature, the vice is a secret one and those who practise it are mutually self-assisting. Neither giver nor receiver is prepared to speak, except in those circumstances when betrayal is advantageous and, without this, proof is always difficult. To establish, in a legal sense, charges of corrupt practice is always difficult, and it was substantially for this purpose that the new administration adopted summary measures.

Moreover, the problem is not just a legal one. The social implications go far wider. It is not merely a matter of what constitutes bribery, and the proof of bribery, in the legal sense. It is the even more pregnant matter of what constitutes, in the mind of the general public, unfair practice, presumption upon official position, and the undermining of efficient and impartial administration through money and gifts in kind, as well as other more vicious forms of gratification.

The point is not easily resolved. What is to the rich man a mere tip given to a flunkey, becomes for the poor petitioner a piece of extortion without which he cannot get past the doorman.[8] The distinctions are not always those of black and white. Between the stringently honest official who resolutely keeps himself above all

[7] See, for example, Wraith and Simpkins, *Corruption in Developing Countries*, George Allen & Unwin Ltd., London, 1963.

[8] See, for example, article on 'Petty Bribery in Mexico' by Paul P. Kennedy, reprinted from the *New York Times* in D, 2 July 1964.

peculation, on the one side, and the ruthless despoiler of the public, on the other, there is the substantial class of grey people who permit their mouths to be sweetened until they reach the stage when they cannot act without this stimulation. These are the hypocrites who comfortably nourish delusions of honesty and bring discredit daily upon the governments they serve.

The new administration, unable to ignore the intense public awareness of the evil, resolved upon an approach which had to do with reputation and general conduct rather than with corrupt acts which had been specifically proved. It was thought that unless there was some method of sweeping away all room for casuistry, legislation and rules would at once become as nugatory as they had been in the past. The obvious risk was that, if pressed too far, this approach might lead dangerously near to the Red Queen's formula[9] and might involve the possibility of abuse by people maliciously inspired.

Reform of the public service was not, furthermore, a simple question of eliminating bribery, although this loomed largest in the public mind. There were other forms of misconduct. There were the inefficient men who had found their way into the service and, by various devices, had even secured advancement. There were the troublesome men and there were men who, quite against the spirit of the service, had allowed themselves to become too closely attached to political interests. Moreover, the question was not only that of punishing notorious offenders for past misdeeds, but also of providing adequate machinery for dealing with offenders in the future.

On the purely criminal aspect of bribery, Regulations[10] were published, in January 1959, providing for punishment of up to fourteen years' rigorous imprisonment for public servants found guilty of obtaining, or trying to obtain, material advantage by corrupt means or, at any rate, by abuse of their position in the service. These Regulations made it possible to deal with persons charged with such crimes by Special Military Court and were, therefore, all the more impressive. A convicted person might suffer not only imprisonment, but confiscation of all his property. The Regulations also stated that, if the accused could not account satisfactorily for the possession of property disproportionate to his

[9] 'Off with his head!'   [10] MLR No. 62.

known resources, the Court was to presume acquisition by illegal means unless the contrary were proved.

For government servants whose reputation was that of being, or having been, corrupt or inefficient, or of having misconducted themselves, an Ordinance[11] of a different character was published at the same time. This Ordinance set up machinery and procedure by which the past conduct of public servants could be looked into, and committees for this purpose were appointed by the Central Government. These committees, variously consisting of Cabinet Ministers and senior government officials, depending upon the rank and category of the official whose conduct was to be scrutinized, were to inquire into past behaviour. The tribunals were quasi-judicial and were armed with the powers of a *civil*[12] High Court enabling them to compel the attendance of witnesses and the production of documents, and to take evidence on oath. They could make rules regulating their own procedure and could order police investigations. Their proceedings were not held in public and could not be questioned in any other court.

Any civilian official deemed to possess an undesirable reputation, was to be informed in writing and was required to explain—either verbally or by written communication—the facts and the circumstances adduced against him. After studying what he had to say and, if necessary, pursuing the inquiry further, it was the duty of the committee to state its findings and recommendation in each case. The appropriate authority would pass its orders on these, but before any order was passed the official concerned could, if he wished, submit an appeal based on whatever further explanation he desired to put forward. Punishment could take the form of dismissal, compulsory removal from the service, retirement, or reduction in rank. At the same time as this machinery was established, all Class I officials and certain groups of Class II officials were required to give statements of their assets in the form prescribed.

So much for the past. A new Regulation[13] was published in March 1959 making it compulsory, on pain of fine or jail sentence, or both, to report any known case of bribery, smuggling, or black-marketing. The law regulating the behaviour of civilian officials in the future was strengthened by new Orders which made it possible

[11] Public Conduct Scrutiny Ordinance 1959 and Rules made thereunder.
[12] i.e. not criminal. Author's italics.   [13] MLR No. 65.

to deal administratively with government servants found guilty of corruption, misconduct, subversion, or inefficiency.[14]

It needs scarcely be said that, at the time, interest centred mainly on the activities of the scrutinizing committees charged to look into the past conduct of certain people whose names had not yet been disclosed. These committees were first constituted in January 1959 and were reconstituted in the April following. Altogether, some fifty-seven committees were set up by the Central Government from which it was inferred that quite a large number of civilian officers were, for one reason or another, faced with the prospect of having to give an account of themselves. That may have been so, but it was also the intention of the Government to have done with these scrutinies as quickly as possible, for which purpose a sufficient number of committees was required. Before the end of June 1959, the screening process had been completed and orders passed by which 1,662 Central Government officials, in the Class I, II, and III categories were found guilty of one or more of the following: misconduct, corruption, reputation for corruption, or inefficiency. The punishments varied from compulsory retirement to a simple expression of the Government's displeasure.[15]

In all this there is much that recalls such tribunals as the Star Chamber. No one really knows on what basis members of the services were invited to come forward and explain allegations as to their past misconduct. No one really knows what went on at these swiftly organized inquests. It is, perhaps, not surprising that people are unwilling to talk about their experience, either as committee-members or as scrutinees and, since it may be hoped there will be no cause for these summary methods to be repeated, it may well be suggested that the matter should be left where it is.

Certainly, it would be useless and improper to resurrect cases, whether individual or *en masse*. The whole thing is *res adjudicata* and there it must be permitted to remain. It may well be that justice, although rough, was by and large done in the sense that no one was the wholly innocent victim of simple malice. At that time, when the results became known, the principal difficulty that clouded the public mind was the knowledge that others, not above

[14] Laws (Continuance in Force) [Amendment] Order 1959 and Laws (Continuance in Force) [Second Amendment] Order 1959.
[15] See Appendix IV.

reproach, had luckily escaped attention. It could, of course, be argued in a pragmatic way that the purpose was achieved and, since nothing in this world is perfect, it should not cause surprise to any sensible person that some guilty men escaped. To look behind all this serves no useful purpose now and, in fact, only two questions need be asked. Were these men adjudged through an ill-advised or unfair procedure? Have the public services improved in consequence of these measures?

As to the first, it is evident that the process did not fail for lack of effort. Excluding all those who were examined and acquitted (as to which no figures or other details, if they exist, seem to have been published) it appears that, in a period of six months, fifty-seven committees dealt with 1,662 cases in which adverse reports were made. A substantial number of cases were screened a second time to ensure that no injustice was done.[16] Thus, excluding the second screening, it follows that on the average each committee screened in a month five cases in which punishment followed. Bearing in mind that all the committee-members were either Cabinet Ministers or senior civil servants, with other responsibilities and duties, the time allowed for these inquiries was not excessive, particularly when it is remembered that a man's career and reputation were at stake. On the other hand, in the case of the lower, clerical grades, where in most cases only a simple question of efficiency was involved, it is probable that no prolonged investigation was needed.

But although it may be true that none of the scrutinees could complain of having been kept waiting, no one can say to what extent the inquiries were fairly conducted and this is the main reason for saying that the chief demerit of the whole method was that it formed no precedent for the future. As we have said, it is a thing that could be done once, but not a second time. It is, to say the least, most unlikely that the public would accept these methods yet again. With whatever sincerity the new régime might be credited, there could be no perpetuation of that peremptory, drum-head system and so the problem of dealing effectively and comprehensively with such offences in the future was left unsolved. If cases were to arise again, there would have to be recourse to the old departmental or legal methods of inquiry. This being so, it

[16] President's statement dated 27 June 1959.

could well be asked why, on this occasion, those methods were abandoned.

Probably the Government was aware of these possibilities of criticism for President Ayub, while regretting the number of able men lost to the service, gave promise of generous treatment,[17] and this they certainly received. Every compulsorily retired official was allowed such proportionate pension as was due to him and nothing was done, directly or indirectly, to place obstacles in the way of obtaining other employment. The fact of removal from service by this screening procedure does not seem to have been treated as involving any moral obloquy and not only did most of these people proceed to obtain other satisfactory occupation, but some have since risen to positions of considerable eminence in finance, industry, and commerce. Those for whom the problem of readjustment was difficult or whose qualifications, branch of knowledge, or experience were not easily marketable outside the service, in some instances found themselves confronted with an irksome problem. And for those obsessed with a sense of status and with the *cachet* which is said to be attached to government service, it was a bitter blow to be hurled summarily from the pinnacle they had imagined for themselves.

As to the second question—whether the public services were improved—the considerations range far more widely. In the early days of Martial Law, it did not really need any threat of screening to dampen enthusiasm for corrupt practice or to arouse negligent government servants from a chronic indifference to their duty. With the threat of summary correction, through a military court, hanging over the head of every civilian, officials behaved with zeal and circumspection. Those who were corrupt but nervous gave up their activities and devoutly hoped the past would not reveal itself. Bolder spirits simply raised the fees in view of the extra risk involved. But the real question, both difficult and delicate, is that of the extent to which the grosser forms of misconduct, particularly corruption, had actually permeated.

This is something on which it is useless to speculate. No doubt the view held generally by the public indicated belief in corruption on a massive scale, but it is certain that much of the talk that circulated was exaggerated gossip. For a very long time it had become the habit to ascribe everything to someone's malpractice and to see

[17] President's statement, 27 June 1959.

dishonest gold at the bottom of every well. Indeed, if all the money that was alleged to have changed hands actually existed, then the only inference was that, compared with the wealth in Pakistan, the gold at Fort Knox was so much small change. Nevertheless, it is indisputably true that most branches of the civilian services were infected to some degree, in some way or another and, in a few instances, corruption was not only widely practised, but was systematic and had become almost ineradicable.

From these generalizations, we must proceed to a close study of such figures as are available, at any rate so far as concerns the Central Government services. Unfortunately, it does not seem that information as to the actual number of people employed in the various categories has been published, and one is confined to approximations. On the basis of 2,800 Class I officials (which includes the top-ranking Civil Service of Pakistan and the Pakistan Foreign Service),[18] barely five per cent were found guilty of any charge and, of this percentage, rather less than half was punished for corruption or the reputation for it. Among 5,500 Class II officials (2,600 gazetted and 2,900 non-gazetted), the percentage declines to four out of which slightly less than one was punished for corruption. Out of 87,000 Class III officials, the percentage incurring any form of punishment was 1·5 and in this case, only fifty-five persons (0·06 per cent) were deemed guilty of corrupt practice. The fact that the lowest percentage of corruption is found among the clerical grades need not surprise us. It is, after all, a question of opportunity as well as integrity.

Bearing in mind all that has been said here on the subject, as well as the constant references in Pakistan, year after year, to corruption and unsatisfactory conduct in the public services, the figures disclosed are not striking. Indeed, one may well inquire what all the fuss was about. A Class I group of public officials, including not only the top administrative service and the foreign service, but also the police and engineering departments, in both of which the opportunities for corruption are numerous, can hardly be described as riddled with this evil when only 2·5 per cent of its members are found guilty of it, or the reputation for it, and

---

[18] Twelve members of the Civil Service of Pakistan were retired: six for corruption or reputation for corruption combined with misconduct, three for misconduct, and three for inefficiency. Three members of the Pakistan Foreign Service were retired: two for inefficiency and one for misconduct.

even then by summary process. Idealistically, it is doubtless argu-
able that in the top-ranking services there should be no instances
whatsoever or, at most, no more than an isolated case here and
there, but we are not dealing with idealistic circumstances. In
short, in view of what the screening procedure apparently disclosed in the Central Government services, were these diseases as
widespread as people had for so long been claiming? And, whether
they were or not, did the screening procedure effectively suppress
them?

These questions present a formidable dilemma for, if we conclude that the screening process was, in all respects, only partially
successful, then obviously much injustice has been done.[19] Nor
does it help to say that if *more* people had been expelled from the
service, administration would have been crippled. If, on the other
hand, we conclude that the scrutinizing committees were effective
in removing *most* of the troublesome, corrupt, and inefficient
people, then so far as corruption is concerned, there are many
Pakistanis today who, as we shall shortly have occasion to see,
would conclude that their successors did not take long to learn
the arts of exploiting their position as government servants.[20]

Two years later, in 1961, the Governors' Conference set up a
Committee to review anti-corruption measures. This Committee
prepared a scheme for dealing with corruption in the public services and the scheme was approved by the Governors' Conference
held in the following year, but the constitutional changes of 1962
necessitated reconsideration of the proposals from the legal and
constitutional aspects. In 1961 we find the President calling for a
termination of corrupt practice and suggesting that a special watch
should be kept on high officials.[21] Meanwhile, departmental
machinery was set up in Rawalpindi, Karachi, and Dacca to inquire into charges of corruption made against public officials.

Having gone so far on the subject of the screening methods of
1959, it is unfair to evade the real issue. Looking back, it does not

---

[19] On the basis of published results, it would appear that in some departments of the Central Government, no one was guilty of misconduct, corruption,
or inefficiency!

[20] The reader must again be reminded that this analysis and discussion are
based on the Central services. Figures in respect of the Provincial services are
not included as the comprehensive data is not available. It is doubtful if this
exclusion vitiates, in any way, the conclusions reached.

[21] *D*, 7 September 1961.

now seem that the scrutiny of that year did much towards the permanently effective elimination of corrupt practice and inefficiency. As soon as the hand of the Martial Law administration was lightened, these evils quickly germinated afresh,[22] although it may well be that these measures did not fail altogether in their purpose. Apart from the removal of unsatisfactory people, there were doubtless others rudely awakened to the possibilities that might confront *them* if they did not mend their ways and, for a time no doubt, the general level of integrity and efficiency was raised.

But we should remind ourselves, also, that in the last anlysis the question is not one of legal process, regulation, and conduct rules. Laws against stealing have their uses, but it is doubtful if a single thief was ever reformed by them. Integrity in public, as well as in private life is ultimately a moral question for which education and example are likely to do more than conviction by the court. Not that anything is ever done by pious language; determination and act must go hand in hand, but these, too, can only have their origins in the sense of values which a man is brought up to and with which he credits himself. The dreary verbiage of the statute book never inspired anyone to a better way of life.

To turn now from public officials to those who held public office, in March 1959 the new administration published the Public Offices (Disqualification) Order.[23] The terms of this Order followed, substantially, those of PRODA and it applied to men who had held public office and been found guilty of misconduct, as already defined.[24] Any inquiry under this Order was to be conducted by a tribunal of not less than two members of whom one had to be, or have been, a Judge of the Supreme Court or a High Court. Any person found guilty of misconduct by the tribunal could be disqualified by the President or by a Governor of a Province from holding public office for a period not exceeding fifteen years and could also be ordered to make good any loss to the public revenue, or forfeit any gain to himself, arising from his misconduct.

Two months later, three inquiry committees were set up (one

---

[22] See *D*, 22 and 25 September 1959. The authorities threatened to recall troops and reopen the information centres.

[23] *Gazette of Pakistan (Extraordinary)* 21 March 1959. This Order became known as 'PODO'.

[24] The definition was similar to that in PRODA.

for the Centre and one for each of the two Provinces) to deal with inquiries against former ministers. Rules made under PODO made it possible for members of the public to apply for the institution of an inquiry against a former holder of public office, but, unlike PRODA, no cash deposit was required as earnest of good faith. The Martial Law authorities probably considered that no one would dare to flout Orders made by *them*.

But, as an instrument for dealing with persons who had been active in politics and who were thought to have used that position in an irregular way to their own personal advantage or to the detriment of the State, it appeared that PODO was inadequate. It was feared that its procedure would be lengthy and cumbersome and, in any case, it only applied to men who had held public office. It did not apply, for instance, to men who had merely been members of a legislature. In consequence, some five months later, a further Order was issued—the Elective Bodies (Disqualification) Order[25]—which applied to any person who had held any public office or position, including membership of *any*[26] elective body in the country. Again, three tribunals were instituted—one for the Centre and one each for the Provinces—and their duties were to inquire into allegations of misconduct[27] such as might be referred to them by any authority appointed by the Government for the purpose. It was not open to the public to submit applications for inquiry under this Order.

The intention was, no doubt, to sweep into the net every person who had been active in politics and against whom some misconduct could be established. Unlike PODO, a person appearing before an EBDO inquiry tribunal was not entitled to the assistance of counsel and was required to appear personally. A further interesting distinction is that the tribunal, hearing a complaint under PODO, was invested with powers under the Code of Criminal Procedure, whereas, for the purposes of EBDO, the powers were those of the Code of Civil Procedure. The summary intentions of EBDO were made very plain by the then Minister of the Interior,[28] and, as an interim measure adopted simply for this

[25] *Gazette of Pakistan (Extraordinary)* 7 August 1959. This Order became known as 'EBDO'.
[26] Author's italics.
[27] Bribery, corruption, nepotism, favouritism, wilful administration, &c.
[28] Lieutenant-General K. M. Sheikh.

chastening purpose, EBDO stood automatically repealed on 31 December 1960.

The consequences to a person charged under EBDO were different from those suffered by a person charged under PODO, and were slightly curtailed in that any guilty person was automatically disqualified from membership of any elective body until after 31 December 1966 and might also be required to make good any loss to the public revenue as a result of his misconduct, or make restitution of any wrongful gain. The provisions of the Order applied retrospectively to 14 August 1947 and they applied automatically to any person who had been removed from Government service on any charge other than that of inefficiency. The purpose was frankly one of expedition and there was a further section by which anyone served with a notice of inquiry under EBDO could, if he chose, elect to retire voluntarily from public life (at any rate, until 31 December 1966) in which case the inquiry would not proceed against him.

The exact number of persons who became, in the cant of the times, 'ebdoed', does not seem to have been published. In 1960, it was reported that in East Pakistan alone, some 3,000 persons had been proceeded against under EBDO of whom the majority either opted to retire or were disqualified.[29] If this is so, then it seems that about 6,000 persons laboured under the EBDO disqualification. The question of whether any cash restitutions were actually called for and paid does not seem to have been disclosed, nor does it seem to be known how many persons charged under EBDO elected to retire rather than face the tribunal. Indications are that a substantial number preferred to retire since this would avoid embarrassing questions. Partly for this reason, perhaps, the Martial Law authorities announced that inquiries were being made as to the misconduct of 'former politicians' and that the results would be published in the form of a White Paper.[30] This interesting publication has never appeared, but it seems certain that minute and extensive inquiries were, in fact, made and that a good deal of information has been collected and is on record somewhere.

[29] *D*, 17 January 1960. The number seems very high and is difficult to reconcile with such other information as is available. If, however, 'screened' public officials are included (since these, if dismissed, removed, or made to retire from Government service or from the service of any public statutory body, became liable to EBDO disqualifications) the figure becomes feasible.

[30] *D*, 15 May 1962.

At the time, the fact of retirement or disqualification had little significance for there was no public life in the sense of there being legislatures or local government bodies to which a man could seek election. The problem would only arise when Martial Law was withdrawn, a new constitution promulgated, and elections held. The dates on which those things happened, and the period specified between elections would, therefore, be crucial for persons disqualified until the end of 1966 under EBDO. If, for instance, it happened that elections were to be held in 1965, for a term of (let it be said) four years, the effect of disqualification under EBDO would be to make it impossible for a man to seek election until 1969. Hence age and health also became important factors. In some instances, disqualification involved virtual loss of all prospect of reappearance in public life. So far as younger men were concerned, they could only await the future. The considerations involved here were purely personal to the individuals concerned, whereas in the case of the public services, there was not only the question of the individual's right and interest under his terms of service, but the wider question of the nation's administrative needs.

On the other hand, politics and public life being what they are, the sentence of disqualification was by no means as final as that of removal from service. It is not surprising that, as the prospects of a new constitution showed signs of maturing and as the days of Martial Law seemed to be numbered, efforts were made, by private persuasion and by public propaganda, to influence the administration to remove the EBDO disqualification. These attempts were resisted all along and, clearly, unless the events of 1958 were to be rendered farcical, the administration had no option but to resist. In 1963, however, after the new Constitution had been brought into effect, the President issued an amending Ordinance by which persons labouring under an EBDO disqualification could apply for relief. This Ordinance became the object of controversy, however, and did not receive approval in the National Assembly.

It must also be borne in mind that those who were disqualified under EBDO were not restrained from participating in any form of political activity whenever that should become possible. The announcement of a new Constitution and the withdrawal of Martial Law opened the way to a renewed political life in the country. Those disqualified from direct participation could take an indirect interest by financing and working on behalf of their own nominees, usually close relatives. Thus the old political interests were neither crushed nor dissipated. Like the land reforms and the reform of the public services, the ultimate effect of EBDO was moderate and the general issue involved here will be considered later.[31]

[31] See Appendix V.

VII

Social Reform

IN the new Government's approach to social problems, part of the activity of an exceptionally busy first year included an attempt to redirect and revitalize the attitude of the public to these and other matters, and a Board of National Reconstruction was established with President Ayub Khan at the head. With him were six other members of the Cabinet, and the Director of the Bureau of National Reconstruction, operating on the instructions of the Board, was its Member-Secretary. By national reconstruction was meant the inculcation of ethical and civic values; the development of a character-pattern; a raising of the cultural and intellectual level, assisting women to overcome the social handicaps that confronted them; encouragement of a healthy national spirit; the elimination of sectarianism, regionalism, and provincialism, and the teaching of simplicity, frugality, and good taste in living standards.[1]

In June 1959, an 'all-out' austerity drive was announced to cover all aspects of life 'right from the use of cars to simple and common dress'. The movement had been somewhat anticipated by the Women's Voluntary Group, formed in the preceding March, which, under the leadership of the President's wife and wives of other Cabinet Ministers, renounced, among other things, the use of cosmetics and foreign cloth and resolved to purchase the simplest kind of cotton materials woven in Pakistan. The slogan for these self-denying aims was 'Austerity is our national style', a somewhat naive piece of self-deception for a nation of people who like to live well. The drive for plain-living did not, in fact, last long. It received at its commencement some scattered applause which died early, perhaps because 'austerity' and 'belt-tightening' had been the common catchwords of almost every government preceding that of President Ayub Khan. There was hardly a

[1] *D*, 18 June 1959. The Bureau was part of the Ministry of National Reconstruction and Information.

Prime Minister, Chief Minister, or any other Minister who had not, at some time or another, appealed for just a little more tightening of the belt, for just a little longer.[2] In September 1959, the Central Government issued a circular detailing measures by which all civilian officers were to 'cast off all pomp and show', but the result of these instructions is not very clear.

As a component of the Ministry dealing with information, the work of the Bureau principally took the form of issuing printed propaganda explaining the intentions of the new Government, its achievements and aspirations. However, the association of the Bureau of National Reconstruction with the former Ministry of Information and Broadcasting cannot go unnoticed and, indeed, in any age of brain-washing and mind-bending, there is an immediate tendency to suspect organizations set up to reconstruct people nationally. However, it deserves to be said that in Pakistan there was no compulsory listening to radio harangues, no forcing of ideas, and no ramming of uncongenial pabulum down unwilling throats. Probably the worst crime against truth consisted either in the suppression of, or slants given to, the news, but as these are the regular preoccupations of all governments, there is no need to single out Pakistan on this ground.

More ominous, perhaps, was the undertaking to rewrite history so as to correct the bias said to have been introduced by British and Hindu scholars. Certainly there is nothing to be said against the idea of re-examination, while there is something to be said for the suggestion that some material, used in less authoritative volumes of Indo-Pakistan history, has been uncritically adopted. It does appear, moreover, that there are aspects of British-Indian history requiring fresh evaluation.[3] Nevertheless, the sense of caution suggests itself most strongly and, for this, there are at least two cogent reasons.

In the first place, the resurgence of nationalism springing from the creation of numerous independent nations following World War II, has led to the re-writing of history in a way that will gratify not only truth, but also the vanity of newly-formed patriotisms, sometimes to the detriment of unflinching his-

---

[2] See appeal by the then Minister of Industries for 'tightening the belt' in the interests of industrial development. *D*, 21 February 1959.

[3] See, for instance, Brijen K. Gupta's paper on the affair of the Black Hole of Calcutta, (*Journal of Asian Studies*, Vol. XIX, No. 1, November 1959) where this celebrated incident is fairly and critically reassessed.

torical accuracy. There may be no actual perversion of specific fact, but much can be done with the shifting of emphasis. Thus it is quite possible to find two independent nations, which share a common past, writing the history of that past so as to produce results distinguished for their differences rather than for their similarities.[4]

In any case, the prerequisites for the task of writing history, particularly when new evaluations are in question, are inexhaustible zeal, a sense of dedicated scholarship, and unswerving fidelity to comprehensive fact. In Pakistan, the results achieved so far under official auspices are meagre[5] and, with regret it must be added, there is, as yet, little promise of any useful or weighty addition to our knowledge.

The Bureau of National Reconstruction made little impact on the public consciousness because, in all probability, there was no impulse towards any forcible bending of the public mind. Whether, since 1958, there has been an elevation of values, of character, and in intellectual stature, is a question it is hazardous to answer—not merely for fear of giving offence, but because the problem is so intimately related to economic circumstance and standards of education. It is foolish to expect illiterate people who are, most of the time, semi-hungry to respond eagerly to an appeal for a finer view, a nobler ethic. No doubt it is often said that the humble and impoverished millions of Asia have an innately higher sense of spiritual values than the men and women of western conturies who are corrupted by too strong a devotion to material things. This may be so, but the explanation can only be that, having little to hope for in this world, the same impoverished millions are obliged to pin their expectations on the next.

Perhaps the new administration felt disposed towards a similar interpretation for a great deal more energy was very properly devoted to a programme of rehabilitation and resettlement of displaced persons, a problem that stemmed from the days of partition when some 8,000,000 persons, mostly poor agriculturalists, entered Pakistan. In 1958, eleven years afterwards, it was ascertained that in Karachi alone there were still some 600,000 persons

---

[4] On this important matter see Smith, op. cit., Chapter III under the sub-heading *Apologetics*.

[5] In 1964 it was announced that a Board would be set up to write history text-books. *D*, 4 June 1964.

living on pavements, in ramshackle huts, canvas shelters, or wherever they could find a place to lay their heads. This census of shelterless people was carried out by students and it was a solid, workmanlike gesture undertaken on the initiative of the new régime.

The refugee problem throughout the country had been shamefully neglected and the President did not misrepresent the case when he said it had been used (abused would have been a more appropriate word) as a means of political exploitation.[6] The existence of a large body of refugees from India and the idea of their solitary helplessness had long been recognized as a useful counter in a heartless game of political manoeuvre. It was the old story of preserving a troubled situation so that, at any decisive moment, merit could be acquired in the pose of champion of the unfortunate.

Under the energetic direction of the Minister for Rehabilitation, Lieutenant-General Azam Khan, the resettlement authorities pressed firmly on with provision for the homeless and land for the landless. On 29 January 1959 orders were issued conferring proprietory rights on 1,420,000 allottees of rural land, in areas which formed part of what was earlier known as the Punjab. Both at Karachi and at Dacca colonies of cheaply constructed dwellings were set up, the work being pushed forward at unprecedented speed—unprecedented, at any rate, in Pakistan. At the Karachi colony, located near the Landhi Industrial Trading Estate, work started in December 1958 and, within five months, 15,000 dwellings had been completed. On 1 August 1959 the first batch of 200 homeless families moved in. No such attempt had previously been made and the goodwill that accrued to the new administration was justly earned. At the same time, other colonies of dwellings were organized where people of limited resources could acquire a home by means of purchase on the instalment system.

Simultaneously, another problem—also stemming from the migrations of 1947—was for the first time tackled in a resolute manner. The movement of communities from Pakistan left an immense volume of abandoned property, both movable and immovable, which required to be administered fairly, both in the interests of the State and as a means of compensating those who

[6] Speech made on 5 December 1958 at the Foundation Stone-laying ceremony at Korangi Colony.

had lost what they possessed in India. It requires little imagination to perceive here the vast possibilities of dishonesty, perjured claims, corrupt practice, not to mention downright looting. Nor does it take much effort to visualize the usefulness to those having, or seeking, power. What can be easier than to gain support by a gift, or the promise of a gift, from so great a reservoir of abandoned wealth? Many had, indeed, endeavoured to dip their hands into this pool of gold by making fictitious or grossly exaggerated claims relating to property alleged to have been lost in India. On this subject, the new Government instituted punitive legislation so that many claims were promptly withdrawn altogether or else reduced, the total value of these modest changes being estimated at Rs.79 crores.[7]

No one in Pakistan would trouble to deny that the administration of evacuee property, as it was termed, constituted a long-festering grievance which interested people never wished to see healed. Apart from its usefulness as a political counter, the question of redistribution afforded remunerative occupation to a large number of government employees as well as to the officers and staffs of what were called 'Custodian Courts'. In addition, lawyers found new avenues for worthwhile practice. The proceedings of the Custodian Courts were both fantastic and interminable and when the new régime announced its intention of reaching a final solution of the problem of evacuee property, doubtless many hearts were chilled.[8]

That solution was not so easily achieved and, as I write now, it has not yet been achieved. Nevertheless a great deal has been done to satisfy small claims by the satisfactory method of payment in full, by payments on account in respect of larger claims, and by means of transfers of evacuee property into the names of claimants in possession. Finally, by determining the value of claims in respect of property left behind in India, it was possible to solve once and for all the plight of many people who, in earlier days, had no hope of any tangible answer. At the same time, many kinds of valuable property, deteriorating for want of interested ownership, were put into active use.

---

[7] D, 21 July 1959. The amount equals £59,250,000 or US$165,900,000.

[8] The resettlement and rehabilitation organization's existence holds sanction up to June 1965. Whether it will continue thereafter can only be seen in due course. No doubt the nation as a whole would like to see the end of it.

In March 1959 the new Government announced its labour policy, a subject that had been somewhat put aside in favour of more urgent concerns. With the promulgation of Martial Law, strikes and agitations in educational institutions and public utility installations were forbidden.[9] The effect of this prohibition was to create a moratorium in relation to labour problems of which there were many. The labour situation had been uneasy for a considerable time and, in favour of maximum tranquillity while the nation settled down under the new dispensation, these problems were temporarily put into cold storage, as it were, and obviously they could not indefinitely remain there.

The President had something to say about Labour-Management relations in an address given on 19 December 1958 when inaugurating a conference on Labour-Management Co-operation. His brief speech foreshadowed no particular measures of reform but tended, mainly, to reflect his aversion for needless political interference leading to exploitation and intrigue. A year later, speaking on similar matters, he expressed a belief in the possibility of solving labour problems by the 'spirit of mutual understanding, goodwill, and co-operation'.[10] There was also, however, a passing reference to trade unionism which showed that, even if strikes were then illegal, trade unionism was certainly accepted by the new Government as a legitimate form of labour organization.

A few months later, in March 1959, the new labour policy was announced,[11] founded upon eleven principles which aimed at increased production from the labour force, an equitable distribution of wealth, better working conditions for labour, and development of trade unionism founded upon the ILO Conventions. These pious and pleasing aspirations were received with much gratification, but nowhere is it more difficult to transform hope into reality than in respect of labour in poor and relatively backward countries.

To some extent, the existence of a sterner régime where private influence, if not nullified was at least diminished, itself provided an amelioration of the labourer's condition. The negligent factory

---

[9] MLR No. 29. This was later reconstituted so as to make illegal only those strikes and lockouts which were prohibited under the Industrial Disputes Act, 1947. With the promulgation of the Industrial Disputes Ordinance of 1959, a further amendment, on corresponding lines, became necessary.

[10] President's address at Labour Rally held at Karachi on 4 November 1959.

[11] D, 1 March 1959.

owner now thought twice about his duties towards his work-force, and did not rely upon a tip to the factory inspector in order to escape the consequences of ignoring statutory obligations as regards safety, working conditions, and so on. But the mere effect of that kind of unseen moral pressure could not, by itself, suffice and, in order to restore the right of bargaining between management and labour, and to provide machinery for the settlement of disputes, an Industrial Disputes Ordinance was published some eight months after the announcement of the new industrial policy.[12] This Ordinance was, substantially, a re-enactment of the Act of 1947 and provided for the appointment of conciliation officers whose duty it was, if possible, to settle disputes between employer and employee. If the dispute could not be resolved by this means, recourse was then possible to the Industrial Court on which both sides were represented. The whole purpose was to provide machinery for the peaceful settlement of labour disputes, for the minimizing of time lost by reason of strikes and other forms of work stoppage, and for the prevention of such abuses as illegal strikes, illegal lock-outs, and the subsidizing of illegal cessations of work.

In the following year, an Industrial and Commercial Employment (Standing Orders) Ordinance was promulgated in the interests of less well-paid categories of employee.[13] This Ordinance was principally directed towards the elimination of those abuses to which illiterate and semi-educated factory-workers tend to be particularly subject. Rules were made relating to worker-classification, the payment of wages, the publication of wage-rates, the elimination of prolonged working-hours and unfair shift arrangements. Onerous fines on workers and the abuse of the fine-system were regulated and provision made to prevent wrongful and unjust termination of services, along with the misuse of 'probationary' employment by which the lower ranks of clerical workers, in particular, could be kept on 'probation' for months and then dismissed without notice.[14]

It would be foolish to pretend that this elementary labour legislation brought about any sustained period of industrial peace, since

[12] Ordinance No. LVI *Gazette of Pakistan* (*Extraordinary*) 21 October 1959.
[13] Ordinance No. III of 1960.
[14] Lieutenant-General W. A. Burki (a doctor by professional training) prescribed 'shock-treatment' for mill-owners in order to make them treat their workers better. *D*, 20 August 1961.

tranquil conditions in industry depend not only upon fair terms of service and good wages, but on other considerations with which the law is not concerned and on the existence of grievances for which the law can offer no remedy. Rising prices, irregular employment, unfair overtime, prolonged periods of unemployment, unwelcome migrations of industry with which are associated problems of housing, education for children, and the availability of essential amenities such as hospitals—all these make their contribution to recurring discontent. Far more sinister, of course, is the tendency to foment labour disturbances for political reasons and this particularly difficult form of political subversion has been common in Pakistan.

I must here introduce a digression concerning the transfer of the federal capital of Pakistan from Karachi to the Pothwar Plateau, about seven miles north-west of Rawalpindi. Dacca was to become the second capital of the country.[15] This decision appears to have been taken on the initative of President Ayub Khan, but was approved at the Governors' Conference in June 1959. In September a four-man Commission was appointed to prepare plans for the setting-up of the new capital, to which the name Islamabad was later given. Meanwhile, Rawalpindi was selected as the interim seat of the Central Government and, in a very short time, the first echelons were on the move from Karachi.

The question of location of the federal capital had been a source of controversy with previous governments, although it appears always to have been assumed that, whatever the decision, the site would be in or near Karachi. This assumption, however, seems to have been founded upon sentimental and historical grounds rather than upon the suitability of the geographical location, which is at any rate questionable. Karachi's climate is somewhat enervating and the city is sealed off from the rest of West Pakistan by arid desert. Immediately upon partition, the city's population multiplied several times, almost overnight, and it became not only the seat of government and of the central administration but also the country's largest industrial centre and principal seaport. In consequence,

[15] In the 1962 Constitution, Article 211, the areas reserved for the two capitals are respectively referred to as the 'Islamabad Capital Territory' and 'the Dacca Capital Territory'. The former is the principal seat of the Central Government and the latter is the principal seat of the National Assembly.

[16] See *The Forward March*, Government of Pakistan, Department of Films and Publications, Karachi, no date, p. 13.

Karachi has laboured under the serious disadvantages of inadequate planning to accompany so hasty an expansion, insufficient water supply, and a sewage system totally inadequate to its purpose. It was also observed that by centralizing his Government at Rawalpindi, the President could preserve a more intimate contact with the Army whose General Headquarters are located there.

This was a bold decision and one not unanimously acclaimed. To begin with, the association with Karachi, as birthplace of Mohamed Ali Jinnah, founder of Pakistan, was too close to be lightly ignored.[17] A number of foreign missions (notably that of the United States of America) had either constructed or had acquired property in Karachi, not to mention the large number of Pakistani civil servants who had built houses suitable for themselves and their families. It was felt, particularly in commercial circles, that the transfer of certain branches of the Ministries of Commerce and Industries would involve needless waste of time and money in visiting the new capital in order to settle comparatively minor problems relating to day-to-day affairs.[18] Among the people of East Pakistan it was apprehended that Rawalpindi's winter climate might be too severe for Bengalis accustomed to seasons of far less rigour. Lastly, there was criticism on the ground of needless expense at a time when the country urgently required money for more immediate concerns.

No doubt all these reasons have their substance, but apart from the weighty convenience of being close to Army headquarters, it is difficult to understand why, in 1959, President Ayub Khan should have felt so pressing an urgency to transfer his seat of Government from Karachi, with all the attendant expense and inconvenience. But, because so much inconvenience was in any case inevitable, it may be he considered 'if it were done, when 'tis done, then 'twere well it were done quickly'.[19]

From a long-term point of view, it could be argued that Karachi was simply developing into another great wen. It is undeniably true that some time before this decision to transfer the capital lock, stock, and barrel, certain measures of decentralization had

---

[17] It is interesting to speculate where Pakistan's first capital would have been located if Mr. Jinnah had been born, in, say, Chittagong.

[18] Rawalpindi is 937 miles from Karachi by rail and the time required to make the journey (by air), in a Trident aircraft is about $1\frac{3}{4}$ hours with no stops. About the same time is needed to make the journey from Dacca to Rawalpindi.

[19] *Macbeth* I, vii.

been going on. For instance, limitations had been placed on further industrialization around Karachi, and in other parts of the country, industrial trading estates were being promoted. It is also true that there had been unending controversy as to the manner of developing Karachi as a federal capital and as the centre of national administration. The transfer to the north put a summary stop to that apparently unending and entirely unproductive debate.

If the decision to transfer the capital aroused misgiving—albeit, during 1959, mainly inaudible—the establishment of a Central Institute of Islamic Research possessed far greater controversial potentiality. The purposes of the Institute were explained by the Government to be: first, 'to define Islam in terms of its fundamentals in a rational and liberal manner and to emphasize, among others, the basic Islamic ideals of universal brotherhood, tolerance, and social justice'; secondly, 'to interpret the teachings of Islam in such a way as to bring out its dynamic character in the context of the intellectual and scientific progress of the modern world'; thirdly, 'to carry out research in the contribution of Islam to thought, science, and culture with a view to enabling Muslims 'to recapture an eminent position in these fields'; and fourthly, 'to take appropriate measures for organizing and encouraging research in Islamic history, philosophy, law and jurisprudence'.[20]

The Institute defined itself as an organization whose 'duty is as academic as it is ethical' and, in its academic aspect, it organized a curriculum which extended over a period of four years after the degree of Master of Arts (Humanities). This curriculum is strictly related to Islamic learning, but includes the Arabic and Turkish languages and either French or German. A knowledge of English is evidently presumed. It publishes quarterly journals in Arabic and English along with monthly journals in Urdu, Bengali, and English. It has projects for studies in Islamic jurisprudence (on which subject it also gives advice to the Government on specific questions referred to it)[21] and for producing translations of

[20] *The Forward March*, op. cit., p. 19. Article 207 of the 1962 Constitution provides that the President shall establish an Islamic Research Institute whose 'function' shall be 'to undertake Islamic research and instruction in Islam for the purpose of assisting in the reconstruction of Muslim society on a truly Islamic basis'.

[21] Articles 199–206 in the 1962 Constitution provide for the establishment of an Advisory Council of Islamic Ideology.

classical Islamic works of particular worth and relevance to modern times. It is interesting to observe that the works of distinguished non-Muslim scholars of Islamic studies are included.

Although this programme may appear unexceptionable, it seems unlikely that the career of the Institute will be untroubled. There is little doubt that its terms of reference are viewed with suspicion, or at any rate, dislike, among those for whom the works of the old classics, as they understand them, suffice. Indeed, in 1963 an unedifying controversy took place on the subject of an essay entitled *Riba and Interest*, prepared by the Director of the Institute.[22] *Riba* is virtually a term of art in Islam and relates to the difficult problem of interest and usury on which there is a Quranic prohibition. The precise nature of this prohibition is a question to which, for centuries, Islamic scholars have ceaselessly applied their minds without, it appears, achieving unanimity of view.[23] The particular relevance today is whether in Islam, or in any country which claims to pursue the Islamic way of life, interest on money, in any form and in any circumstances, is permissible.

This single instance serves well to illustrate a profound and often irreconcilable diversity of approach. On the one hand, there are men like President Ayub Khan whose personal belief in the progressive, dynamic, and modern potentialities of Islam and Islamic teaching have been stated by him on so many occasions that no doubt is left where he stands on that issue.[24] On the other hand, it is decidely another question whether everyone in Pakistan accepts these possibilities. Of the religious obscurantists, some of whom possess considerable powers of rabble-rousing, we need not trouble to say much here, but Khwaja Nazimuddin evidently

[22] Dr. Fazlur Rahman, M.A. (Punjab), D.Phil. (Oxon.). The English version of this paper appeared in *Islamic Studies*, Vol. III, No. 1, March 1964. Some of the less savoury aspects of the controversy will be found in *O*, 26 October 1963. See also *D*, 9 October 1963.

[23] The question has, of course, two aspects: (*a*) the doctrinal and (*b*) the economic feasibility. The literature on the first aspect is enormous. On the second, it is not quite so copious but in Pakistan some professional economists and bankers have written books purporting to show, for example, that interest-free banking is perfectly feasibly in the present-day world.

[24] See, for instance, his address to the Darul Uloom Islamia, 3 May 1959; 'Id-i-Milad-un-Nabi message dated 4 September 1960; broadcast to the nation on 26 October 1960; speech delivered at the University of Cairo on 9 November 1960; inaugural speech at the sixteenth All-Pakistan Science Conference on 24 March 1964.

clarified the viewpoint of his party, the 'Council' Muslim League, when he roundly condemned all attempts to modernize Islam which, he said, would lead to *kufr*.[25] It is significant that in the Law Commission Report, to be discussed shortly, there is a passage referring to a survey and reassessment of Pakistan's legal heritage in the light of the requirements of a modern state and so as not to be 'inconsistent with the truly dynamic spirit of Islam',[26] but, the Report goes on cautiously to add, any commission set up for that purpose should be 'fairly representative of the old learning as well as of *modern enlightened*[27] opinion'.

To pursue this important topic further now would take me too far from the central purpose of the present narrative, but further consideration should be given to the Report of the Law Reform Commission, which I have just mentioned. This Commission, set up in November 1958, produced a Report that turned out to be a good deal less epoch-making than had once been expected and the authors of the Report themselves stated that the Commission was not 'directly concerned with the substantive law obtaining',[28] although its business was certainly to suggest how justice might be better and more speedily done and, for that purpose, to examine the hierarchy of the courts and their powers, the law of procedure and evidence, the state of the legal profession, cost of litigation and related matters. Like most of the state papers issued at this time, the Report, if not adequate for its purpose in all respects, nevertheless repays reading for the information it contains, especially that which is relevant to the administration of justice among mainly uneducated people whose code of social behaviour is noticeably different, in some respects, from its western counterpart.

The Commission attended to its task in assiduous fashion, putting forward no less than 368 recommendations, of varying weight, which had to do with legal procedure, simplification of legal business, and the efficient conduct of the legal profession. It contained recommendations for the relief of harassed litigants and the reduction, if not the elimination, of such evils as perjury and corruption. Its most concrete proposal was for the establishment of special family courts where, by means of a simplified procedure,

[25] *Kufr* signifies heresy, unbelief. *D*, 14 December 1962.
[26] Law Commission Report, 1959, p. 6.
[27] Author's italics.   [28] Law Commission Report, p. 5.

problems relating to marriage dower, divorce, and children could be effectively decided.[29]

While, therefore, it was a workmanlike contribution to sound legal administration, it left untouched any question of far-reaching change in the legal system and, in fact, the Report expressed a clear opinion that the sweeping and often ill-advised criticism of the existing system had less to do with the system itself than with the manner of its operation.[30]

In March 1959, after a long period of internal wrangling, there appeared the Report of the Press Commission. The history of this Commission forms an interesting and curiously apposite instance of the kind of internal intrigue and conflict so often bedevilling much that has been attempted in Pakistan. The story goes back as far as September 1954 when the Press Commission was first set up. It then comprised a Chairman (a former High Court Judge) and, after various additions and changes, thirteen other members of whom nine were newspaper editors. Unfortunately, these editors were divided in opinion by their membership of two rival professional bodies, namely, the All-Pakistan Newspaper Editors' Conference and the Council of Pakistan Editors. Differences of view between these two organizations led to protracted delays in the work of the Commission and, eventually, because of the improbability of any positive conclusion to these disputes, it was decided that the Commission should be reconstituted.

Thus four years almost to the day had elapsed when the Government decided, on 5 September 1958 (about a month before Martial Law was declared), upon the desired changes. The new Commission, consisting of a Chairman and five other members of whom only the Member-Secretary was a professional journalist, was now able to go about its business unhindered by professional disagreements. The establishment of the Press Commission, therefore, does not represent any act of initiative on the part of the new dispensation, but in the prevailing atmosphere of drive, the Report

[29] A proposal to this effect had been made, some nine years earlier, by a Commission set up to consider marriage and family laws in Pakistan. The recommendations of this Commission were substantially followed in the Family Laws Ordinance of 1961. See Chapter X. In July 1964 West Pakistan's Family Courts Act implemented the Law Commission's proposal for family courts. By October 1964 East Pakistan had not given effect to the recommendation.

[30] Law Commission Report, p. 6, on the subject of 'Wholesale Drastic Changes Not Necessary'.

came out eight months after reconstitution. There is no doubt that the public had long been interested in problems relating to the Press, which was by no means in a satisfactory state, either in the conduct of its work or the conditions of service of journalists.

In these circumstances, it was left to the new Government to adopt measures, based on the Report's recommendations, for the advancement of conditions of service among journalists, including the establishment of a Wages Board to determine fair rates of pay and allowances, and the compulsory setting-up of Provident Funds for the benefit of professional staff. Such legislation had not hitherto existed in Pakistan and there can be no doubt that the Ordinance[31] which introduced these reforms was particularly welcome to a profession with so many inherent risks and financial limitations—risks and limitations all the more severe in a country where illiteracy prevails, where several written languages are in use, and where, because of these circumstances, newspaper circulations are trifling by comparison with those achieved wherever the majority of the population can read and write.[32]

In the same year, a Press and Publications Ordinance[33] was issued whose purpose was to revise and codify the existing law relating to the proprietorship and editorship of newspapers and other periodicals, as well as the control of printing-presses. The outlines of this Ordinance substantially followed existing legislation, taking into account the views of the Press Commission, including the thorny topic of Press supervision and control. It did, however, introduce an important and liberalizing change by which questions of financial security (which might be required from a newspaper or from a printing-press as guarantee for satisfactory conduct) as well as forfeiture of that security (in the event of a breach of the guarantee) became subject to the powers of the judiciary rather than of the executive.

The last, and in some respects the most important, of the state papers I propose to comment on in any detail is the Report of the Commission on National Education, appointed by the Martial Law

[31] Working Journalists (Conditions of Service) Ordinance, 1960.

[32] In Appendix VI will be found a note on the Press in Pakistan, with particular reference to the Martial Law period.

[33] Ordinance No. XV of 1960. In 1963 this Ordinance was replaced by Ordinances issued by the Provincial Governments exercising powers conferred by the new constitution of 1962. The change created considerable dissatisfaction. See Appendix VI.

Government on 30 December 1958. The Report was presented to the President on 26 August 1959, and is a document of some 336 pages, prepared after eight months of inquiry and an extensive tour of the principal centres in both wings of the country. It constitutes an important and valuable review of the conditions of education in Pakistan, the particular problems that stand in the way of transforming a people, about twenty per cent literate, into a nation possessing the means of acquiring essential primary education and of imparting adequate instruction in advanced forms of learning as well as professional studies. It endeavours to face—not, perhaps, as explicitly as would have been useful—some of the difficulties and abuses that have undermined, and continue to undermine, the national system of education,[34] as well as some of those particular difficulties associated with the existence of more than one national and regional language and more than one national and regional script.

On some points the Report was very clear. It recommended 'most strongly that the Bachelor's degree course should be extended from two to three years'.[35] It considered there should be a system of monthly examinations conducted by teachers and that the results of these monthly examinations should be taken into account when determining the final result of the student's university career.[36] It was concluded that a high proportion of students are 'altogether unsuited for university education' and that 'we are allowing into our colleges and universities many thousands of students who are foredoomed to failure and who know they are'.[37] On the basis of this plain-speaking, the Commission produced detailed proposals for a general raising of educational standards along with revised syllabuses intended to promote a better standard of instruction and knowledge. As a result of these efforts, a Curriculum Committee was established with the object of giving further effect to the Commission's recommendations. The President's own interest and approval of the Commission's work were stated in such addresses as that to the University of Cairo,[38] and in his inaugural speech at the Conference of Heads of Universities of SEATO member countries.[39]

[34] These include, for example, the textbook trouble, p. 293; political interference and student unrest, pp. 37 and 39; inadequacy of libraries; trafficking in university places. The college admission problem also manifested itself in the earlier days of Martial Law. *D*, 3 September 1960.
[35] ibid., p. 20.   [36] ibid., p. 23.   [37] ibid., pp. 36 and 37.
[38] 9 November 1960.   [39] 25 January 1961.

Surprising as it must doubtless appear, the most significant consequence of this Report—certainly the most widely publicized consequence—to manifest itself, was a determined opposition which, after the withdrawal of Martial Law, disclosed itself in violence and student-strikes in September and October 1962. The measures proposed by the Report, and those adopted in pursuance were, it appeared, totally unsatisfactory to the student-body and to university teaching-staffs also. Agitation centred on the proposal to introduce a three-year Bachelor's degree-course conjoined with other grievances such as the expense of text-books, the difficulty of obtaining them, and the unnecessarily frequent changes in book-prescription. The high cost of tuition fees and similar complaints were added to the more prominent issues.

Since this book is, primarily, to do with the Martial Law period, it is not necessary to describe in detail the tragic episodes that ensued. It is enough to say that in Karachi and Dacca student demonstrations and strikes led to loss of life and damage to person and to property. In Karachi, the police had recourse to tear-gas. In Dacca, the Army was called upon to assist in restoring order.

The outcome of this resistance to change was a complete victory for those in opposition and this opposition included, moreover, members of university teaching-staffs who were threatened, under the new proposals, with a great deal more work. The three-year degree course was put into abeyance[40] and, in Karachi, externment orders, imposed for a period of one year on a group of students who had been fomenting agitation, were withdrawn unconditionally.[41] In Dacca, all police cases pending against riotous students were withdrawn and the families of people who had been injured in the disturbances were to be compensated. Not content with this, there was a recurrence of trouble in Dacca a year later, when students demonstrated and again demanded that the entire Education Report be scrapped.[42]

Stated thus, the impression may well be conveyed that, on the one hand, the labours of the Education Commission were totally wasted and, on the other, that the students were entirely and unreasonably unco-operative. There may be some truth in this, but it is by no means the whole of it. The Education Report was, after all, a comprehensive survey of educational needs from

[40] D, 1 October 1962.   [41] D, 16 October 1962.
[42] D, 18 and 20 September 1963.

primary schooling upwards and much of the Commission's work turned out to be valuable guidance for subsequent measures. And, so far as concerns the attitude of the students, this sprang from causes with which, fundamentally, the Education Report had little concern and for which the Commission was by no means responsible.

The Report was the victim, in short, of a situation that extended far beyond educational reform in a purely pedagogic sense. For years—from the very commencement of Pakistan's existence— student unrest had been a significant aspect of the national life. The opposition and disturbance that crystallized around the Report and the changes it proposed, had their origins in causes far more deeply rooted. To be sure, the Education Commission itself had touched upon the subject of student indiscipline and its beginnings in pre-partition days, but the reference was perfunctory and made no attempt to trace all the causes and contributory factors.

It is quite erroneous to suppose that, in the sub-continent, students, as a whole, are simply a difficult lot, factious and quarrelsome. Quite apart from the exuberant idealism of youth, they have laboured under serious grievances for years. The subject of student-unrest, both in Pakistan and India, is a complex one, worth a book of its own that would in parts make ugly reading. No doubt, there are undesirable elements among the student-body, including a number of apparently 'professional' students who seem to hang permanently around the colleges whispering discontent and inducing opposition to authority, but there are serious and genuine problems which have gone unredressed for years, and abandonment of the Education Report or, at any rate, some of its provisions, was the propitiatory sacrifice demanded.

Although the successful opposition to some of the Report's recommendations came after Martial Law was withdrawn, it must be remembered that whereas, during that period, the authorities were successful in silencing politicians, they were never quite able to quell demonstrations of active protest on the part of younger people at college. In Lahore in 1960 the students staged a walk-out from the the examination hall, complaining that the Constitutional law paper was too difficult and too long. There had previously been similar incidents in Karachi and Hyderabad and the Education Minister issued a statement to the effect that this kind of behaviour, and the hooliganism which accompanied it, must stop.[43]

In February and March of the following year a much more serious situation sprang up in Karachi when students took out a procession, in defiance of Martial Law Regulations, and proceeded to the chancery of the Indian High Commission, to demonstrate there against the communal riots in Jabalpur. Outside the chancery, inflammatory speeches were made, stones were thrown, windows broken, and eventually the police had to use tear-gas to break up the demonstration. In consequence, 179 students were charged with a breach of Martial Law Regulations and eight were convicted by a Military Court.[44] At this point there was a general absence from classes and the situation became somewhat tense. The President issued an appeal, calling upon the students not to become the victim of the machinations of others. More significant was the pre-censorship of news touching student affairs imposed by the Chief Commissioner of Karachi.[45]

These incidents, and the part played by the police, were not forgotten and the memory of them must account, in part, for the determinations of the student community in 1962, which I mentioned earlier. It is, of course, also evident that the events of 1962 owed much to the withdrawal of Martial Law and to the fact that a National Assembly had come into existence whose members, although not immediately faced with election prospects, were nevertheless sensitive on this point. Finally, it is more than probable that some of the angry resistance which these young men and young women were led to demonstrate in 1962, on the Education Report question, had its origin in some very direct and purposeful political inspiration.

I end this chapter with a brief mention of those other Commissions which, however important in themselves, are of too restricted an interest to warrant longer notice here. A Maritime Commission, appointed on 19 November 1958 to inquire into Pakistan's commercial maritime affairs, led to the establishment of a shipping corporation which acquired several brand-new vessels and entered the international trade. In February 1959 a Credit

[43] *D*, 12 and 13 May 1960.

[44] Four students were sentenced to one year's rigorous imprisonment, one to nine months, and three to six months. About four months later, in July 1961, they were all released.

[45] *D*, 28 February, 1 and 16 March, 6 and 8 April 1961.

R.P.—8

Inquiry Commission was appointed to study the situation concerning monetary credit and, in the same year, Commissions were set up to study the cotton yarn and textile industry and the equally important jute industry. In November 1959 the Government appointed a Medical Reforms Commission and, in the following month, a Commission to inquire into the country's sugar requirements and indigenous production from the country's own sugarcane resources.

Since the Companies' Act of 1913, which regulated the formation and operation of joint stock companies, had become obsolete in many respects, a Commission was set up to inquire into this aspect of commercial law. The Company Law Commission submitted a Report in 1961, but no legislative action, in response to its recommendations, was pursued—a point which later became a source of criticism.[46]

Lastly, I must mention the Pay and Services Commission, appointed in September 1959, under the chairmanship of Mr. Justice Cornelius, at that time a Judge of the Supreme Court of Pakistan and later Chief Justice. Assisted by seven members and a secretary, the Commission was to inquire into the structure of the civilian services and their emoluments. There had been, at various times, both criticism of the structure of various branches of the public service and, more particularly, of their emoluments which, it was recognized, had fallen out of step with prevailing economic conditions. The general feeling was that increases of pay were necessary and inevitable.[47] Although certain interim measures were adopted (presumably in the light of the Report's recommendations) to ameliorate the condition of the lower ranks of public servant, the Report has not yet been published. This circumstance also provoked discontent, particularly in view of the fact that, in 1964, increases of pay were promptly sanctioned for members of the Armed Forces.[48]

[46] This, at any rate, was true until October 1964. See article entitled *Big Business Killings, O*, 8 August 1964.

[47] See statement by President Ayub Khan at the National Press Club, Washington D.C., 13 July 1961.

[48] Until October 1964 the Pay and Services Commission Report had not been made public. Civilian employees of Government earning up to Rs.500 a month received interim increases of pay, however.

A list of Commissions set up and Reports published during the Martial Law period is in Appendix VII.

VIII

Basic Democracies

THE first measure of representative government established in Pakistan by the Martial Law administration bears the description 'Basic Democracies', and its introduction deftly coincided with the first anniversary of President Ayub Khan's assumption of complete power.[1] The phrase signifies a political conception and a way of life as well as a political institution. In its singular usage—'Basic Democracy'—it also denotes the small political unit in a system of local government.[2] Undoubtedly, this was the first clear step towards conferring upon the citizen a right of participation in the government of his country and, in a land where circumstances admittedly contribute little towards the successful exercise of that right, this institution has been variously hailed as the ultimate in political wisdom on the one hand and, on the other, as a mere sop to democratic sentiment at home and abroad.

Without pursuing verbal niceties too far, the expression 'Basic Democracies' falls somewhat awkwardly upon the ear, perhaps because of the clumsy application of the word 'democracies'. This has given rise to the suspicion that it was pressed into use for its propaganda value rather than for its material relevance. Secondly, it is exposed to the Orwellian gibe that all democracies are basic, but some are more basic than others. It must be added, however, that President Ayub Khan has provided an explanation for the adoption of this terminology and it is only fair to reproduce it here. He said: 'We have given [the scheme] the name of Basic Democracies for the obvious reason that we want it to grow and evolve from the very first rung of the political ladder so that it finds its

---

[1] Basic Democracies Order, *Gazette of Pakistan* (*Extraordinary*), 27 October 1959. This auspicious occasion was also marked by the promotion of General Ayub Khan to the rank of Field-Marshal.

[2] Basic Democracies (Federal Capital) Election Rules, 20 November 1959.

roots deep among the people starting at the village level in rural areas and at the mohalla[3] level in towns.'[4]

At any rate, whatever one may think about this coinage, such was the phrase contrived and such is the description of the system of local government introduced after one year of Martial Law. This, too, describes the method of selection of an electoral college by which a referendum was held in February 1960 when President Ayub Khan was approved and endorsed as holder of that office. The same electoral college was employed, later, for the purpose of electing candidates to the National Assembly. As we shall see, it is doubtful if the system enjoys universal and unqualified approval in Pakistan, but this circumstance in no way diminishes its importance in the country's historical and political development, nor are its implications to be underrated.

All this we shall, in due course, come to. First, we should see in what this system consists and what this enlargement of individual political responsibility involved.

At the initial level (or 'tier' as it has sometimes been called) the scheme envisaged units of local self-government which, in the case of urban areas, were called 'towns' and, in the case of rural areas, are called 'unions'. These units were demarcated on a population basis in the order of 10,000 to 15,000 people. Big cities with large populations were divided for this purpose into units on a similar basis. Each such unit was to elect its representatives, say one representative for every 1,500 electors, and these people, chosen by simple majority vote, were to sit on Union Councils for these primary units, for a term of five years. In scope and duties there is a marked similarity to the parish council as it once existed in the British Isles.

Along with these elected members, others could be nominated by the Government to represent special interests, for example, women, or minority religious communities, or classes of people who might find it difficult to secure election for one of themselves. The case of the labourer whose illiteracy might make it difficult for him to advance his own interests adequately was instanced.[5] The number of nominated members could not exceed one-half of the total number of elected members.

[3] Parish or quarter within a township.

[4] President's broadcast from Dacca, 2 September 1959.

[5] See pamphlet entitled *Basic Democracies*, published by the Bureau of National Reconstruction, Government of Pakistan, no date, p. 12.

From its own body, the Union Council was to elect a Chairman[6] who was entitled to receive an honorarium. Subject to the supervision prescribed in the Basic Democracies Order and to the general supervision exercised by the normal administrative machinery of the Government, the duty of this Council was to execute the functions allotted to it and it could raise money for that purpose by certain forms of local taxation. Thus it could provide and maintain public thoroughfares, open spaces and gardens. It could undertake duties connected with local sanitation, water supply, burial places, disposal of animal carcasses, and 'any other measures likely to promote the welfare, health, safety, comfort or convenience of the inhabitants of the Union or of visitors'.[7] In all, no less than thirty-seven forms of local activity were listed and in these the Union Council could interest itself,[8] but in the case of large cities, possessing a corporate existence and corporate machinery, the new councils[9] could not encroach on the rights and duties of the existing corporations.

The chairmen of the Union Councils automatically became representative members at the next stage—the Thana or Tehsil Council. To this Council could be nominated official and non-official members to a number which did not exceed the total number of representative members from Union Councils. In addition, the sub-divisional officer and the circle officer, within whose executive jurisdiction this unit lay, became *ex officio* members of the Thana or Tehsil Council. The Order allots no specific functions or duties to this Council whose purpose was to ensure and promote co-ordination among the Union Councils within the Thana or Tehsil.[10]

On similar, but not identical principles of construction, the pyramid rises through the District Council to the level of the Divisional Council, itself the largest administrative unit within the Province and comparable with the county in the United Kingdom. However, at the District Council level and upwards, the

[6] Under the original Basic Democracies Order, chairmen of Union Councils might be either elected or nominated members. Under the new arrangements, which came into force in June 1965, the Union Councils will have no nominated members and therefore all chairmen will be drawn from elected members.

[7] Basic Democracies Order, Third Schedule.

[8] The functions were not stated to be mandatory.

[9] In this case 'township committees' would be the correct terminology.

[10] Thana and Tehsil signify administrative sub-units in East and West Pakistan respectively.

pattern changes. The representation, as well as the power, of elected members tends to diminish and the power, as well as the supervision, exercised by administrative officials tends to expand.[11] In both District and Divisional Councils there were to be official and appointed members. At least half of the appointed members were to be Chairmen of Union Councils within the District or Division. Presiding as Chairman of the District or Divisional Council was the District Magistrate (or Collector) and the Divisional Commissioner respectively.

The functions of the District Councils were extensive, comprising no less than twenty-eight compulsory duties relating to education, libraries, hospitals, roads, sanitation, agricultural and industrial development and, along with these, seventy optional functions were specified. Thus the District Council became the effective executive instrument of local government. The Divisional Council was not assigned any specific functions under the Order, but co-ordinated the activities of its District Council and maintained a general watch on their zeal and competence. In addition, there were, of course, the usual arrangements for audit of accounts and the customary measures of control to ensure there was no abuse of power or public money.

Finally, provision was made for the establishment of two Provincial Development Advisory Councils, one for each Province. These Councils were to consist of official members and non-official members appointed by the President on the recommendation of the Governor of the Province. These two categories were to be equal in number and, of the appointed non-official members, at least one-third were to be selected from among Chairmen of Union Councils and Committees. These Provincial Advisory bodies, each consisting of forty-eight members, with the Provincial Governors as Chairmen, were set up for the first time in May 1960.

From this brief summary of the first measure of political representation to follow the abrogation of the 1956 Constitution, one aspect stands out very clearly. No one who wished to enter, or re-enter, this aspect of public life, could do so unless he offered himself as a candidate for a Union Council,[12] or unless he obtained a

---

[11] In his Dacca broadcast of 2 September 1959 the President indicated the hope that, in due time, this trend would reverse itself.

[12] It will be understood that persons disqualified under the terms of PODO and EBDO could not offer themselves as candidates.

nomination, a far less satisfactory expedient for anyone with an eye to the future and certainly a less likely prospect, if only on mathematical grounds.

This circumstance undoubtedly introduced something fresh and important, leading to a new and more active political consciousness among the people. In the past, the bigger magnates, especially among the landed gentry, had aimed at membership of the National and Provincial Assemblies. For that purpose, they had to tour the countryside and address the electors or, if the candidate possessed no fluent eloquence, there were others to do it for him. Now they had to be content, if they wished to remain in public life, with making a public appearance at a low and much more intimate level and, if they were tongue-tied on the platform, so much the worse for them. In this way, it may be true, a premium was thereby placed upon the glib speaker, and the man with the tradition of centuries behind him, who knew the people and their problems but was no orator, was at a disadvantage. It perhaps did no harm for the scions of old and influential families to find themselves competing with humbler members of society for the privilege of participating afterwards in the deliberations of what was not much more than a meeting of village elders.[13]

The Basic Democracies scheme is intimately associated with the name of President Ayub Khan and he is credited with having devised it.[14] From its inception it has been treated by him as an article of political faith and he has, in numerous references, made clear that from it he expected to see a fabric woven that would clothe the administration in a type of democracy best suited to Pakistan. At Ankara, he said: 'Elections to Basic Democracies . . . would give our people an opportunity to work out for themselves the way of life best suited to promote their common weal.'[15] At Belgrade: '. . . we believe we have found the answer to our problems through our system of Basic Democracies',[16] and at Bonn: 'Our system of Basic Democracy has been devised to ensure this

[13] It was reported that at the Dera Ghazi Khan election a local landlord was defeated by a cobbler. It also appears that both had the same name! However, conclusions should not be too hastily drawn. In these elections candidates choose a simple object by which the illiterate elector can identify him, for example, a tree, or a lantern, or something equally recognizable. These symbols appear on the ballot paper and the voter puts his X where he chooses. See D, 8 January 1960.

[14] D, 16 December 1959.   [15] 18 November 1959.
[16] D, 13 January 1961.

participation (i.e., in major development at all levels of work and responsibility).'[17]

Not only so, but the scheme was adduced by him as evidence of sincerity in promising a return to representative, democratic government[18] and as his conception of a pattern out of which could be moulded the type of democracy which would work best, at any rate in Pakistan. And it has further been suggested that it contains an approach to the problem of representative government in countries where a large part of the population is illiterate and politically unsophisticated.[19]

All this I shall examine in more detail, but, first, would touch on what followed the promulgation of the plan. In order to explain and popularize the new concept, the President undertook, in the December following its announcement, a week's tour of the West Pakistan countryside in a train called *Pak Jamhuriyat Special*.[20] He addressed many gatherings and submitted to much questioning on the nature and merits of the Basic Democracies scheme. It was during this campaign, also, that he began to give clearer expression to his own constitutional ideas and began to indicate, in greater detail, the type of constitution that he would favour for Pakistan.

Later, in January 1960, he carried out a similar countrywide tour in East Pakistan, but, meanwhile, elections were being held in an orderly manner and in an atmosphere of public interest. Since, under Martial Law Regulation No. 55, there existed a prohibition on meetings for political purposes, a relaxation was authorized. Since, also, political parties had been dissolved and their existence had become illegal, the elections were conducted on a personal basis, the idea being, as the President had repeatedly urged, that electors should vote, not for a party-machine, but in order to get the right man to represent the people's best interests. Thus candidates presented themselves at the hustings, made their speeches, answered questions and, generally, did their best to impress the voter with a sense of their individual merits.

As a result, some 80,000 persons became members of Union Councils and, on 23 January 1960, these Union Council members —Basic Democrats, as they were called—were invited to state

---

[17] *D*, 17 January 1961.   [18] Speech at Lyallpur, 12 October 1959.
[19] See *D*, 17 December 1959, in which Mr. Jaiprakash Narayan is reported to have agreed with Presidendent Ayub Khan's views on this aspect.
[20] Pakistan Republican Special.

by secret ballot whether or not they placed their confidence in Field-Marshal Ayub Khan as President of their country. The ballot paper contained squares in which the voter could signify either 'Yes' or 'No'. Against the 'Yes' square was a photograph of Field-Marshal Ayub Khan and against the 'No' square was a patch of solid blue, and the result of the ballot showed 75,084 votes in the affirmative, with 2,829 against. There were 608 invalid votes and 150 votes could not be cast as the seats were lying unfilled. Thus, by an overwhelming majority, President Ayub Khan was vouchsafed this expression of approval. He was then, somewhat euphemistically, termed Pakistan's first 'elected' President[21] and an oath of office was administered to him by the Chief Justice of Pakistan.

Thanking the Basic Democrats and the people for the trust placed in him, the President stated that, at an early date, he would set up a Constitution Commission to devise a suitable political structure for the country.[22] He said that he preferred to do this *after* there had been some expression of the people's will. In his own words, he wanted the people 'to have a say in it at every stage'. As to the type of Constitution which the President favoured, there could not be much doubt in anyone's mind since he had already given so much expression to his views.

Much of what the President had to say on constitutional matters is very relevant to the evolution of the Constitution of 1962, but his utterance on this subject belongs historically to the whole period of Martial Law, during which time he gave expression to his ideas and the reasons for his conclusions. Because of this I must now consider his views on the constitutional problems of Pakistan.

He had, to begin with, become convinced that the British type of parliamentary democracy, whose foundations and approach had guided all previous constitution-makers in Pakistan, was unsuited to the country, not because he saw anything inherently wrong with it, but because he felt that the circumstances which had led to the development of this form of government in the United Kingdom and elsewhere, did not obtain in Pakistan. It was his belief that his

[21] *D*, 16 February 1960.
[22] What follows is taken from President Ayub Khan's statements, as reported in *D*, 16, 17, and 18 December 1959 and from his address to the Basic Democrats' Convention, *D*, 17 June 1960. References to Basic Democracies are numerous in his various public statements and speeches, the volumes of which, published by the Government of Pakistan, should also be consulted for the *ipsissima verba*.

constitution-devising predecessors had failed, among other things by reason of slavish copying, although he conceded there was reason for that, too. 'We adopted the British parliamentary form of political system . . because that was the only thing we knew.'[23]

There were further reasons which he and other members of his Government stated at various times. All stressed the low level of literacy in the country; the ease with which the masses could be persuaded, excited, and exploited by unscrupulous party-men; the general lack of political sophistication. These were conditions that made it necessary to devise a constitution which would safeguard the public from its own shortcomings, and ensure stability in government. In attempting to do this, President Ayub Khan was not setting out upon something quite as novel as he may have thought and, like others before him, he was to learn that this was a difficult and even dangerous business.

Now, since it could not reasonably be disputed that Pakistan's earlier constitutional experience (if it can be so described)[24] had been neither smooth nor markedly democratic, the President was by no means necessarily in the wrong when he began to look in new directions for a solution. Nor is it surprising that it was precisely this experience that had contributed so much to the conclusions he had reached. He had therefore come to hold that what the country needed was a presidential form of government, with a strong Centre, based on indirect elections to the national and provincial legislatures, for which purpose citizens elected as Basic Democrats were to form an electoral college which would also serve to elect a President.

He did not believe in political parties, not even in a single political party such as prevails in Communist countries. He desired what he described as the Islamic method and he instanced the case of the Advisory Council set up by the Caliph Hazrat Umar in which a number of persons of wisdom and high moral character are brought together, as independent men free of party restraints and affiliations, to act solely in the best interests of the people. In this way, they did not create, said the President, 'one-party dictatorship nor did they entangle themselves in the vicious circle

---

[23] Address at a Joint Session of the Congress of the United States of America, 12 July 1961.

[24] The Report of the Constitution Commission, 1961. Chapter I is illuminating on the nature of this experience.

of the majority and minority. The Islamic type of constitution demands that every member of the Assembly or Parliament should express his opinion on national problems as a free member and should not be influenced by any nation or group.' Election of these men should likewise not be held 'on a party ticket', but should be based on the needs of different sections of the population. 'This is the real Islamic method of election.'[25]

In due course, we will have to consider how far the President has been able to persuade his countrymen of the weight of his political conclusions. Three points, however, were immediately made plain. The first was that the President was totally committed to the Basic Democracies scheme. In his own words, these institutions were the 'foundation-stone of a new political system' in the country. Secondly, there appeared in his speeches and addresses an ever-increasing emphasis on Islamic values and on 'reflecting the spirit of Islam' in the Constitution.[26] Thirdly, from this time on, his political preoccupations (in the sense of responding to politically-felt sentiments within the country) began to grow and his position as a military ruler tended to diminish.

It must not be thought that the Basic Democracies scheme was accepted without adverse comment, and public criticism of it, even under Martial Law, was not disallowed. This criticism by Pakistanis was itself a part of political maturation and must therefore be treated with the consideration that its usefulness deserves. The critics held that the elected members (the Basic Democrats) would be subservient to administrative officials who enjoyed a considerable ascendancy in terms of power. It was thought that situations might arise in which cleavages of opinion between official and non-official (particularly non-official) members would be irreconcilable. Some people said that here was nothing more than an imitation of the *panchayat*[27] system and still others said that it had been evolved simply in the interests of President Ayub Khan and his government. Lastly, it was suggested that the electoral college,

[25] President's address at Lahore, 15 June 1960. Cf., Joseph Conrad, *Under Western Eyes*, where Miss Haldin says: 'We Russians shall find a better form of national freedom than an artificial conflict of parties—which is wrong because it is a conflict and contemptible because it is artificial.'

[26] Later he claimed that the presidential system was nearest to the Islamic tradition. *D*, 7 October 1963.

[27] A body of village elders, or the elders of a particular community of people, which meets to settle disputes. A *panchayat* has the function of a court of arbitration rather than that of administration, but the latter is not excluded.

consisting of citizens elected as Basic Democrats, was a more easily manœuvrable body of men than the entire electorate and that their votes could more easily be purchased.[28]

The President's refutation of these criticisms sprang largely from his belief in the possibility of dispensing with political parties, his belief in the Basic Democracies system as a training-ground for citizenship and the discharge of civic duties and, thirdly, in his belief that a solution of these problems must be sought in the country itself. 'People ask me in which book one can find our system. My reply is . . . I have read it in the book of Pakistan.'[29] Moreover, according to these views, time and experience would make it possible to enlarge the scope of responsibilities entrusted to Basic Democrats and, as elected and official members continued to work together, so the question of subservience would pass. Working 'as a team, most of their mutual misunderstandings, difficulties, and suspicions would automatically disappear'.[30] 'Can't we adopt,' he said, 'the sensible alternative of going by consensus of opinion for the common good instead of creating hard and fast cleavages in our ranks based on majorities and minorities?'[31]

As to those who made comparisons with the *panchayat* system, the President roundly declared that such people were not only not conversant with that system, but had not honestly pondered 'the philosophy underlying the Basic Democracies'.[32] He dismissed as ridiculous the suggestion that the system was designed to make his Government and himself secure and, as for the suggestion that the votes of Basic Democrats could be bought, he considered it would be so expensive a business that rich people would not be interested 'in such a heavy bargain'.[32] Moreover, he believed that the 'Basic Democrats are good people. It is a wild allegation to suspect them of bargaining in votes'.[32] Finally, he reiterated the view that the system he had introduced was fundamentally and

---

[28] President's address at Lahore, 15 June 1960. It is fair to add that the use of the expression 'Union Panchayat' had an official origin. In his Dacca broadcast of 2 September 1959 the President used the phrase 'Union Panchayat' when making his first official pronouncement regarding the Basic Democracies scheme. In reporting a proposed plan for a measure of 'basic democracy', *Dawn* used the phrase 'Union Panchayat' (14 and 18 June 1959). The same newspaper used the phrase when reporting a proposal for advisory bodies for Provincial Governors (2 July 1959).

[29] *D*, 13 July 1964.   [30] Address at Lahore, 15 June 1960.
[31] Broadcast to the nation, 26 October 1960.
[32] Address at Lahore, 15 June 1960.

genuinely Islamic and derived from the teachings and traditions of Islam.

Now the importance of all this can scarcely be overstressed and although it takes us somewhat further ahead than was intended at this stage, and even, perhaps, outside the frame of the Martial Law period, it seems to be convenient to consider briefly the validity of the Basic Democracies scheme and President Ayub Khan's political testament as he has at various times expressed it.

It does not seem at all open to argument that, as a system of local government, there is nothing defective in the Basic Democracies scheme, nor is there any reason to suppose that it will fail to ensure fair participation by the elected citizen in local administration. Participation is not, after all, solely a question of being elected, or nominated, or even of being an official member. It is also a question of capacity. Where the elected members are weak and of limited ability, it follows that official members will dominate the deliberations and will exercise the greater influence in formation of decisions. Where the elected members are of equal or greater competence, their share will be correspondingly larger. This is simply a matter of reason. It is reasonable, also, to assume that as these combinations of elected and nominated members acquire knowledge and stature, so will they acquire maturity and respect. Ultimately, they will be looked to as the natural holders of authority at all levels of local government.

This kind of political evolution seems to hold good everywhere. It stands to reason that not every citizen elected to these bodies will necessarily be capable, honest, or useful, but a substantial proportion should justify the confidence placed in them and out of those can be expected to emerge men of experience and mature capacity. This need not be doubted and whether the system owes anything to the older *panchayat* does not seem to matter.

But the question whether the elected Basic Democrats can, and should, form an electoral college for the selection of a President and members of the legislatures is a vastly different matter.[33] Nor is it clear that the nation was, or even is, in agreement with President Ayub Khan, or his Government, on this matter of indirect elections. Although the Constitution which he gave to the country in 1962 maintains this approach, it is far from certain that the nation as a whole approves. Indeed, it has not been established

[33] *O*, 8 August 1964.

that the nation agrees with him in his view of the unsuitability of the British parliamentary method of government. Mr. Mohamed Ali Choudhury, the principal architect of the 1956 Constitution, in his exhaustive replies to the questionnaire issued by the Constitution Commission, firmly joins issue on this question.[34] The Constitution Commission held the view that the defects of the 1956 Constitution were not such as could have prevented its successful working.[35]

Thus it may have been with a sense of this division of opinion that, after the 1962 Constitution was promulgated, the President felt the need to set up, in August of the same year, a Franchise Commission of five members to examine (in the light of circumstances and conditions obtaining in the country) the electoral system prescribed in the new Constitution, and to say if it was an efficacious and appropriate instrument for realistic representation of the people. Depending upon the answer to these questions, the Franchise Commission was asked to give its views on the electoral college, on a possible limited extension of the franchise, and on the question of the qualification of electors in the event that universal adult suffrage was recommended.

The Report of the Commission showed that on these issues there was a difference of view, with a majority favouring universal adult suffrage and direct elections for both President and legislatures.[36] Consequently, the Ministry of Law 'thought it expedient to set up a Special Committee to examine the recommendations of the Franchise Commission, keeping in view the socio-economic and administrative requirements of the country and to analyse the various issues dispassionately. The Committee was assisted by some experts in the field of law, political science and administration.'[37]

The Special Committee's Report is an uneasy and somewhat

[34] Reported verbatim in *D*, 17 June 1960.
[35] Constitution Commission Report, 1961, Chapter I.
[36] The Franchise Commission Report was submitted to the President on 12 February 1963. It was published in the *Gazette of Pakistan* (Extraordinary), dated 23 August 1963, on the eve of prorogation of the National Assembly. This circumstance aroused considerable ill-feeling on the part of Opposition members.
[37] Preface, dated 16 January 1964, to the Report of the Special Committee, published by the Ministry of Law with comments by 'a Professor of Political Science', 'a Lawyer', and 'an Administrator'. So far as can be traced, the names of these gentlemen, and the names of the members of the Special Committee have never been made public.

muddled document, which surveys the arguments in favour of direct and indirect elections. It also surveys the inescapable conditions in which elections have to be conducted in Pakistan, with an electorate which is mainly illiterate, although it does not follow than an illiterate man is necessarily stupid or less able than another, who can read and write, to judge what is in his best interests. Among the difficulties to be faced are dense populations, climatic conditions which can be obstructive (as in East Pakistan), and the problems associated with a sparse population scattered over wide areas (as in West Pakistan). The Report suggests that not only can the voter be unduly and unwisely influenced by noisy party propaganda, but he loses contact with, and therefore interest in, the man he sends to the National or Provincial Assembly, often hundreds of miles away. Because he cannot read the newspapers it is difficult for him to know and understand what is happening to the government of the country. On the other hand, he is always in touch with the man who can vote on his behalf, the Basic Democrat.[38] It is significant that the Special Committee's view seems to have been founded largely upon the unwisdom of cutting 'Basic Democracies adrift from the mainstream of political and constitutional activity' and circumscribing 'their functions merely to local government'.

At the same time, the Report contained this statement: 'The concept of universal adult franchise has been recognized in clear terms and whatever its merits and demerits in our present-day conditions, this must be accepted as a fact of life.' Notwithstanding this observation, the Special Committee favoured the election of a President and of members of the National and Provincial Assemblies through an electoral college composed of elected members of the Basic Democracies. It was argued that since the Constitution gives every adult (with certain obvious exceptions such as lunacy, etc.) a vote, and as that vote is exercised by electing Basic Democrats who, as an electoral college, proceed to vote for a President and members of the legislatures, there is, in effect, universal adult suffrage. The Governor of East Pakistan went so far as to say that under the Constitution of 1962, the elector in Pakistan enjoyed the maximum right of suffrage.[39]

[38] Whether the Basic Democrat was any closer to the representative in the legislature or could himself read the newspapers is not clear.

[39] D, 18 June 1964.

It is doubtful if most Pakistanis would agree with this and events since the abrogation of Martial Law have shown that a substantial minority, at any rate, is in clear disagreement. The difficulties of administering direct elections, based on universal adult suffrage, are recognized; likewise the fact that in western countries, education and the extension of the franchise virtually went hand-in-hand and, if either lagged, it was certainly not education. But, as the authors of *Corruption in Developing Countries* have pointed out, the fact is that new countries are having to live in several centuries at the same time in terms of literacy, education, superstition, way of life, and economic circumstance.[40] It is 'metaphorically possible in many parts of Africa to span the centuries in the course of a short walk' and this is true of Pakistan.

Wraith and Simpkins go on to say:

In this situation, it has become necessary to give every person the vote. This is not questioned, at any rate by us. It is no argument to say that in Britain it took more than a century after the first Reform Bill to achieve a democratic franchise for that sort of process will never happen again. Attempts have been made in some parts of the world to devise a qualitative franchise which would give the vote to those capable of exercising it; some of these have been ingenious and sincere and have, looked at objectively, corresponded to the commonsense facts of the situation. But the forces working against such attempts are overwhelming.[41]

Those who share President Ayub Khan's assessment may well reply that even if unqualified universal adult suffrage and direct elections are not to be questioned now, a time is coming when that question will be put; and that the forces to which Wraith and Simpkins refer will, themselves, one day be overwhelmed by the powers of confusion and darkness they have themselves engendered. Certainly, the bulk of recorded experience, in nations newly emerged since decolonization started after World War II, sustains no hopes for democracy as it has grown up in Anglo-Saxon countries, yet— and here is a paradox whose truth is incontestable—the more successful the Basic Democracies scheme turns out to be, the more certain is the prospect of an election system in which each individual possesses the right to vote, without intermediary and without restraint, for every political office in the land.

Even if there is doubt as to the success of President Ayub Khan

[40] Wraith and Simpkins, op. cit., p. 197.   [41] ibid.

and his administration in convincing their countrymen of the efficacy of these methods of choosing a President and members of the National and Provincial Assemblies, there need be no doubt as to the fate of his opinion on the undesirability of political parties. During the whole period of Martial Law, he pursued the non-party theme, stressing, in a way that seemed sometimes naive, the need for selecting the individual on the basis of individual worth, but it was doubtful if at any time he succeeded in carrying his countrymen with him. He was not the first man to inveigh against the evils of party government; doubtless he will not be the last, but the institution, for all its faults, survives.

Soon after the withdrawal of Martial Law and the installation of a National Assembly in 1962, the existence of political parties was recognized and made legal. In July of that year a Political Parties Act was passed which permitted the creation of parties subject to some fairly pedestrian sections about holding no opinions or pursuing such activity as would be subversive to Pakistan or repugnant to Islamic ideology. The most important feature was the prohibition on members of the legislatures from changing their party allegiance on pain of having to give up their seats. In most countries a change of party usually involves, by convention, resignation and fresh election, but in Pakistan convention has been honoured more in the breach than in the observance. In the past, capricious crossing of the floor had done much to mar the working of previous legislatures and the Act aimed at putting an end to this particular kind of flighty political self-seeking. But the most obvious and immediate consequence of the Act was the re-appearance of the old organizations. No sooner was the Bill made law than the former political parties which, evidently, had been dormant but not destroyed, sprang into life.[42] About a year later, the President himself joined the Muslim League and became its head.[43] In July

[42] This did not cause surprise. It was already well-known that these parties existed and were active in a quiet way. Some weeks earlier, the Prohibition of Unregulated Political Activity Ordinance was issued. In this, certain well-known party names were listed and ordered not to be used until the National Assembly had had time to consider the position. *D*, 11 May 1962.

[43] *MN*, 23 May 1963. As a result there was a schism in the Muslim League. The 'old guard'—members of the Council of the Muslim League when it was dissolved in October 1958—claimed to be the true and rightful heirs and their organization became known as the 'Council' Muslim League. The organization presided over by President Ayub Khan is called the 'Convention' Muslim League because a convention of former Muslim League members was called to revive

1964, when addressing a gathering of his countrymen in London, he said experience had shown political parties to be a necessity.[44]

It is only just to add that although President Ayub Khan had displayed so strong an aversion for political parties and had repeatedly expressed the belief that the country could, and should, be governed without them, he was not, at the outset, so sanguine as to think they could easily be dispensed with. In fact, at a very early stage he had foreseen difficulties and had said as much.[45] Later, he became more confident, and the fact that so much play was made of a Constitution[46] in which parties would have no place seems to indicate that he had been encouraged by others to think that National and Provincial Assemblies could be set up and worked without recourse to the party system and that they could function successfully in that somewhat amorphous condition.

It seems probable, moreover, that having gone so far in the exposition of this gospel, the abandonment of a non-party system (however illusory the idea of such a system may have been) was unwelcome to the President and was a reversal of his constitutional aims. It had the effect of reopening criticism of his own political ideas, which criticism had been earlier brushed aside by the simple assertion that under the new dispensation, the corrupt and disruptive influence of party could be absent. Moreover, however much the President kept himself aloof, he might at any time find it necessary to connive at the acts of his own party men. In politics there is much that a leader must go along with, if he is to survive, no matter how irreproachable his personal conduct, and there is no better example in recent history than that of India's Jawaharlal Nehru.

As I have indicated, the Political Parties Act of 1962, in restoring their legal existence, was intended also to restrain some of the wilder excesses witnessed in earlier years, but the President admitted that the law on the subject was not perfect.[47] More important, perhaps, was the effect on the Basic Democracies

---

the organization after Martial Law was withdrawn and parties again permitted to function.

[44] *D*, 13 July 1964. In 1964 nine members of the National Assembly changed their allegiance from opposition to independence to support the Government's Second Amendment to the Constitution Bill, without which the amendments could not have passed the House. It is not clear whether any penalty under the Political Parties Act was exacted.

[45] *D*, 21 December 1959.   [46] That of 1962.   [47] *D*, 13 July 1964.

scheme since it became apparent immediately that, with or without restraints, the party-machines would find it easier and more convenient to their purpose to deal with small groups of Basic Democrats, as members of the electoral college, amounting to no more than a few hundred in each constituency. Could it reasonably be asserted that the old, familiar methods would have any less place among these groups where each vote was, mathematically, a much more significant factor? Could it reasonably be asserted that the cost[48] of running an election would be prohibitively greater than had been the case in constituencies with electorates comprising tens of thousands? As it was, in the party-less election of 1962, for the purpose of electing members to a National Assembly comprising 150 seats, there were nearly 100 election disputes afterwards, for which it was necessary to set up tribunals. The disposal of these complaints against successful candidates occupied approximately two years.

There remains the question of the Islamic authority which President Ayub Khan claimed for the Basic Democracies scheme and the constitutional structure with which it has been so closely associated by him and those who think with him. Indeed, the question is so intimately bound up with Pakistan's emergence as an independent nation, and the pursuit of its own ideals, that some consideration of it is inescapable, notwithstanding the acute sense of trepidation that any mention of it induces. It is a matter fraught with complication, not to mention the emotional response inevitably provoked, but if we can only explore the limits within which it can usefully be spoken of at all, that, too, is important since it has meaning for Pakistanis, as well as for the outside world, whether Muslim or not.[49]

It is a wider issue that concerns us and, although President Ayub Khan has made unequivocal claims of Islamic validity for all his political conceptions, it would be both inadequate and unfair to treat the whole problem as if it were a personal responsibility resting solely on his shoulders. To be sure, he did give undertakings of that sort,[50] but who is to say whether the responsibility has been sufficiently discharged or not? Therefore, while

---

[48] The word is intended here to bear a very wide connotation.

[49] The whole question of Pakistan as an Islamic State is deeply and sympathetically considered in Smith, op. cit., Chapter 5.

[50] See his address to the nation, 15 February 1960.

no doubt need be attached either to the sincerity of purpose or belief, his measure of success may well become the object of controversy among those who feel deeply about such things.

From that particular point of view, therefore, there is nothing further to be said. The President has stated the basis of his ideas and the foundation of his claims. Those learned in Islam can endorse or contest as their understanding may direct. The broader aspect, with which everyone is concerned, touches the abiding and, in the circumstances, necessary insistence upon an Islamic emphasis in all the institutions of Pakistan, an aspect which cannot be ignored or silently passed over because it is thought to be inconveniently delicate. The fact is that Pakistan was brought into existence to enable Muslims of the sub-continent to live according to their ideals and way of life. Therefore, the repeated insistence upon Islamic ideals and Islamic values is scarcely surprising and appropriate weight must be attached to it.

The question is not only difficult in itself, it is multi-dimensional. It can even be said that there is a sense in which any claim to Islamic authority is not open to discussion. There is, as one might say, a presumption in favour of anyone by whom Islam is confessed, since to impugn the claim of adherence to the tenets of the faith may well lead to assertions of *bid'ah* (innovation) and, perhaps also, of *kufr'* (unbelief or heresy).[51] To call in question another's claim to Islamic validity may be as serious as—or even more serious than—accusing a member of the Politburo of deviation from the party line, or of suggesting to a Daughter of the Revolution that she has been guilty of conduct which is not precisely American.

For anyone not within the fold of Islam there is a very real sense in which the question of what is, or what is not, Islamic, cannot exist. Similarly, for the non-Christian, there is a sense in which the question of what is Christian conduct, and what is not, cannot arise. The questions envisaged here are not simply intellectual tests. They involve matters of faith and belief which transcend intellect and anyone who has not been vouchsafed the necessary illumination is, from this aspect, not qualified to speak.[52]

---

[51] There are injunctions against accusing a fellow-Muslim of *kufr'*. The whole question is extremely difficult and by no means free of embittered controversy, as the history of Islam amply proves.

[52] See also Smith, op. cit., Chapter 1.

Parallel with this are those conditioning factors of heredity, environment, and upbringing by which values are acquired and an approach to life is learned. It is presumably not denied that most people who call themselves Christians, or have become Christians, do so because such was the faith of their parents. The same appears true of other religions and even political attachment. But it is important to remember that even where belief and attachment are denied, those early influences are not, *ipso facto*, shed by that denial. People who regard themselves as belonging to no religion[53] and consider themselves detached from religious influence, or as having shaken off its influence, may yet be conditioned to a degree they do not suspect, much less be ready to admit.[54] Looking at this point, in reverse as it were, Uncle Peregrine, in Evelyn Waugh's novel, says: 'Personally, I find it very difficult to regard converts as Catholics.'[55] Acceptance is there, but not the background.

Of course, in matters of Islamic history, tradition,[56] and law, there is nothing which stands in the way of a non-Muslim speaking with as much authority as a Muslim, given the necessary application to those branches of learning. By a parity of reasoning, a man may well be an authority on the canon law without being a Roman Catholic. It is quite possible for a lawyer, whose spiritual ancestry is traceable to some obscure, nonconformist tabernacle, to rule with felicitous accuracy upon the legality, or otherwise, of ornaments inducted into an Anglican place of worship and, after all, not every member of the Privy Council is required to be in communion with the Established Church. This is why, in Pakistan, it is possible for non-Muslims to sit on the judicial benches.

It is only within the limits of these ideas that the problem can be spoken of at all, for, outside them, there is no room for useful discussion. Having said this one is then confronted with the vast body of Islamic learning and wealth of ideas. Nothing is easier, nor more harmless, than to declare that within Pakistan there is

---

[53] The word is used in the sense of denominational or institutionalized religion.

[54] The classic case of our time is James Joyce.

[55] Evelyn Waugh, *Unconditional Surrender*, Chapman & Hall, London, 1961.

[56] In Islam, the word 'tradition' has a technical meaning and the 'traditions' not only contribute much to Islamic conduct and the way of life, but form a distinct branch of study.

a preponderating wish to have the nation's affairs conducted beneath the aegis of Islamic belief and teaching, but the matter does not, and cannot, end there. Even if the intensity of this wish neither waxes nor wanes, its orientation can still swing between the out-an-out traditionalism of men like Maulana Maudoodi and an approach governed by the terms of reference of Pakistan's Institution of Islamic Research. The possibility of this ambivalence is implicit in the remarks of the Law Reform Commission, as we have seen. The difficulties are neither few nor simple. Islam has never been, and is not now, free from sectarianism, as the President himself has pointed out.[57] Like other great world religions, Islam possesses sharp divisions, as well as a vast body of learning into which some plunge deeply, eyes wide open, while others immerse themselves in the word but are impervious to the spirit. Others again skim with facile ease across the surface, their prolific utterance reminiscent of the mosquito's hum and about as useful.

No one supposes that to look for inspiration and guidance in Islam will be dangerous, but specific danger seems possible from obscurantism, over-simplification, from the introduction of controversy where it should have no place, and from the exploitation of irrelevant sentiment. This is a kind of destructive experience with which the whole world is only too familiar. In Pakistan, it seems there are too many people who, worthy as they may be as Muslim citizens, possess no great understanding of their faith, yet are among the most vociferous on the subject. They compare with the type of Christian who goes to Church at Christmas, Easter, and the day he marries, but is ready at the drop of a hat to take up the doctrinal cudgels.[58]

When all is said, there remains the obstinate question whether, in the twentieth century, a preoccupation with religious doctrine serves any useful purpose in organizing a constitution or system of public administration. No doubt it would be very foolish to dispute the debt that is owed, by every category of scholarship, to man's spiritual yearnings and the outward shape that they have taken, whatever may be the criticism that can be directed against all forms of institutionalized religion. Perhaps this difficult question can only be answered by those who feel the need for a back-

[57] Address to the Darul Uloom Islamia, 3 May 1959.

[58] cf. proceedings in the House of Commons on the subject of a proposal to revise the Book of Common Prayer, 1927–28.

ground of religious sanction, since others can only conclude that such a preoccupation does not make life any easier for those devising constitutions. It is certain that the day Henry VIII appointed himself Head of the Church of England he did nothing to simplify the position of the Throne nor to advance the cause of Christianity.[59]

Nevertheless, the same obstinate question also involves a fact of political life. If the Islamic sentiment or aspiration is there, it cannot be ignored, or is ignored only at peril. President Ayub, like all his predecessors, has been confronted with it, at various times, in terms which cannot possibly be misunderstood and which are, to put it plainly, difficult.[60] It is unfortunate that there have been too many instances in which the Islamic appeal has found more applications in the field of demagogy than in sober study and spiritual progress.[61]

When we read of a Bill being introduced into the West Pakistan Provincial Assembly whose object is to punish married adulterers by stoning to death and unmarried adulterers by flogging,[62] we may pause to wonder. It is, to say the least, unlikely that legislation of this character will ever find a place on the statute-books of Pakistan, but it is evidence of an approach and of a state of mind which the administration cannot simply disregard.[63] We remember that it is but forty years since William Jennings Bryan, in the defence of Biblical fundamentalism, used his great and undoubted gifts in the prosecution of a schoolmaster in Tennessee and the echoes of that controversy are still not fully silent.

[59] It is not intended to suggest that anyone in Pakistan aspires to follow the example of Henry VIII in any aspect.

[60] See editorial in *D*, 24 February 1953, entitled *Ulemacracy*; also two speeches by the Governor-General, the late Mr. Ghulam Mohamed, on 12 February and 12 May 1953.

[61] On this, the Report of the Court of Inquiry into the Punjab Disturbances, 1953, is instructive, as also is the presidential election of January 1965.

[62] West Pakistan Prevention of Adultery Bill, 1964. *Gazette of West Pakistan*, 1 July 1964. The Bill made no progress for want of support.

[63] At the Commonwealth Law Conference, held in Melbourne in August 1965, the Chief Justice of Pakistan, in the course of an address on *Crime and the Punishment of Crime* referred to the usefulness of inflicting physical disability as a form of practical deterrent. It seems clear he had in mind certain aspects of the Islamic code, at any rate as practised in earlier centuries. It was not clear, however, whether, to prevent theft or escape, the Chief Justice was actually prescribing amputation or simple immobilization of a limb by severance of a nerve or tendon.

Whether, therefore, President Ayub Khan's claim of Islamic validity for his political conceptions is sound, and whether they satisfy the Islamic aspirations of the nation, I do not feel competent to pronounce. Such issues tend always to be highly controversial and the experience gained during Pakistan's presidential election of 1965, when Miss Jinnah's candidature was challenged on the ground that, under Islam, a woman cannot be the Head of the State, shows how widely ranging these questions may be.[64] The essential point is that what may be termed, perhaps, the Islamic aspect in Pakistan's affairs is important and likely to remain so. In assessing how those affairs are managed, or are likely to be managed, the weight and significance that this aspect deserves must unquestionably be allowed.

[64] It is by no means clear that this challenge was initiated by any of the other three candidates. Miss Jinnah remained a candidate and was the only effectual opponent against Field-Marshal Ayub Khan.

IX

Enforcement: Economic Planning

FROM the preceding chapters it will have been understood that, in its first year, not only did the Martial Law administration introduce reforms as rapidly and as extensively as possible, but did, in fact, accomplish much. It will, however, have been noticed that, in reviewing this many-sided achievement, nothing has been said of foreign affairs, a major aspect of the nation's business in which President Ayub Khan enjoyed possibly his principal success. Similarly, neither the sensitive problem of East Pakistan–West Pakistan relations, nor the difficult question of reform in matrimonial and family law have been touched upon. These are matters of great importance, yet it seems advisable to leave them to a later stage. At this point it is desirable, in the interest of historical continuity, to observe the ability of the new administration to enforce its initial changes. The implications here are political, social, and economic and I will consider them in turn.

I mentioned earlier that not a whisper of dissent was audible upon the declaration of Martial Law, and, while this continued to be generally true, there were one or two incidents of little importance in themselves so far as can be traced, but with consequences that certainly call for notice.

On 13 August 1959, the day preceding the anniversary of Pakistan's independence, seven people were arrested in Karachi and a quantity of cyclostyled posters, written in Urdu and Bengali, were seized. The contents of the posters have not been made public, but a doubtless unauthorized reference to Miss Fatima Jinnah, sister of the late Quaid-i-Azam Mohamed Ali Jinnah, was quoted as having figured there. The arrests were made under Martial Law Regulations 24 and 51, which dealt with the spread of alarm and despondency among the public and the creation of dissatisfaction with the Armed Forces. Among the arrested people was a compulsorily retired member of the Civil Service of Pakistan, one of the six who had come before the screening committees, with results adverse to themselves.[1]

The object of this affair, now generally known as 'the Poster Case', is not really clear, but during the proceedings, so far as these have been publicly reported, it was suggested that the principal participants expected that these posters (which were to be distributed in Karachi, Lahore, and Dacca) would find such a response in the public mind that a collapse of the Martial Law administration would follow. What substance there could possibly be in this extraordinary assumption, and equally extraordinary performance, it is difficult to assess, but it is worth noting that the ex-civil servant concerned, Aftab Ahmed Khan, had, in his official capacity, served as private secretary to the late H. S. Suhrawardy when the latter was Prime Minister of Pakistan. It seems that Aftab Ahmed Khan had allowed himself to become concerned with the political aspects of his position beyond the necessities of his duty. It was also observed that two of the other accused were members of Suhrawardy's party, the Awami League, and one of them had been President of the League's Karachi organization.

I do not mean to suggest here that Suhrawardy, who was alive when these incidents occurred, was in any way privy to what was planned. The most that can be inferred is a clear political intention on the part of the arrested men. However, before their barrage of paper could be let loose, the authorities came to know of it. Arrest and seizure followed. Shortly after, there were other arrests and, as a result, seven people were sentenced to ten years' rigorous imprisonment and two were sentenced to seven years. After serving portions of their sentences, however, the balance was remitted and all were released although not, it seems, with a pardon.[2]

A somewhat similar case occurred in April 1960, when four men were arrested under Martial Law Regulations 24, 55, and Section 121A of the Pakistan Penal Code for activities stated to be treasonable. They comprised two former Ministers of an earlier West Pakistan Provincial Government, Muzaffarul Haq and Ismail Burhani; M. H. Gazdar, a former Deputy Speaker of the National Assembly; and Aslam Murad, an executive of the

[1] See Chapter VI.
[2] See *D*, 13 August, 30 September, and 25 October, 1959.

Burmah-Shell Oil Storage and Marketing Company of Pakistan Ltd.[3]

As in the Poster Case, the precise nature of the accused's intentions and activities does not seem to have been made public, but they were sentenced, in due course, to varying terms of imprisonment ranging from five to ten years and, in the case of Muzaffarul Haq, to a fine of Rs.60,000 in addition. Although information on this particular matter is somewhat unclear, the fine was not, so far as is known, recovered and all the convicted men, after serving a part of their sentences, were released.[4]

This pattern of severity followed by lenience found a kind of capricious usage which will have to be considered. To be sure, in the case of political offences where violence has not been used or moral turpitude is not involved, it is generally understood that liberality of attitude on the part of the government in power is justified. Like men in most callings, politicans have their own freemasonry. Under President Ayub Khan's administration, however, this was exercised in cases which, on the face of it, were considerably less deserving.

In 1959 Azizullah Hassan, a member of the Civil Service of Pakistan and, at one time, Karachi's Municipal Commissioner (a civil service post), was found guilty by a Military Court of offences under Martial Law Regulations 5, 30, and 32, which related to illegal gratification and abuse of official powers. The sum involved was said to be Rs.5 lakhs and Azizullah Hassan was sentenced to seven years' rigorous imprisonment. However, after serving a part of it, he was released.[5]

An even stranger instance is that of one Malik Habibullah, arrested in connexion with smuggling. This man was stated to have had no less than nine aliases and had succeeded in ingratiating himself with such senior officials as a former Inspector-General of the Karachi Police, a former Collector of Customs and Excise, officers of the Intelligence Bureau, and the Deputy-Inspector-General of Police (Anti-smuggling).[6] He was sentenced by a

[3] See D, 6 April 1960. These conspirators do not seem to have been any more competent than any of their predecessors, even after allowing due credit to the Intelligence Bureau, the Police, and the Martial Law authorities.

[4] In 1963 the indefatigable Mr. Gazdar was arrested on charges of sedition. See D, 22 August 1963.

[5] D, 21 November 1959. The amount equals £37,500 or US$105,000.

[6] See D, 8 July 1959.

Military Court to imprisonment for life, but after serving a portion of his sentence, he, too, was released.

Throughout 1959, there was a series of sensational smuggling, hoarding, and food adulteration cases in which substantial terms of imprisonment, along with fines involving lakhs of rupees, were awarded, but it appears that most of the convicted people were released after serving in jail for a time and that the fines imposed were not recovered.[7] Perhaps, therefore, it is not surprising that in October 1961, three years after Martial Law had begun its anti-smuggling activities, fifteen men were arrested in connexion with the smuggling of gold, who stated that during the three months preceding their arrest, no less than 300,000 tolas of gold had been smuggled into Pakistan.[8]

There is an attitude involved here which it is difficult to understand. In those attempts at political subversion (the Poster Case and the case of Muzaffarul Haq and Others) it may be that the administration attached no importance either to the attempted offences or to their participants, since it is very noticeable that where there was reason to apprehend active opposition on the part of someone who could be credited with real influence in the country, detention was immediate and continuous. Thus Abdul Qayyum Khan, a Frontier politician, was arrested in September 1960.[9] Abdul Ghaffar Khan, an old Frontier stalwart who had done much in the cause of independence, was arrested in April 1961.[10] Sheikh Mujibur Rahman, a turbulent figure in East Pakistan politics, was held for a considerable time under the Pakistan Security Act in the very early days of Martial Law.[11]

It has already been indicated that upon the introduction of the Basic Democracies scheme, the President had provided himself with political preoccupations that, with the passage of time, must become increasingly weighty. In those days the full significance of the move was not so easily discernible and it does not follow that there was any connexion between the move and a diminution in the severity of the régime. It is clear that vigilance in political matters was never relaxed and, as we shall see when considering

---

[7] Whether this is true of the adulteration cases is not certain.

[8] This is equal to 3·34 tons of gold whose value, at Pakistan's internal gold prices, was Rs.40,000,000. The statement may well be exaggerated.

[9] D, 27 September 1960.   [10] D, 13 April 1961.

[11] He had been arrested on other charges also. See Chapter I.

the evolution of the 1962 Constitution, whenever political activity seemed to be surfacing, warnings to desist followed speedily.

Moreover, if the Martial Law administration were indeed lightening its hold, it could well claim that this was to be attributed to the success of its earlier measures and to the confidence that the people placed in it. It is evident that without undue effort on its part, and certainly without any oppressive show of force, the administration was able to maintain civic discipline and to contain whatever tendency there might be towards an active and effective opposition. Indeed, except towards the end of its time, when a resumption of representative government in some form or another appeared inevitable, there was almost no interruption of civic tranquillity.

However, as to the lenience extended to people convicted of serious criminal offences (and we must presume quite properly convicted) by a Military Court, that is quite another matter and far less easily understood.

Although it is true that the Martial Law administration was able to maintain order without undue repression, the same success was not, unhappily, reflected in its administration of economic affairs, to which we now must turn. This is not altogether surprising since it has long been known that the principles of economics are a good deal less malleable than those of the people politically concerned, and men as a rule can be ordered to do things with much greater prospect of obedience than can fortune's presiding goddess. Hence, it does not altogether follow that between the easier tendencies of the Martial Law administration and the difficulty of stabilizing prices at congenial levels there was a precise correspondence, but the problem was there, clear enough.

As an encouragement and as a sign, price controls were lifted, at an early stage, on a wide variety of consumer goods, but it was noticeable that soon after prices began to rise.[12] As early as February and March 1959, complaints of black-market activities increased and the authorities announced a drive against the revival of these practices. Yet, it seemed, the tendency towards a rising price level was beyond restraint and could not be entirely explained by the pressure of external circumstance. In June 1960 President Ayub expressed his anxiety that prices should fall, and

[12] There are many newspaper references. See *D*, 1 September 1959; 17 June 1960; 14, 15, and 25 February, and 6 June 1961.

the Finance Minister, in his Budget speech immediately following, made reference to a persistently rising trend. In February 1961 there were greater signs of exasperation at the apparent inability to hold prices down. The Minister of Industries threatened indigenous industries that, if they could not bring the prices of their products into line, he would invite foreign industrialists to come in and show them how. At the same time, the Finance Minister said he was ready to make foreign exchange available for the import of consumer goods as a corrective to the situation. In the middle of the year, textile mill owners were given an ultimatum that prices must come down within a month. Meanwhile, in February 1960, a Price Commission was appointed to investigate this disturbing situation.

Whether these circumstances are to be regarded as a failure of the Martial Law administration or not, all available evidence makes clear a rising price-trend that was both consistent and irreversible. Thus, the Statistical Tables published by the State Bank of Pakistan in its *Report on Currency and Finance*[13] show that, during the period 1952 to 1963, the consumer's price index (clerical) for Karachi rose steadily from 96 to 121.[14] In the same period wholesale prices for selected commodities rose in a similar manner. Some of the contrasts are startling, even allowing for circumstances of extraordinary fluctuation. Thus jute rose from 46·7 in 1952 to 116·1 in 1963. The price of rice rose from 70·7 to 115·2; wheat from 96·5 to 116·9; hides from 137·1 to 246·3.[15] The only exception was cotton which maintained a steady level. During the same period, the national income *per capita* in Pakistan, taken at constant prices, rose from Rs.235 to Rs.259.[16] The conclusion seems to be that, with the passage of time, the average Pakistani, if not exactly growing less prosperous, was hardly any better off in a situation that no amount of Martial Law could, *per se*, change for the better.

There is, however, another aspect of the situation which deserves to be mentioned. The rising trend in prices, which the Martial Law administration was unable to arrest, continued during the years that followed and this uninterrupted tendency, with its

[13] For 1962–63. Published in Karachi, undated.
[14] Base: 1956 equals 100.
[15] Base: April 1948 to March 1949 equals 100.
[16] Based on average prices for the period 1949–50 to 1952–53.

adverse consequences upon salary and wage earners, has not seriously been disputed. However, it is argued that notwithstanding difficulties of this sort, the economy of the country has developed, and is developing, favourably, and that much, if not all, of this development is owed to the impetus provided during the Martial Law régime. With that initiative given to economic planning and with the general determinations of the people and of the Government, the gross national product is expanding.

No doubt there is evidence to support this view. Figures taken from the same State Bank Report on Currency and Finance show that on the average for the period 1949–50 to 1952–53 (equals 100), the agricultural production for all crops in the year 1957–58 was 109 and, for the year 1961–62, was 131. From the same authority we learn that on the basis of 1954 (equals 100), industrial production (mining and manufacturing), the index for 1957 was 150·9, for 1958 it was 161·4 and, for 1961, was 203·2. Revised indices show somewhat better results.

The position is further, and more recently, discussed in the Mid-Plan Review to which reference was made earlier. Here it is shown that in the first three years of the Second Five Year Plan, the gross national product, at factor cost, increased by more than thirteen per cent over the 1959–60 level. But it is recognized that agriculture showed a decline in production and that the biggest contributor to the gross increase was construction. It is not easy to determine how much of that construction is itself productive. The Mid-Plan Review adopted, justifiably, a tone of sober optimism, and anticipates better results, but so long as agriculture fails to make its indispensable contribution, the economic planners of Pakistan are not likely to feel complacent.

There are complex problems involved here which are really beyond the scope of this narrative—problems that belong to the immensely difficult question of raising economic standards in countries which start economically handicapped and educationally backward, whether or not they possess exploitable raw materials or, for that matter, whether they possess raw materials at all. The economics of development programmes in such countries seem scarcely to have been elucidated or, if they have, the authors are very reticent about their conclusions since it is clear enough that, in terms of more and better food, more and better shelter, more and better clothes, development projects have not done much. In

Pakistan, as with other countries in similar circumstances, it is doubtful whether the average man (and that means a poor man) is getting a half-ounce more of foodgrains to eat today, than he was fifteen years ago, fifty years ago, or a hundred years ago.

However, that is another problem. So far as concerns Pakistan's Martial Law administration, there was nothing that could be done inside that framework beyond the strict application of the law intended to buttress and defend the economic structure. No doubt the régime started with a distinct bias in the poor man's favour. There was a noticeable accent on the interests of the under-privileged and the less well-to-do, which encouraged the im-poverished majority to feel that even if the new dispensation was absolute and non-representative, it genuinely had the interests of that majority at heart.

It may well be that that interest was preserved during the entire forty-four months of Martial Law administration, for as late as 1961 President Ayub Khan and his Cabinet colleagues were calling for a war on poverty and ignorance, but there can be no doubt that the economic policy of this administration, for which the two Finance Ministers (Mr. Mohamed Shoaib and Mr. Abdul Qadir) seem principally responsible, led inevitably to a shift in emphasis. It is evident that, notwithstanding 'the public sector' and the 'semi-public sector' (of which the latter, according to the Second Five Year Plan, exists to supplement and encourage private enterprise and not to replace it),[17] confidence is entirely reposed in the ability of a wealthy bourgeoisie to develop indigen-ous banking, insurance, industry, and commerce. I do not intend to discuss here the extent to which these vital branches of the economy are concentrated in the hands of small groups, or of 'communities'[18] within the community, nor do I suggest that confidence has necessarily been wrongly placed. The question is whether the system is realistic and will work.

A study of the economic development of countries like Pakistan and India since their emergence as independent nations reveals a pattern which conforms with remarkable closeness to the nine-teenth-century situation which prevailed in western countries when political, followed by economic, liberation, filtered down to the working-classes from the more prosperous middle-class. This

[17] *The Second Five Year Plan*, Government of Pakistan, 1960, p. 38.
[18] See article by Dr. Gustav Papanek, op. cit.

became possible after the land-owning class had been disarmed. In the same way, in the Indo-Pakistan sub-continent, independence was followed by a liquidation of the princely interests and a reduction of the land-owning influence. Both have been replaced, in accordance with this classic liberal process, by a concentration of power in the hands of a capitalist class in whose ranks the dispossessed aristocracy and landlords tend to enlist themselves. In both countries there has been much talk of secular, or Islamic, socialism, but no one really doubts that what prevails today in both is a well-entrenched capitalism which, admittedly, does not breathe quite the same unsullied air of *laissez-faire* and *laissez-aller* as existed in the nineteenth century, but which is pretty free, notwithstanding.

It is difficult to say whether, in accordance with the same pattern, the political and economic emancipation of the under-privileged section of Pakistani society will follow just as inevitably. It seems unlikely, although it may well be argued that, in a political sense, success has been achieved. This brings me to the question of whether a man living in a state of poverty and under-nourishment, but having the right to cast a vote every five years, is, in any true sense, politically free.

The political solution is not, moreover, conclusive. Every inch of land can be put into national ownership and it does not follow that the agrarian problem is thereby solved in terms of food and cash crop production. The Soviet Union is a well-known case in point. What is more, the fact that through a policy of *laissez-faire* the western nations were able to industrialize themselves successfully may well be a reason which interdicts that policy for the newly emerging countries.[19]

It is, at any rate, certain that the circumstances are not the same. The economics of Adam Smith and Marshall, applied in the new countries, no longer have as their secret weapon and resource the advantage of colonial possessions and virgin territories. These things may have been in President Ayub Khan's mind when, addressing the Far East–America Council of Commerce and Industry, he said: 'Your industrialization or your internal industrialization took anywhere from seventy to a hundred years. We

---

[19] See article in *Trade Journal of the Chamber of Commerce and Industry*, Karachi, June–July 1964, based on an address by Mrs. Joan Robinson at the Economic Development Seminar, Lahore, March 1964.

cannot afford to do that. Time will overtake us if we go by that base.'[20] It is upon considerations of this kind that Pakistan and countries in similar circumstance lay strong claim to the generosity and help of the developed, western countries, and although the case has sometimes been overstated, and even unfairly stated, and although the principle of self-help has been applied with insufficient resolution, the substance of the position deserves recognition.[21]

It is against this background that, on 21 June 1960, the Economic Council of the Government of Pakistan gave its general approval to the objectives, principles, and programmes of development contained in the Second Five Year Plan. The first of such Plans was born in some respects a crippled child for it was not approved by the National Economic Council until 1957, two years after the Plan period had ostensibly begun.[22] The First Plan, as set out, has been very fairly described as a classic analysis of the long-term requirements and potentialities of Pakistan, yet, notwithstanding so much careful study and its modest aims, the Plan was judged, on the whole, to have failed. This failure seems to have sprung, primarily, from a lack of faith in the ability of Pakistan to execute the Plan and realize its targets. This, not surprisingly, led to a want of determined effort. It was remarked that 'the failures... are a sad commentary on the mode of implementation of the Plan, not on the Plan itself'.[23]

The Second Five Year Plan aimed at an increase in national income of twenty per cent, but when the Plan was published the 1961 Census had not been taken and the rate of population growth was estimated, in the Plan, to be in the order of 1·6 per cent in 1960, rising to 1·8 per cent by 1965. As it turned out, the 1961 Census disclosed the alarming rate of population growth of approximately 2·2 per cent per annum. It was expected that the Plan would cost Rs.19,000,000,000, equal to £1,245,000,000, or US $3,990,000,000, but these figures were much increased as time went on. The objectives concentrated on self-sufficiency in food-grain production; optimum utilization of existing industrial capa-

---

[20] 14 July 1961.

[21] On the question of self-help, the President urged its necessity very early in the Martial Law period; for example, at Lahore on 25 February 1959.

[22] It was also the victim of a very unkind cartoon. See *D*, 17 May 1956.

[23] See Report of the Panel of Economists on the Second Five Year Plan, Government of Pakistan, Karachi, 1960.

city which, with additional investment for balancing and modernization, was to increase by sixty per cent in the case of large and medium scale industry and by twenty-five per cent in the case of cottage and small-scale industry. Maximum possible employment was to be created along with further development of water and power resources, transportation and communications.

The Plan partly depended for its success on foreign financial assistance and, in the following year, the World Bank organized a Consortium, consisting of the United States of America, some of the wealthier European countries, and Japan, with the object of finding ways and means of raising financial aid. A high level delegation visited the United States to present the case for assistance, with results that greatly disappointed the people of Pakistan. The reaction was immediate, with resentment particularly expressed towards the United States[24] on which, it was felt, Pakistan had strong claims. As we shall later see, this was not the first occasion during the Martial Law period that Pakistan found cause to criticize its ally. President Ayub Khan, in a television interview in London on 9 July 1961, expressed the opinion that, whereas the United States had made a special effort to help India, none had been made to help Pakistan and that while some of the objections raised against the Plan were genuine, others were spurious and designed to put Pakistan off.

It is difficult to assess the truth of the situation. It was no doubt certain that American interest in India had increased in direct proportion to the developing ill-will between India and China, but why that should lead to a diminution of interest in Pakistan is less clear. There seems to be ground for suggesting that the Pakistan delegation did not present its case with the force and knowledge necessary to persuade bankers to part with money. Certainly, when Pakistan's irritation became fully manifest, the attitude of the Consortium changed and, in August, the Finance Minister was able to announce the likelihood that the needs of the Plan would be met.[25]

The Second Five Year Plan, although the product of the Martial Law administration, was afterwards much expanded, and its execution belongs, for the most part, to the administration that followed the withdrawal of Martial Law in June 1962. It is generally claimed that the objectives have been substantially achieved, but

[24] *D*, 9 and 13 June 1961.   [25] *D*, 13 August 1961.

the extent to which real advance has been made is difficult to ascertain. At the risk of appearing to disparage a great deal of commendable effort, positive results in terms of living-standards seem slender for reasons I have already touched on. Perhaps, at this point, two comments are admissible. The first comes from the Chairman of Pakistan's Eastern Federal Union Insurance Company Ltd., who said: ' . . . any claim to affluence is a far-off cry. Many a Five Year Plan will have to be implemented before we can turn our backs on want and poverty.'[26] The second comes from President Ayub Khan in an outline of the Second Five Year Plan, broadcast on 30 December 1959. He then said: '. . . . if the present rate at which the population is growing continues, it will undermine all our efforts to uplift the nation', and this grim assurance conveniently brings me to my next chapter.[27]

[26] Address to the shareholders of the Company, 26 June 1964.

[27] It would take me too far from my brief to consider the extent to which economic development in Pakistan has been hindered by the outbreak of hostilities with India in September 1965. The actual period of fighting does not, in itself, appear to have been economically crippling, but the implications are important. They have a direct bearing on the cost of defence as well as on the attitude of countries whose financial assistance is indispensable to the success of economic plans.

X

Family Laws

IN a speech broadcast on 23 July 1959, the President said: 'In the race between food supply and a progressively growing population, we know who will be the loser. At best, we may find that we have to run twice as fast merely to stay where we are. Family-planning is a long-term process, so the sooner we address ourselves to it, the better.' The population explosion, as it has come to be called, is by no means the sole concern of Pakistan, but it occupies a position of political (as well as social) importance due to the attitude towards family-planning.

The political implications arise from the views which are variously held as to the Islamic validity of this practice, but it is clear that the Martial Law administration showed itself favourable to the idea of properly organized methods of advice and guidance on planned families, and clinics were established where women could obtain the desired advice and help. By the middle of 1961 it was estimated that some 800 such clinics had been set up. The leaders of the new administration, in frequent references to the subject, urged parents to see the wisdom of adopting well-advised measures, and propaganda was encouraged to stimulate a widespread realization of the dangers of a totally uncontrolled population growth. In an earlier reference to the subject, the President had said that he believed in family-planning, 'otherwise the battle for progress may be lost'.[1] In a broadcast speech in March 1961 he went further, suggesting that a time might come when man would start eating man and (very much more to the point) that it was not a matter of religion, but of simple economy. This indicated the political crux of the matter.

Before the advent of Martial Law, official sources of family-planning guidance had been sporadic and inadequate. There were, of course, both professional and voluntary workers giving advice to troubled women, but their work was frequently obstructed by

[1] *D*, 25 February 1959.

prejudice which sometimes took an actively hostile form, while the attitude of the previous governments had tended to be lukewarm at best. It is noticeable that the First Five Year Plan, notwithstanding its comprehensive nature, had nothing to say on the subject and, apparently, apprehended no danger from a rapidly growing population. The Report on the 1951 Census, published some three years before the First Five Year Plan started, disclosed a rate of population growth calculated at 1·4 per cent. In that Census Report it was stated that 'if this rate were to continue steadily, the population would reach 90,000,000 by 1965', a forecast which erred only because it was too little. The Report went on to say that the rate of growth is 'about double the rate at which the United Kingdom had been increasing during the same period'. Nevertheless, in spite of its concern with under-employment and inadequate utilization of man-power, the First Five Year Plan made no reference to population problems and no provision for family-planning, unless it was to be tacitly understood that maternity and child-welfare centres would deal with that delicate topic.[2]

The question of limitation of birth is, in Pakistan, a sensitive one because of the widespread belief, that human interference with, or regulation of, conception is an interference with the Divine will and, therefore, contrary to Islam. However, in 1964, the West Pakistan Provincial Minister of Health[3] stated, with some boldness, that family-planning was not contrary to Islam, a statement which indicated the importance of the Islamic viewpoint in Pakistan's affairs.

It is worth adding, perhaps, that according to the learned translator of, and commentator on, the *Mishkat-ul-Masabih*,[4] the Arabs used to practise a kind of *coitus interruptus* called *azal* which had for its object the prevention of conception. It was practised by the Prophet's companions and, when the Prophet came to know of it, he did not disapprove. The same commentator is, however, guarded enough to add that the practice was not encouraged; it could only be followed with the wife's consent;[5] it was to be resorted to in those cases where the wife's health was

---

[2] The Second Five Year Plan made a specific provision of Rs.30,500,000 for family-planning. See p. 360.

[3] Begam Mahmuda Salim Khan. See *D*, 27 June 1964.

[4] op. cit., Vol. II, p. 673.

[5] Consent, in the case of a slave-girl, was not necessary. Ibid.

involved; and the commentator adds in a footnote, the great jurist, Abu Hanifah, considered it abominable.[6]

According to the same commentator, any other form of birth control is forbidden in Islam and, in another section of his work, he mentions the traditions which enjoin restraint on passion, including sexual passion,[7] but the idea of continence as a way of restricting conception is not mentioned and Islam does not, in general, encourage monasticism or celibacy. It seems fair to say that, on the whole, the traditional[8] Islamic attitude towards birth control is an adverse one, even if it can be shown that there is no specific prohibition and that it is not, in the Quranic sense, unlawful.

The reservation of attitude is made clear by the results actually achieved by the administration's adoption of a positive policy towards family-planning. The Mid-Plan Review, published in 1964, states that in the first three years of the Second Five Year Plan, 938 clinics were opened in East Pakistan and 1,032 clinics in West Pakistan. The Review adds that during this period 902 doctors, 3,224 village workers and volunteers, and 1,191 Basic Democrats and Union Council secretaries were trained in family-planning, and four films on the subject were produced. With the assistance of the Population Council of New York, two medico-social research projects were started, one at Lahore and one at Dacca. This reads well enough, but the same Review also states that out of 30,500,000 rupees to which I have referred, only Rs.8,600,000 had been used by 1962–63, leaving Rs.21,900,000 to be utilized before the Plan expired in 1965.

In a largely illiterate society, where an infraction of custom, even if not of law, may carry with it a charge of heresy, it is no small matter to educate people in a social change of such a delicate and far-reaching nature. Certainly, it was not easy for the new administration to come out, four-square, on this uneasy subject, laying up possibilities of serious opposition and criticism in the future.[9] It was one thing for President Ayub Khan to assert that

[6] The majority of Pakistanis are governed, in personal law, by this Imam's canon.

[7] Vol. I, p. 553.

[8] Here the word is not used in its technical Islamic sense, but as signifying what has become accepted social usage among Muslims.

[9] It should be mentioned that a few months prior to the elections, President Ayub Khan announced a Commission on the subject of family-planning: *D*,

this was not a religious question at all; it was quite another to convince his countrymen of the accuracy of this assertion and, what is more, to retain their goodwill at the same time. This being so, the fact that at no time during the Martial Law period was there the least indication of the administration changing its position on the subject of family-planning, was the all the more creditable.

It was against a similar background that the new Government introduced, in 1961, one of its most courageous and far-reaching measures which, with its importance to married women and families, bears relation to the encouragement given to population control. This piece of legislation, the Muslim Family Laws Ordinance,[10] represents a significant step in the social evolution of Pakistan. To be able to grasp that significance, however, it is desirable to know something of the legal background relating to marriage and divorce in Islam, as well as the social picture that exists in Pakistan in relation to these important institutions.

In Islam, a marriage entered into by a legally competent man and a legally competent woman forms a contractual relationship between them, and is not treated as a sacrament. This does not mean that the marriage-tie is regarded with less seriousness than in those communities and religions where marriage is vested with a sacred meaning.[11] A declaration and acceptance of the contract, and its terms, must be expressed by the parties, or their appointed agents, in the presence of witnesses. In the case of Shia communities, and of those Muslims whose personal law is governed by the school of Imam Malik, the presence of witnesses, while desirable, is not absolutely enjoined. However, there must be a clearly expressed contractual intention and, furthermore, there are traditions to be observed as to the giving of a marriage-feast with its attendant publicity. Anyone with experience of eastern hospitality will understand the degree of publicity involved. It is the custom to record the marriage contract in written form termed *nikahnama*.

31 August 1964. To date, it does not appear that this announcement has been implemented. On the subject of opposition to family-planning see also an interesting letter in *D*, 23 June 1965.

[10] Ordinance No. VII of 1961.

[11] Legal competence means that the parties to the marriage must not be within the prohibited degrees of consanguinity. They must be of sound mind, have attained puberty, and have the consent of parent or guardian where necessary. A Muslim man can marry a Christian woman or a Jewess and she may continue to follow her religion. He cannot marry an idolatress or fireworshipper. A Muslim woman can only marry a Muslim man.

Since Islam does not have priests or ordained ministers of religion, the question of any such sacerdotal presence does not arise, although it is usual for some person, learned in Islam, to prepare the *nikahnama* and, perhaps, recite some appropriate Quranic verses. These things, however, are not indispensable in the legal sense.

A man may lawfully be the husband of not more than four wives at any one time, subject to certain rules about consanguinity among the wives. This is the law, as stated in the books, but the subject has become surrounded with controversy partly because of the interpretation put upon some qualifying verses (which we shall come to), partly because of the general and world-wide tendency towards monogamous practice, and partly because of the efforts to justify this particular Islamic institution.

The Quranic texts certainly indicate that a man may have not more than four wives at any one time, but they add that if he cannot do equal justice to all, he should confine himself to one only. It is not difficult to see that on the question of what constitutes just and equal treatment there is room for infinite debate. Indeed, it is sometimes said that since equality of treatment includes con-jugal rights, and since this may well be impossible on more grounds than one, there is, in effect, a total, if roundabout, prohibition on polygamous marriages. The force of this type of reasoning may appeal to some, but the classical view seems to be that if a husband gives reasonably equal companionship, food, shelter, and similar necessities, he has discharged his duty sufficiently.[12]

There is another form of marriage, recognized by the Ithna Asharia law of the Shia community called *muta'*. This form, for a fixed term only (which may be a day, a month, a year or whatever period is previously agreed to by the prospective wife and husband), comes to an end upon expiry of the agreed term whereupon the marriage stands dissolved. It is doubtful if this system of marriage is ever practised in Pakistan, but that it is part of the prevailing system of Muslim personal law cannot be doubted. The commentator on the *Mishkat-ul-Masabih* makes the somewhat

---

[12] *The Hedaya*, a work of considerable authority, states that a man must divide his time equitably among his wives, but recognizes that it is not within a man's power to divide his affections, a point which also has bearing on the question of connubial duties. (Second edition, translated by Charles Hamilton, edited by Standish Grove Grady, The New Book Company, Lahore, 1957, p. 67.)

controversial assertion that *muta'* marriage is '*absolutely illegal*' and claims it is founded upon a tradition reported by Ibn Masud and subsequently retracted.[13]

Divorce is permitted in Islam although, as in other societies, it is considered unfortunate and undesirable. A marriage can be dissolved by the husband without reference to a court of law, provided certain legal forms are observed. These forms define the method of pronouncement of the *talaq*[14] which the husband is to follow. The idea seems to be that nothing should be done hastily and that the contending husband and wife should have time in which to think over their differences or their motives. Moreover, this approved method of pronouncing the *talaq* gives some protection to a woman who may be pregnant.

There is, however, a form in which the husband pronounces the word *talaq* three times in succession and the wife then stands irrevocably divorced. This method, termed *talaq-i-ba'in*, is highly disapproved by all schools of Islamic jurisprudence and is considered sinful, yet, as the author of *Muhammadan Law*[15] points out, it is perhaps the most prevalent. Considering that a substantial part of the Muslim Family Laws Ordinance was aimed at this, it is interesting to see that the commentator on the *Miskhat*, although generally of conservative attitude, remarks that the sooner this method of divorce is abolished by legislation, the better.[16]

There are other methods of divorce which rarely occur in Pakistan and, when they happen, are of limited social consequence, except, of course, to the parties themselves. A man may, for instance, take an oath to abstain from intercourse with his wife; he may, by implication, assert that she is related to him within the prohibited limits; there may be an accusation by the husband of adultery and a denial by the wife. In such cases, the dispute is then submitted to the court. In addition, there are the obvious cases in which something turns out to make the marriage void or irregular —the cases of impotence and so on.

Generally speaking, the power to divorce by means of *talaq* lies with the husband, but the wife can stipulate in the marriage contract that she will also have the right. There are cases, also, where

---

[13] op. cit., Vol. II, p. 685.
[14] *Talaq* is an Arabic word signifying divorce.
[15] op. cit., p. 221.   [16] op. cit., Vol. II, p. 700.

she may derive such an option from her husband, or be appointed his agent to exercise his power of divorce as regards other wives. These are all exceptional and somewhat abstruse matters and the rulings vary according to the school of Islamic jurisprudence which governs the case.

However, the most usual method by which a wife frees herself of an undesired marriage tie is termed *khul* in which she asks her husband for a divorce and he agrees upon a consideration. In many cases where the marriage has obviously gone astray, agreement is readily forthcoming. In other instances, the husband may agree provided the wife forgoes her dower, but it is also possible he will refuse or fix the consideration at an impossible sum in which case the wife is helpless, unless she proceeds under the Dissolution of Muslim Marriages Act, which is not founded upon Islamic law. It enables a Muslim woman to obtain from the Court a decree of divorce on any of the grounds prescribed in it. The utility of this legislation is limited by its cost and the difficulties involved for women who are uneducated and whose lives have been sheltered and who are, for this reason, unacquainted with legal business. Sometimes difficulties arise from the practice of *pardah*.[17]

This brief survey of Islamic marriage and divorce law is the minimum guide to understanding the family aspect of social life among Pakistanis, at any rate up to the time that the Muslim Family Laws Ordinance was promulgated. The subject is a complex one on which the legal and sociological literature is extensive, but the few facts set out here may help to explain the social consequences of the law. It is also true to say that those consequences, where they are open to criticism, have as much, and perhaps more, to do with poverty, illiteracy,[18] and selfishness[19] than with the law itself.

It is not difficult to see that in a society where illiteracy prevails, where less than ten in every hundred females above the age of five are educated enough to be able to read 'a simple letter in any

---

[17] The word means 'curtain' but signifies here the seclusion of women.

[18] According to the 1961 Census (Bulletin No. 4) the percentage of literate females, above the age of 5 years, was 9·3 for the whole of Pakistan. For East Pakistan, the figure was 10·7 and in West Pakistan 7·4. In the rural areas of West Pakistan, the figure is only 3·2 per cent.

[19] Tyabji, op. cit., p. 221, quotes Maine's dictum: 'Men have always moulded the law of marriage so as to be most agreeable to themselves.'

language',[20] where marriages can be contracted by simple declaration, where a husband is free to contract polygamous marriages and, if he wishes, can divorce his wife, or wives, by uttering the word *talaq* three times, there is room for social injustice to both women and children. Bearing in mind also that before the Ordinance of 1961 there was no registration of marriages, divorces, or of the documents in either case, it is clear that the position of the people concerned—especially wives and children—could be difficult and even disastrous.

In sanctioning a simple form of marriage (which has the merit of protecting the wife's title to her own property and carries with it a right by which the wife inherits a specified share in the deceased husband's estate), and in providing for a simple form of divorce and, in certain circumstances, a measure of polygamy, it may well be that Islam imposes a full sense of responsibility concerning these matters. It is fundamental to any religious teaching, or to any social system, that what it sanctions or enjoins is necessary to a well-ordered society, since any other proposition is quite unthinkable. It must also prescribe the manner in which its institutions are to be observed. Unfortunately, as has long been noticed, the observance does not always correspond to the doctrine.

On the difficult question of polygamy, the institution, as Islam permits it, is defended on a number of well-known grounds, beginning with the assertion—doubtless well-founded—that in Islam monogamy is preferred. It is argued that Islamic polygamy simply regularizes and limits a practice which has existed from time immemorial and certainly was widespread in the East in the day of the Prophet himself. It is claimed that it has the merit of diminishing prostitution; that it provides a way of protecting helpless and unguarded women. It reduces irregular unions and illegitimate births.

Such are the arguments in its favour, and that they possess historic substance can be conceded, just as it can be conceded that right-minded Muslims do not wish to abuse, and do not abuse, the rights which religion confers upon them. The social evil springs from the exercise of these rights by the weak, the vicious, and the grasping. The point was stated by President Ayub Khan when he

---

[20] This was the test of literacy adopted for Pakistan's 1961 Census. See Bulletin No. 4, p. iii.

declared that the provisions of the Family Laws Ordinance were not in conflict with the Quranic injunctions. The following quotation is fairly representative of the tone:

... untold miseries and cruelties ... are commonly perpetrated in our country under the cover of indiscriminate polygamy. This does not only result in embittering and ruining the lives of innumerable tongue-tied women and innocent children, but it also brings in its wake the social, moral, and economic collapse of thousands of families.[21]

It should be made clear that the Muslim Family Laws Ordinance deals with other things besides polygamy, but before I go on to consider the provisions of this important measure, there are reasons for glancing at its historical background. The Ordinance is expressly stated to give effect to certain recommendations of a Commission on Marriage and Family Laws, set up some six years earlier, well before the declaration of Martial Law. These recommendations are contained in the Report of the Commission, whose terms of reference are set out as follows:

Do the existing laws governing marriage, divorce, maintenance, and other ancillary matters among Muslims require modification, in order to give women their proper place in society according to the fundamentals of Islam? The Commission was asked to report on the proper registration of marriages and divorces ... maintenance ... women's rights.[22]

A later paragraph purports to state the reasons for the formation of the Commission, although it is difficult to trace, from a study of that paragraph, what those reasons were, and the impression is left that the true purpose is to conceal, rather than reveal, the circumstances in which the Commission was originally set up.

The unfortunate fact is that however desirable such a Commission was, its terms of reference were very loosely worded and it was left to the Commission itself to frame the questions whose answers might help in elucidating a difficult social and legal problem. It is these circumstances which helped to make the Commission's Report a disappointing and unsatisfactory document, and these circumstances in all probability sprang from the events which led to the appointment of the Commission in the first place.

Early in April 1955, the Prime Minister of Pakistan, the late

[21] In a letter addressed to Mufti Mohamed Shafi, dated 11 June 1961.
[22] *Gazette of Pakistan (Extraordinary)*, 20 June 1956.

Mr. Mohamed Ali (of Bogra), while still in office, married a second wife in the lifetime of his first. The circumstances in which he did so, whether in compliance with Islamic injunctions or not, are of no present concern to us, but it is undeniable that this second marriage, when it came to be known, excited a good deal of unfavourable feeling. This was particularly true among the educated classes of Pakistani women, and protesting delegations met the Prime Minister to impress upon him the unfortunate example he was setting. It is fair to his memory to add that he was by no means the only Pakistani of his time who, while holding high office, had contracted a polygamous marriage, but it was his misfortune to do so when the movement towards women's emancipation and the enforcement of their Quranic rights, was gathering strength. Expressions of disapproval concerning the Prime Minister's conduct were vigorous.[23]

The upshot of all this was a promise by the embarrassed leader that a Commission would be appointed to go into the problems of Pakistan's marriage and family laws and, shortly before he resigned from the prime ministership (on 4 August 1955) this Commission was appointed. It consisted of a former Chief Justice of Pakistan (who replaced the first Chairman who died suddenly), three women, a well-known figure among the 'ulema,[24] and two other men. One of these two[25] did not attend a single meeting of the Commission (although the Report stated that he approved the draft before publication), and Maulana Ehtishamul Haq expressed dissenting views in a Minute written in the Urdu language.

The Report, which includes the recommendations on which the Family Laws Ordinance is stated to be based, is a document of some thirty-five printed pages of which nine, amounting to about 7,000 words, constitute the Report itself. For the most part, this comprises some neither new nor profound observations on the nature of the Quranic injunctions and the Sunnah,[26] as well as the machinery of their elaboration into the Islamic legal system. Had the terms of reference, notwithstanding their admittedly cloudy nature, been imaginatively and adequately responded to, the result could well have been a thoroughly comprehensive and

[23] Relevant references are in *MN*, 8, 16, 17, and 20 April 1955.
[24] Maulana Ehtishamul Haq. '*Ulema* is the plural of '*alim*. It signifies a person learned in Islam.
[25] Mr. Enayat-ur-Rahman.
[26] *Sunnah* signifies traditions in the technical sense.

worthwhile contribution. We might then have had a valuable survey of marriage, divorce, and family problems, viewed in the twentieth century, in the powerful light of Islam. As it turned out, the substance of these nine pages amounted to little more than a condensed version of what could be extracted from any standard textbook of Islamic jurisprudence, along with some vague historical generalizations.

The balance comprises answers to a number of questions framed by the Commission within the terms of reference and circulated to members of the public in order to elicit opinion on as wide a basis as possible in both wings of the country. Out of these answers the Commission synthesized its recommendations which, summarized as concisely as possible, stated that there should be compulsory registration of marriages and that marriage contracts should be signed by the parties to the marriage or, if illiterate, that their thumb-prints should be affixed. Limitations of age were suggested below which males and females should be deemed not competent to marry and penalties were suggested to prevent sale of daughters. Restrictions on the husband's power of divorce and power to contract plural marriages were recommended, along with measures for registration of divorce documents, as well as for maintenance for divorced wives and their children, and for safeguarding the right of a wife to her agreed dower. There were suggestions for safeguarding the property of wives and minors and for the setting up of matrimonial and family courts. In brief, they form proposals which to an outside observer would go far towards ensuring reasonable justice in respect of those problems which sometimes spring from the marriage tie, the raising of a family, and the inheritance of property.

The misfortune was that, however worthy these proposals might be, they did not rest upon any adequately stated foundation of Islamic scholarship and it did not call for much intelligence to find flaws in the reasoning by which these recommendations were ostensibly justified. This the dissenting member, who was sufficiently well qualified for the purpose, proceeded to do in a Minute whose English translation is forty-three pages long. Whatever may be thought of the dissenting member's opinions and conclusions, it has to be acknowledged that the Minute of Dissent was a better performance than the majority Report and it showed that, in terms of Islamic learning, the recommendations were not fully secure.

The reception accorded to the Report upon its appearance in 1956 was lukewarm with a distinct note of opposition. The evident lack of scholarship attracted immediate notice, and in conservative quarters the attitude was clearly adverse. At least one well-known and well-educated Muslim woman, Princess Abida Sultana, daughter of the late Nawab of Bhopal and, at one time, Pakistan's Ambassador in Brazil, published an article in which the Report and its recommendations were criticized and condemned.[27] And, finally, when the dust had settled and interest had passed to other things, the Report was permitted to lie, unused and unadopted, until the Martial Law régime utilized it for the purpose of the Ordinance we are discussing.

The effect of the Ordinance was to set up Arbitration Councils whose business it was, if possible, to bring about a reconciliation between husbands and wives, and to which a notice had to be sent when the husband pronounced a *talaq*, or when either of the parties to the marriage sought a dissolution in any other way. Every marriage solemnized under Islamic law had to be registered and these records were to be preserved by the Union Councils. Copies could be obtained on payment of the prescribed fee. No man was permitted to contract a further marriage so long as a previous marriage subsisted, except with the permission of the Arbitration Council to which an application had to be submitted. In this application it was necessary to state whether the consent of the existing wife, or wives, had been obtained. Equitable maintenance of wife or wives could be compelled and the age limit, under the Child Marriage Restraint Act of 1929, was raised from fourteen to sixteen.

Unlike the reception given to the Report, publication of the Ordinance was received with much acclaim, as indeed it deserved, but it is open to question whether this cordial welcome was attributable so much to its merits as to a form of adulation. One must not carp, however, at a decisive and progressive change, representing one of the principal achievements of President Ayub Khan and his colleagues. Nevertheless, while there can be no doubt of its social importance, the Ordinance laboured beneath the misfortune of being founded upon an ill-contrived Commission and a poorly worked-out case.

----

[27] *D*, 5 August 1956. Her opinions on polygamy had been repudiated earlier by other Pakistani women. See *MN*, 23 April 1955.

For this reason, no sooner was Martial Law abrogated a year later, than a Bill to repeal the Ordinance was introduced into the National Assembly.[28] Considerable effort was made to whip up support among Assembly members for repeal, while women's organizations agitated strongly for its retention and their delegations met the President to elicit his assurances. Heated feelings were displayed. Eventually the President made it known that no proposal for repeal would be countenanced and the Bill failed. Nevertheless, opposition to it remained. Later in the same year Maulana Maudoodi, head of the Jamaat-i-Islami, one of the more formidable of those organizations in Pakistan which aim at the restoration of pristine Islam (as understood by those organizations), called afresh for repeal of the Family Laws Ordinance, and he uttered words of caution to those women who supported its retention and continuance.[29]

One further point should be mentioned in connexion with these questions of social life and conduct and the controversy which surrounded the endeavours of the Martial Law administration in these respects. The history of these developments and the accompanying opposition to them point very clearly to a measure of anti-feminism of a kind with which western countries have, in their time, also been familiar. The question at once arises whether this springs from anything inherent in Islam or the intellectual climate that its teaching produces. The answer seems to be that it does not. Islam certainly does not require that a woman, venturing forth into the street, should do so swathed from head to toe in an unsightly and unhealthy garment called *burqa*. It does not permit a man to debauch himself with wives capriciously married and, with equal caprice, divorced. It does not enjoin that he should invite ruin by undertaking to pay dower artificially assessed to gratify false social aspirations.[30] These things are not matters of religion at all, but social evils and social practices which take root with the passage of time and which most people have neither the courage to resist nor the strength to destroy.

Bearing in mind the claims that have been made for the protection that Islam affords the rights of women, this note of anti-

---

[28] *D*, 4 July 1962.   [29] *D*, 12 November 1962.

[30] President Ayub Khan expressed the view that the prevailing dowry system was ruinous. *D*, 24 May 1961. The effect of Section 10 of the Ordinance is adverse to the practice mentioned in the text, although it does not specifically prevent it.

R.P.—11

feminism in Pakistan calls for a word of explanation. It seems fair to say that the apparently wilful denial of reasonable liberty to women, the exercise of their social rights, and the liberty to develop their natural talents, as it has expressed itself, for instance, in the opposition to family-planning and the Family Laws Ordinance has, in reality, very little to do with religion, however much a religious cloak may be employed. Anti-feminism, whether in Pakistan or elsewhere, springs from considerations that have nothing to do with religious sanction, whether Islamic or otherwise. In Pakistan, the blinkered state of mind is passing and is bound to pass entirely. It has long since been proved that any nation which fails to utilize its woman-power to the best possible advantage simply divests itself of half of its human assets, in both physical and intellectual terms.[31]

[31] During registration of voters, some male heads of households declined to give the names of their womenfolk, apparently with the object of denying them their right to vote. D, 27 June 1964.

XI

East Pakistan—West Pakistan Relations

IT has never been seriously denied that differences have sprung up from time to time between the two Provinces of East and West Pakistan, with unpleasant consequences. These are inevitable in a new nation geographically split by twelve hundred miles of foreign territory. Different languages, using different scripts, are spoken and written; the ethnic, climatic, geographic, and economic distinctions are substantial, and the religious minority communities (with all their special implications in Pakistan) are, to all intents and purposes, concentrated in one of the Provinces, namely, in the eastern wing.[1]

Beneath all this lies a basic political problem arising from a considerable disparity in population. According to the Census of 1961, the population of East Pakistan is 50,853,721, and that of West Pakistan, 42,987,261. Assuming, therefore, that the proportion of persons qualified to vote is about the same in each; assuming, secondly, that representation in the National Assembly should be proportional to population, it follows that East Pakistan should have more seats in that Assembly than its western counterpart and should continue to have more seats until the balance of population is substantially changed. If, further, it is assumed that East Pakistan's members of the Assembly tended on the whole to be united by a provincial loyalty, there would be a tendency for the country's policy and administration to be dominated by East Pakistan.

West Pakistan's fear of this contingency has been partly responsible for an undercurrent of mutual animosity and mistrust. Certainly it has never been explicitly stated that the people of East Pakistan or their leaders ever seriously hoped to exercise this kind of dominance (unless it were in private conversation and in lesser politics) and, in any case, it could never be more than an

---

[1] Of the 11,164,000 non-Muslims in Pakistan, 9,950,000 are resident in East Pakistan (1961 Census, Bulletin No. 2).

unrealizable dream. It is true that in an editorial comment upon President Ayub Khan's constitution of 1962, *Dawn*, reiterating a policy publicized some years earlier, wrote: 'We believe in the Grand Conception—One Country, One People, One Government, One Legislature, and One Purse',[2] a conception which may well be interpreted as the abolition of provincial governments and a fully centralized administration. But whatever the meaning to be placed upon this proposal, it is evident that West Pakistan has always been far from accepting the possibility of any such assimilation which, itself, indicates the kind of interpretation that can be put upon this idea. Still more does it reveal the impossibility of West Pakistan's acceding to any constitutional position in which the higher population of East Pakistan is allowed its natural advantage.

Indeed, such a change was so unlikely that at an early stage in Pakistan's constitutional development the 'principle of parity' was tacitly agreed upon and has not since been seriously contested in the process of constitutional evolution. Not, unfortunately, that this ended the matter, particularly in the days which preceded the administrative consolidation of West Pakistan. Prior to this consolidation there were the further complications springing from the claims of the Provinces that made up the western wing.[3] These are not strictly relevant here, but they, too, helped to complicate and obstruct the emergence of any sort of Constitution, for it must be remembered that until 1956 Pakistan was being administered under the provisions of the Government of India Act of 1935, as amended for Pakistan, and the provisions of the Independence Act of 1947.

All this being so, it could not have pleased East Pakistan that, as events turned out, the position was reversed and, at the outset, West Pakistan appeared to acquire an ascendancy in national affairs. This development was not surprising. The fact that Mohamed Ali Jinnah belonged to Karachi and established the new capital there, the fact that world attention was focused at the beginning on the great Punjab migrations and the trouble in Kashmir, the fact that Pakistan's Armed Forces were principally located in (and belonged to) the soil of West Pakistan, and the

[2] *D*, 2 March 1962.
[3] See Callard, op. cit., and Feldman, op. cit. The Provinces in question were: Sind, Punjab, Northwest Frontier, Baluchistan, and the acceded states.

fact that in the superior grades of the public services there were substantially more West Pakistanis than East Pakistanis, all combined to give a prominence and an advantage to the western wing which, to this day, has never quite been effaced. So it was that, in 1950, during a debate on constitutional matters in the Constituent Assembly, Mr. Nur Ahmed, a member from East Pakistan, expressed the apprehensions of the East Pakistani people that moves were afoot which, if successful, would reduce the majority province to a minority one and make a colony out of East Bengal.[4] This, doubtless, was going rather far, but such plain speaking reflected all too clearly the existence of a well-nurtured suspicion as to purity of motive.

By 1950 there were strong feelings in East Pakistan about certain grievances apart from the political problem I have mentioned. It was said that the western province had unfairly dominated policy; that East Pakistan had not received its fair share of the national wealth (notwithstanding its own very substantial contribution made from the sale of jute, tea, and other produce); that its economic and industrial development had been impeded in the interests of West Pakistan. The attempt to make Urdu the national language of the entire country, to the exclusion of Bengali, was fiercely resented and ultimately failed. It was considered that far too many of the best jobs in the services were going to West Pakistanis with consequent prejudice to the interests of East Pakistan and the prospects of men recruited from that wing. The situation was further aggravated by extreme tactlessness on both sides and, as late as 1962, we find a report that while leading 'Id prayers in Karachi, Maulana Ehtishamul Haq[5] charitably included a supplication to the Almighty to 'create love for Pakistan in the hearts of Muslims of East Pakistan'.

Whatever the grievances might be, it is certain they were not weightless and various reasons were advanced, from official sources, to explain them. Thus, in the First Five Year Plan, out of the total public programme of expenditure, 400 crores of rupees were allocated to East Pakistan, whereas to West Pakistan the allocation was 471 crores and, to the Centre, a further 64 crores.[6]

---

[4] Feldman, op. it., p. 28.
[5] The matrimonial law expert. He later expressed regret and claimed to have been misunderstood. *D*, 12 and 13 March 1962.
[6] First Five Year Plan Report, December 1957, pp. 74–6.

Since the Central Government was principally located at Karachi, this last expenditure seemed likely to benefit mainly, even if not wholly, the people of West Pakistan.

The First Five Year Plan Report endeavoured to explain the disparity by saying that West Pakistan was six times bigger in area and that seven-eighths of the refugee influx at the time of partition came into West Pakistan. There was no mention of the departing Hindus and Sikhs. The dependence on irrigation and the pressure on cultivable land in the western province were adduced as further reasons for the high allocation. Historical reasons were also given to explain why the amount allotted to the eastern wing was the maximum considered feasible.

It is doubtful whether this reasoning convinced the people of East Pakistan, where the population is so much greater, and the pressure on land, cultivable or otherwise, is so intense that in some areas the population amounts to 1,600 people to the square mile, with an average for the whole Province of more than 900. It could equally have been argued that even if West Pakistan did not have enough water, East Pakistan, at certain seasons, had far too much and that one of the great necessities of the Province was an adequate system of flood control and the utilization of its great rivers in power, as well as agricultural, projects.

If there was substance in these grievances, they did not go unforeseen. When the British Government, in 1947, announced its intention to transfer power, and when the principle of partition became known, H. S. Suhrawardy raised the cry of a 'sovereign, independent, and undivided Bengal in a divided India'.[7] Suhrawardy, a Calcutta man with a gift of shrewd political evaluation, must have known that neither the prospective Indian Government, nor the prospective Pakistan Government would for a moment countenance the idea, quite apart from the question of viability of any such a republic. But what he said was not uttered without reason, and it may well be he foresaw those circumstances

[7] He was then Chief Minister of Bengal under the British régime. This proposal was made at a Press Conference on 27 April 1947. The newspaper references will be found in *Keesings Contemporary Archives*, 1946–48, p. 8364. In 1960 President Ayub Khan uttered a warning against communist efforts to make East Pakistan part of a separate state. It is unlikely that Suhrawardy was referred to in this connexion. *D*, 26 July 1960. Later, after Martial Law was withdrawn, he said: 'Suhrawardy always led the disruptionists.' *D*, 30 September 1962.

which later combined to give a distinct initial advantage to the western wing.

The people of Bengal have for centuries displayed an attitude of some independence towards the rest of the sub-continent, and upon this, in East Pakistan, reacted the grievances we have mentioned. From it there appeared, from time to time, a form of rancour expressed in some bitter talk, not omitting reference to secession which, on one occasion at least, threatened to become an issue.[8] No doubt any such development was highly improbable, for such a remedy, if it could be so described, would have been more injurious to East Pakistan than the disease of which it complained. Yet such murmurs never evaporated entirely. It is noteworthy that in his address to the nation on Pakistan Day, 23 March 1962, some weeks before the inauguration of the new Constitution, President Ayub Khan made a specific reference to disruption. And again, after Martial Law had been dispensed with, the late Khwaja Nazimuddin, speaking for the Opposition, declared that people who talked of secession would be dealt with as traitors and hanged publicly.[9] Since it is highly unlikely that he meant either President Ayub Khan or his ministers in this connexion, Khwaja Nazimuddin (who belonged to East Pakistan) was either protesting too much or he was making clear to certain groups in his Province just where he and his party stood.

There is no worthwhile purpose to be served here in labouring troublesome matters,[10] although the background is obviously important when considering the impact of Martial Law on East Pakistan and upon the methods adopted later by the new administration to find a solution to the problem of inter-wing relations. It seems evident that the *coup* of 1958 was conceived and planned in West Pakistan by men who were all non-Bengali and, with the possible exception of Mr. Zakir Hussain, who became Governor of East Pakistan immediately after the promulgation of Martial Law, it may well be that no other East Pakistani had any participation whatsoever in the moves that preceded the overthrow of the 1956 Constitution and the introduction of military government.

Mr. Zakir Hussain was a former Inspector-General of Police in East Pakistan, to which Province he belongs. He was serving there

[8] See Feldman, op. cit., Chapter VII.   [9] *D*, 14 December 1962.
[10] References to East Pakistan's problems, and articles on that subject, will be found in Smith, op. cit., Chapter 5.

in the Police force at the same time as Major-General (as he then was) Ayub Khan was commanding the East Pakistan Division. The Martial Law Administrator in East Pakistan was Major-General Umrao Khan, a man evidently capable of doing a sound job.[11] Of the administration of Mr. Zakir Hussain as Governor, and of Major-General Umrao Khan as Administrator, little was specifically heard, and certainly nothing significant by way of criticism, but their work was overshadowed by the more powerful personality of Lieutenant-General Azam Khan who, in April 1960, replaced Mr. Zakir Hussain as Governor. A West Pakistani like General Umrao Khan, General Azam greatly endeared himself to the East Pakistan people. It seems that he possessed a commendable fund of loyalty to any cause he could make his own, and when, in May 1962, he was replaced by Mr. Ghulam Faruque, he left behind a considerable name because of the manner in which he had identified himself with the interests of the Province he had recently been governing.

It is obvious that with the dissolution of political parties and the suppression of political activity, the airing of provincial grievances had no place. Indeed, as in West Pakistan, attention was focused only on the measures of reform which the Martial Law administration had promised and upon those other activities intended to prevent smuggling, black-marketing, and other anti-social offences. In East Pakistan, as in West, screening of officials and disqualification proceedings under EBDO went on. Whatever people in East Pakistan thought of Martial Law, there is nothing to show any greater resistance to it than in the western province, and acceptance—docile or obsequious—was no less evident.

Shortly after the declaration, General Ayub Khan visited Dacca, and it was from there that, on 17 October 1958, he made the observation that 'whereas Martial Law will not be retained a minute longer than is necessary, it will not be lifted a minute earlier than the purpose for which it has been imposed has been fulfilled'. It does not seem that this was uttered especially for the benefit of East Pakistanis but, as I have mentioned, it was probably a rejoinder to Iskander Mirza's statement that Martial Law would be retained for the shortest possible time.

President Ayub Khan did not visit East Pakistan again until

[11] Major-General Umrao Khan came originally from Rohtak which is now in Indian Punjab.

September 1959, and it was probably significant that he chose Dacca as the place from which to make an important broadcast to the nation. In this broadcast he made a clear pronouncement on the subject of Basic Democracies for the first time.[12] It was no less significant that at the end of the same month the editor of *Ittefaq*,[13] a daily newspaper published in Dacca in the Bengali language, was arrested under Martial Law Regulation No. 24. This newspaper had close associations with the Awami League, H. S. Suhrawardy's party, and had at various times published material which exhibited a tendency towards provincial loyalty. Since the Regulation under which the editor was detained concerned the causing of public alarm and despondency and creating dissatisfaction towards the Armed Forces, one can guess the gist of what was published and attracted the displeasure of the Martial Law authorities.

In January 1960 President Ayub Khan visited East Pakistan again and stayed there for some eight or nine days. It was on this occasion that he toured the Province in a *Pak Jamhuriyat Special* train, preaching the basic democratic gospel and revisiting many places with which he had become familiar when he had been commanding the Division stationed in the Province.

During this tour, concerned mainly as it was with propagating the merits of the Basic Democracies scheme, there does not seem to have been any particular emphasis on inter-provincial unity, apart from the customary declarations of brotherly feeling and the common dedication to Islamic ideals and the Pakistan conception. However, in his address at the Dacca University Convocation,[14] the following passage occurs: '. . . nowhere do I feel myself a stranger. It is because we are one. We are basically similar. Our way of life is similar and from that emerges the common ideology of ours. We must always bear that in mind for that is the basis of cohesion.'

The question of similarity in this context does not seem to call for analysis here, but it would have been better logic to have said that the way of life is similar because of the common ideology, the simple fact being that the peoples of East and West Pakistan are united by Islamic belief and ideal. If Islam does not bind these territories together, then it is impossible to know what does. Perhaps it should be added that in an address to the Armed Forces

---

[12] 2 September 1959.   [13] 30 September 1959.   [14] 21 January 1960.

on 23 March 1961, also in Dacca, the President did pursue the more logical line of reasoning I have suggested here.

It has earlier been indicated that in the supervening circumstances of Martial Law and the focusing of attention on other things, the question of inter-provincial difference found little prominence, at least, for a time. Any pursuit of the theme might well have been viewed with disfavour and visited, perhaps, with punishment. All the same, the question was not totally dismissed and at the beginning of 1960 a practical attempt was made to bring the two Provinces together, other than through the medium of fraternal assurances and such contact as springs from the brief visits of government officials. On this occasion, the experiment consisted of a resettlement of East Pakistan agriculturalists on barrage land in West Pakistan, irrigated by the waters of the Indus and distributed through the Ghulam Mohamed Barrage at Kotri.[15]

Apart from the obvious merit of bringing the people of the two Provinces closer together and of creating closer interest in each other's problems and circumstances, the scheme, if successful, could have contributed much to a solution of East Pakistan's population problem and—who can say?—to the political aspect of that problem. Unhappily, the experiment did not succeed. About one hundred families were brought over from East Pakistan and settled on land allotted to them, but they were unable to establish themselves and eventually the majority returned to East Pakistan.

The reasons for the failure are difficult to isolate. As the condition of the settlers deteriorated and as the subject found its way into the newspapers, recrimination developed with blame and counter-blame and, towards the end of the controversy, there was a distinct note of acerbity which did nothing to improve inter-provincial relations. As is usual in such cases, there was doubtless fault on both sides. The West Pakistan Government claimed it had done everything within reason to ensure success, but that the East Pakistan Government had failed to send suitable people, the families chosen coming from a class of fishermen and not from the agricultural class at all. East Pakistan advanced the counter-argument that the land allotted was unsuitable and that the settlers had been treated with neglect and indifference.

The lesson to be learned from this (which was surely obvious at

[15] *D*, 4 January 1960.

the outset) is that, taking into account the problem of language, of difference in habits of life, and in the very circumstances in which the settlers would have to adapt themselves to vastly differing climate and modes of cultivation, it would be no small matter to ensure success. The result is that such unlettered people, impressionable as they are, will not easily be persuaded to volunteer again for such experiments (if, indeed, any such are envisaged) and it is a great pity that this attempt was permitted to languish and come to nothing.

Perhaps, at that stage of the proceedings, the new administration was not much more impressed than were any of its predecessors with the absolute necessity for a solution to the problem of interprovincial relations that would, once and for all, put an end to sporadic bickering. Thus, when one recalls the ill-feeling engendered by the disparity of allocation between East Pakistan, West Pakistan, and the Centre, in the First Five Year Plan, it is curious that no reference to this particular cause of dissatisfaction found any mention in the President's initial statement on the subject of the Second Plan.[16] Nor did the Plan itself, first published in June 1960, make any reference to the need for satisfying the eastern Province's particular needs and aspirations. It is true that the Report of the Panel of Economists on the Second Five Year Plan[17] made special reference to this point and drew attention to the technically complex problems involved. There was substance in what these experts wrote, but it was equally certain that nothing less than an absolute recognition of East Pakistan's claims, in terms of gross allocation, would suffice to extinguish any smouldering discontent. And this became so apparent that, by February 1961, we find the President giving unequivocal promises to hasten the industrialization of East Pakistan;[18] and, with subsequent revisions and expansions of the Second Five Year Plan, the eastern Province became the principal object of development expenditure.[19]

Leaving aside for the moment the question of practical steps, the new administration, in emphasizing the essential unity of the country (divided in a geographical sense though it might be), and

[16] 30 December 1959; 21 June 1960.
[17] Government of Pakistan, 1960.   [18] D, 18 February 1961.
[19] See President's broadcast, 6 February 1962. The same policy is reflected in the Third Five Year Plan. D, 28 August and 5 September 1964.

in calling for a dissolution of local loyalties was, to be sure, doing no new thing. The desirability of all this was a subject on which the ministers of every preceding government had so often been eloquent. President Ayub Khan's various exhortations[20] to abandon provincial notions, and even that clannishness within the Provinces themselves, which leads to nepotism, favouritism, and other forms of unfair discrimination which, in turn, lead to inefficiency and discontent, were really no different from other such exhortations made before him. All the same, as time passed, the day came when the Martial Law administration could justly claim the merit of having taken bolder and firmer steps to encourage these admirable sentiments and to erase, finally, those marks of division between the Provinces which appeared to be so indelibly inscribed.

This gives rise to some interesting questions. How did all this come about? What were these steps that the Martial Law administration adopted, and what was their success?

The facts indicate that the new administration, with President Ayub as principal policy-maker (and, certainly, in this instance, because constitutional questions were deeply involved and because he was about to discard his military colleagues) achieved a compromise involving the Centre and the two Provinces that is not likely to be departed from. The compromise meant that, beneath the aegis of the unifying dedication to Islam, and within the framework of loyalty to Pakistan,[21] each of the two Provinces acquired a very considerable measure of economic and administrative autonomy. The tendencies in this direction became apparent early in 1962, and even before Martial Law was replaced by a constitutional form of government, and it seems probable that this concession, particularly agreeable to East Pakistan opinion, helped greatly to facilitate acceptance of the new Constitution.

That pressures were being exerted in the early months of 1962 cannot be disputed. In East Pakistan, during February and March of that year, there was a series of disturbances in which students were prominent and in which political leaders, particularly of the

[20] See, for example, *D*, 19 October and 8 November 1961, and President's broadcast address, 23 March 1962.

[21] Later, we find President Ayub Khan giving the growth of *Islamic nationalism* (author's italics) as a guideline for the survival of Pakistan. *D*, 27 August 1964.

Awami League party, were arrested.[22] Between 8 and 13 February there were demonstrations in Dacca, Barisal, Kushtia, Chittagong, Sylhet, Khulna, and Noakhali. In the last-named town, a railway train was stoned and passengers injured. More people, principally students, were arrested and it was then asserted that the students were being 'exploited for selfish and nefarious ends'. Although no details were given in the local Press, the only interpretation that could be put upon these words was purely political.

But the authorities pursued the conciliatory theme that the students were innocent dupes and when, in March, the arrested scholars were found guilty and sentenced to hard labour by a Military Court, they were promptly pardoned and released. These acts of condonation did not, however, satisfy either the convicted youngsters or those with whom they were associated. Later in the same month there was a recurrence of trouble; tear-gas was used to disperse the crowd and 200 students were arrested. Undeterred, they demonstrated again two days later, and the Governor of the Province repeated the theme that these young people were being exploited. President Ayub Khan adopted a firmer note. He said that Calcutta and Kabul were being used as bases for disruptive manoeuvres and that students who played into 'undeserving' hands would not have things their own way.[23] The suggestion that Indian agents were using students for their own purposes was repeated soon afterwards[24] and President Ayub Khan uttered a warning that continued unrest within the country would affect the attitude of other countries offering to assist the development of Pakistan.

However, no one was satisfied. In the middle of April the situation became clearer. Dacca University classes were suspended and the students published their demands which included release of their arrested classmates, release of all political *detenus*, withdrawal of warrants of arrest still unexecuted, and, significantly, a guarantee of civil liberties. These demands continued to be pressed with the support of other local organizations including the Dacca High Court Bar Association. An editorial in *Dawn* newspaper, which bore the heading *Incomprehensible*,[25] began with these words: 'The student situation in East Pakistan, instead of getting better, seems to be getting worse', and, in a sense, that was

---

[22] Sheikh Mujibur Rahman, for instance.
[23] Address at the Tenth Convocation of Peshawar University, 28 March 1962.
[24] *D*, 31 March 1962.   [25] *D*, 18 April 1962.

true. However, a month before Martial Law was withdrawn all arrested students received a pardon and an appeal was made to the student-body to eschew politics.

In considering what the happenings really signified, certain things must be borne in mind. To begin with, they took place during the Martial Law period, although by this time Martial Law was only a shadow of its former self, and the country knew, from many published statements and from the fact that the Constitution Commission had completed its labours as far back as May 1961, that it was on the eve of constitutional government. Secondly, although there was no suppression of news of the incidents themselves, there was a general abstention on the part of Pakistan newspapers to give details of what the students were actually demonstrating about. While there seems to have been no formal censorship, it is probable that editors were reminded of the wisdom of discretion when elaborating detail.

However, one assumption was perfectly admissible, namely, that these demonstrations, well- or ill-advised, were not about nothing and, in the absence of more specific information, it was possible to discern three implications in all this unrest which, it must be added, was confined at this time to East Pakistan. The first lay in the grievances of students with respect to education and those grievances reflected themselves in resentment over the Education Report. The second lay in agitation promoted to create ill-will between the two wings of the country, even if not for the purpose of actual secession which is, after all, a very far cry. Thirdly, there was the use of student agitation as a cloak for applying political pressures in relation to the Constitution then under preparation. To assess the relative weight of each is difficult, although it is obvious that agitation undertaken in the cause of any one of them materially assisted the cause of all.

Ingenuous youth has long been made the tool of designing people, but this does not always mean that there is nothing to be indignant about. The tendency in Pakistan has often been for the administration to comfort itself with the thought that such young men and women are being used by the unscrupulous, and to treat them with lenience accordingly, or, at any rate, to back down after giving a demonstration of severity. In this way, genuine complaints could be shifted conveniently out of sight, but not out of the student-mind where they remained to smoulder, sometimes pungently. On such occasions, the only persons actually deceived were the authorities themselves.

During this period of disturbance, it is evident that great play was made of the sense of student discontent in which an appeal to provincial loyalty occupied a large part. The administration tended to interpret these happenings as the work of people primarily interested in disruption. President Ayub Khan's speech made at the Peshawar University Convocation, precisely at the time when these episodes of student violence were going on, is obviously important for it reveals what he and his advisers thought about this subject. His words indicated a recognition of provincial discontent which could only lead to disunity and, eventually, to the destruction of Pakistan.

If this is so, it seems to have been an erroneous appreciation. The moment was too carefully chosen and the form in which the clamour was expressed too relevant to the hour. The major purpose, it seems clear, was simply to bring about a delegation of power and responsibility to provincial governments and to ensure that this received effect in the Constitution that was soon to be announced.

For, if it were otherwise, and if the administration was thoroughly convinced of the disruptive purpose of the agitation, what was the necessity for making the administrative concessions for which East Pakistan had so long been pressing? Indeed, it could even be argued that the administration had sought to forestall trouble by changes that could only be congenial to the eastern wing. At the beginning of February 1962 the Pakistan Industrial Development Corporation, a statutory body set up some eleven years previously for the development of industry in the country, to which it had made a conspicuous contribution, was divided into two such corporations,[26] each under the control of its own Provincial Government. At about the same time the Governor of East Pakistan said that his Province desired a bifurcation of the railway service which, hitherto, had been centrally administered. The West Pakistan Governor said there was no objection from his side, and the railways were then divided on a provincial basis, each system falling under the control of its Provincial Government.[27] Two separate

[26] D, 3 February 1962. They were called East Pakistan Industrial Development Corporation and West Pakistan Industrial Development Corporation, respectively.

[27] D, 15 February 1962.

Railway Boards were set up, in place of the Central Government's Railway Board, which exercised the controlling authority over the country's railway system. The provincialization of the railways was in the circumstances understandable, even if questionable. The necessity for two Railway Boards is quite incomprehensible.

In the first half of 1962 the process of decentralization continued. In June, the Water and Power Development Authority, another statutory organization responsible for irrigation, power-generation projects, land reclamation, river-training, and so on, was divided into the East Pakistan Water and Power Development Authority and, of course, its western counterpart. The Provincial Governments were empowered to take over all development projects in their respective territories. Other branches of the central administration were divided and transferred to the Provincial Governments, or powers delegated to them so that, in effect, each Provincial Government was master in its own house, except for the obvious instances of defence, external affairs, central banking and currency, citizenship, certain aspects of taxation, the central public services, and a number of subsidiary matters with international implications.

The second, and perhaps more important aspect of the compromise, is found in the 1962 Constitution which President Ayub Khan gave to the country. By comparison with the 1956 Constitution, the division of powers, as between the Central and the Provincial Governments, was far more liberal and more favourable to the Provinces. The 1956 Constitution enumerated thirty subjects on which the Central Government had power to legislate exclusively; it enumerated nineteen subjects on which the Central and Provincial Governments had power to legislate concurrently, and it enumerated ninety-four subjects on which the Provincial Governments had power to legislate exclusively in their own Provinces, with residuary powers to the Provinces. The 1962 Constitution enumerates forty-nine subjects on which the Central Government has exclusive powers of legislation and proceeds, in a later Article, to state that the Provincial Governments have the power to make laws on any subject not included in the list of forty-nine reserved to the Centre.

However, the language of Article 131 appears to open the way for the Central Government to legislate on any subject it may choose. An officially sponsored study[28] explains this arrangement as conferring overriding authority on the Centre in matters concerning national security, co-ordination between the Provinces, and economic development. This may certainly be the intention, but the possibilities implicit in the language of the Article appear to go wider. Nevertheless, it seems certain that any attempt at straining the provisions of the Article, and even its utilization, except in the most patent cases of necessity, would provoke controversy. It is, however, improbable that the Central Government would seek to use these powers without good and sufficient reason.

The position can be fairly summarized in the following terms. A unitary form of government would probably be congenial to East Pakistan, and less congenial to the western Province. On the other hand, that form of Federal administration in which the Centre exercises extensive powers of administrative and financial control, especially with reference to trade, industry, and government expenditure generally, is less acceptable to the east wing. This has been substantially recognized in the devolution of powers and duties during the Martial Law period.

Thus it becomes evident that East Pakistan, having won its cultural battle with the recognition of Bengali as a national language,[29] proceeded to win the administrative and the economic. This is a situation that President Ayub Khan's administration came to recognize. Not everyone in Pakistan may have agreed with the solution that was adopted, but it is difficult to see what else could be done. The alternative would have been long-festering discontent, and I conclude that the decision was correct as well as courageous.

Yet if this interpretation is accurate, how is it to be reconciled

---

[28] *The Constitution—A Study* produced for the Bureau of National Reconstruction by the Department of Films and Publications, Government of Pakistan. No date.

[29] This was indeed a victory. In his address at Dacca University Convocation on 24 March 1948, Mr. Jinnah, having conceded that Bengali could be an official language of East Pakistan, went on to say: '. . . they proceeded to demand that both Bengali and Urdu should be the state languages of Pakistan. Make no mistake about it. There can only be one state language . . . and that . . . can only be Urdu.' The Constitution of 1956 (Article 214) recognizes both Urdu and Bengali as 'State' languages. The 1962 Constitution (Article 215) recognizes both as 'national' languages. Even in this change of terminology there is a faint nuance of concession to East Pakistan.

with the necessity, frequently stated by President Ayub Khan, for a strong Centre? During the period of Martial Law the question scarcely arose since all power was in military hands and exercised by the military group that had seized it. There was only one source of power and that lay with the military government. The question became relevant only after the decentralization of power to the Provinces and upon withdrawal of Martial Law. Evidently, some explanation of this apparent anomaly was considered necessary and President Ayub Khan provided it when he said:

I may tell you my interpretation of a strong Centre is . . . a central organization, an organization which should be able to resolve the quarrels between the various parts of the country and the different groups of people. As long as there is no friction, these various regions and different groups should be free to work as they like. But whenever there is a difference of opinion, then it is imperative that a central organization should have the complete authority and the complete responsibility of resolving such differences.[30]

This interpretation of the policy of the strong Centre seems entirely consistent with the policy of decentralization and compromise which the Martial Law administration adopted with respect to the problem of relations between the two Provinces.[31]

[30] Address at Rawalpindi, when inaugurating the memorial to the late Liaquat Ali Khan. Speech quoted verbatim in *D*, 18 October 1964.
[31] The Constitution Commission Report repays study on the entire question.

XII

Foreign Policy

UPON the conclusion of his Asian tour of 1961, Vice-President Lyndon B. Johnson reported to his own President, the late John Fitzgerald Kennedy, as follows: 'President Ayub, in Pakistan, is singularly impressive. He is seasoned as a leader, where others are not, confident and straightforward and, I would judge, dependable . . .'[1]

This seems to be a very fair assessment of the image which President Ayub Khan created for himself at the outset, and possibly represents the view that is still taken of his stature. Certainly, it partly accounts for the success he has had—and it is largely a personal success—in guiding Pakistan's relations with other countries and in restoring to the country that respect and esteem which, in international affairs, it had lost by the time that Martial Law was declared. In short, therefore, the first achievement of the Martial Law administration in foreign affairs was a moral one by which the world quickly became satisfied that a firmer hand, disembarrassed of profitless political strife, was in control. In this swift acceptance of the new dispensation, which was recognized everywhere without hesitation, there was also, perhaps, an element of relief, for there was a time when Pakistan seemed to be degenerating into the status of Asia's sick man.

The impress of this personality which did much towards establishing a new view of Pakistan was not directly felt outside the country until the latter part of 1959, and the first of these occasions was a brief halt at Delhi to meet the late Pandit Jawaharlal Nehru. Since relations with India form the subject of the next chapter, we need not pause to consider that now.

The first specific statement on foreign policy appeared in a speech delivered by President Ayub Khan on 25 December 1958[2]

---

[1] Quoted in *D*, 17 June 1964 from William S. White's book *The Professional*, a political biography of President Lyndon B. Johnson.

[2] Quaid-i-Azam Mohamed Ali Jinnah's birthday anniversary.

at Karachi. In a brief passage of some 150 words, he reiterated adherence to the United Nations charter, abhorrence of colonialism, and friendship with all Muslim countries, particularly those in the Near and Middle East. Pakistan, he said, stood by its commitments and would prove to be a steady and dependable friend, but it would seek new friends in the belief that the more it had, the better it would be. Perhaps the most important sentence in this particular passage of his speech was that with which it began: 'The structure of our foreign policy is based on the fundamental needs of our country.' The accuracy of this statement need not be doubted, but was not, of course, peculiar to Pakistan. Foreign policy, everywhere, must be taken to express self-interest, more or less enlightened.

But, in the ascertainment of where its interest truly lay, and in the development of its policy towards the world at large, Pakistan started with certain initial disadvantages. Some of these were to be expected, while others can only be attributed to an ignorant indifference which was quite inexcusable. The disadvantages to be expected lay in the unfriendliness of India, the pressures created by the migration of peoples into and out of West Pakistan, as well as the necessity for sorting out the confusions to which the partition had given rise. Those less easily explicable sprang from the apparent inability, or perhaps unwillingness, of some other countries to accept the fact of Pakistan as a new and independent state whose sovereignty and existence possessed a title equivalent to that of India and derived from precisely the same root.[3] Perhaps, also, in a world still wondering about the consequences of a war only recently concluded, there was little inclination or time to dwell upon the fate of those first products of decolonization, a process which had its beginnings in the independence of the Indo-Pakistan subcontinent.

If it is accepted that the principles which guide all relations between states are founded upon the necessity for preserving sovereignty, upon the defence of the people and the soil, upon the protection of commerce, currently accepted values, and way of life, then the shape of any nation's foreign policy sooner or later becomes plain. So with Pakistan whose territories are divided and bounded, over great distances, partly by an unfriendly Afghanistan

---

[3] The manner and circumstances in which Pakistan was, for instance, elected to membership of the United Nations, were quite indefensible.

and partly by an India with which relations have waxed and waned in warmth and, at all times, have been greatly complicated by the problems of Kashmir and the river waters. There was a strongly felt intention and desire to pursue the faith and values of Islam, in concert with those other nations where the same belief prevailed. There existed considerable coastlines with seaports through which trade could principally be expanded and local industries, depending upon the wealth of the sea, built up. There was a recognized need for external aid in economic development. These, and these alone, were the facts from which the fundamental requirements of the country could be recognized and upon them the structure of foreign policy was erected.

For a good many years one of the principal components of this structure had been Pakistan's alignment with the western powers, notably the United States of America and the United Kingdom. This alignment found expression in membership of the CENTO and SEATO treaty-groups and in certain treaties of assistance and defence. So long, indeed, has this alignment subsisted that it seems to have been forgotten that this situation did not develop until 1953. Before that year, Pakistan, except for membership of the Commonwealth, pursued no particular affiliations, although the tendency of its world-view had always been pro-west and anti-communist. Even before 1953 it had accepted Point Four aid, which President Truman had instituted within the framework and intentions of the Atlantic Charter, and aid through the Colombo Plan.

It seems to have been during the Governor-Generalship of Ghulam Mohamed that a decision was taken to enter upon closer relations with the United States of America and so, indirectly, with the United Kingdom. The decision was not immediately popular. It was noticed that India was keeping aloof from such alliances[4] and it was felt that having gained, after a long and difficult struggle, its own independence, there was a danger of Pakistan's becoming a subservient client of the powerful Americans. The probability is that Ghulam Mohamed, an able and clear-headed finance man with a considerable fund of determination,

---

[4] Years later, the late Mohamed Ali (of Bogra) in the capacity of Foreign Minister, asserted that as far back as 1951 the United States had entered into a secret treaty with India and had thereby deceived Pakistan. *D*, 22 November 1962.

had reached the conclusion that without closer ties with the United States, Pakistan could not expect to receive, in necessary measure, that assistance upon which economic advancement so greatly depended. At all events, it was after his visit to the United States in 1953 that rumours began to circulate of a treaty of mutual defence between the two countries.

Further than this we need not go. Whatever the circumstances and the merits, it soon became clear that both Governments had made commitments to each other. In May of 1953 a Mutual Defence Assistance Agreement was signed. It was specifically made clear that this Agreement was not a military alliance, nor would military bases be made available by Pakistan to the United States. All this was, apparently, made necessary by the great play that India was then making of Pakistan's entering into a treaty of defence and the obligations that would arise. The day was not then foreseen when India would, herself, be seeking avidly and accepting military aid from both the United States and the United Kingdom. On the signing of the Agreement the Soviet Union entered a protest which was rejected. It was this Agreement which led, in due course, to membership of the CENTO and SEATO groups and no doubt it was to these alliances that President Ayub Khan referred when he said that Pakistan would prove to be a steady and dependable friend.

Indeed, with the onset of Martial Law, there was not the least indication of a change in these cardinal features of Pakistan's foreign policy—the agreements with America and the concomitant features of association with the United Kingdom—beyond and irrespective of the Commonwealth link and, of course, closer relations with Iran and Turkey.

It had happened that some six months before the declaration of Martial Law, an understanding had been reached between the United States, on the one hand, and Iran, Pakistan, and Turkey, on the other, that some closer association could be negotiated, and it is evident that the October *coup* in Pakistan had done nothing to discourage either the United States, Iran, or Turkey. The fact that in January 1959 it became known that some obstacles had developed in the course of the negotiations, indicated that not only were the negotiations continuing, but that the United States, as well as Iran and Turkey, were satisfied about the stability of the Martial Law government. In consequence of this interruption in negotiations, however, there were consultations between the three eastern nations, while the Soviet Union, for its part, showed displeasure over these developments and adopted a minatory attitude. Notwithstanding this, on 5 March 1959, at Ankara, Pakistan entered into a bilateral agreement with the United States with precisely the same terms as did Iran and Turkey.

Consonant with all this was the visit of President Ayub Khan to Teheran and Ankara in November 1959 and, in the December following, the visit of President Eisenhower to Pakistan. Eisenhower received a notable welcome and, on its side, the United States did not omit to indicate in discreet measure to the people of Karachi the extent of its resources and power.[5] Five months later occurred the incident of the U-2 aircraft which was brought down flying over Soviet territory; the American pilot, Powers, was made a prisoner and subsequently tried.

Pakistan was implicated in this incident by the Soviet Government which addressed Pakistan in threatening language alleging that the aircraft had taken off from an airfield at Peshawar. The Pakistan Government disclaimed all responsibility and when, as a result of the incident, the Paris summit conference failed, President Ayub Khan commented that the free world would have to be more alert.[6] This statement was significant for it indicated the attitude of the new régime towards Communism and the eastern bloc. In November 1959 the President had expressed the view that the Communist countries would undertake a drive towards the Indian Ocean and it was in relation to this belief that he suggested the desirability of joint-defence arrangements between Pakistan and India.[7]

The question of Indo-Pakistan relations we can, for the moment, leave aside. The immediate interest is in the implicit opposition to Communism which had always been the attitude of successive governments in Pakistan. It is clear that an alliance with the United States would otherwise have not been possible. In his own pronouncements on the subject, President Ayub Khan was very forthright, even to the point of claiming that to the 'modern

---

[5] All day a procession of helicopters flew over the city, on what business was never really made clear. They were based on a United States warship in the harbour, attending on the President who, himself, travelled in an aircraft of the U.S.A.A.F.

[6] *D*, 20 May 1960.   [7] *D*, 19 November 1959.

slavery of Communism'[8] there was only one answer and that answer was to be found in Islam.[9] Therefore, he continued, to meet the challenge of Communism, 'Islam should be retrieved from the recesses of the past and presented to the world in the light and language of today'.[9] The theme was repeated in an address to the Basic Democrats' convention at Lahore, in June 1960, but there, when asserting the superiority of Islam over Communism and Fascism, he suggested, at the same time, a superiority over western democracy where 'truth and sincerity are thrown overboard due to mutual squabbles among parties.'[10]

This attitude of aversion to Communism continued to be expressed, but, later, from a slightly adjusted angle. As we already know, Pakistan was much disappointed with the financial prospects held out by the foreign Consortium in relation to the Second Five Year Plan[11] and, in the middle of 1961, considerable resentment was shown, particularly towards the attitude of the United States. In July of that year, President Ayub Khan visited America and suggested that unless a fair measure of help was forthcoming, Pakistan's economy might break down with disastrous results, leading inevitably to Communism.[12] In a speech, afterwards described as one of the best ever heard there, at a Joint Session of the United States Congress, he said it would be a calamity if Pakistan were to 'go under Communism'.[13]

From all this, and from what has been said in earlier chapters, it is evident that Communism was not acceptable doctrine to the Martial Law administration, but while to reject Communism is one thing, to reject the friendship of, or useful relationship with, countries where that scripture prevails, is quite another. There are various ways of combining strange bedfellows and politics is one of them. Contemporaneously with all this talk of Communism and ties with the United States of America, other events were in the making.

There has always been, in Pakistan, a body of opinion unfavourable to the treaty commitments made with the United

---

[8] Address at Dacca University Convocation, 21 January 1960.

[9] Address to Darul Uloom Islamia, 3 May 1959.

[10] At this time, he was, of course, still pursuing the idea of a non-party system of government.

[11] See Chapter IX.

[12] Address to the Far East-America Council of Commerce and Industry 14 July 1961.   [13] 12 July 1961.

States and to membership of the CENTO and SEATO Pacts. This body of opinion could be divided into those who not only doubt the wisdom of these commitments, but also possess left-wing sympathies and desire to see considerable change in internal policy. The second sub-division is solely concerned with the rather more cynical view that Pakistan had gone too far in its attachment to the West and pointed to the adroit and successful manner in which India, apparently without undertaking commitments of any sort, had been able, so it appeared, to make the best of both worlds—the American and the Russian. Why, it was argued, should not Pakistan do the same?

Setting aside the question of whether the respective situations of Pakistan and India are so identical as to ensure that the same policy could be pursued with the same success, the idea that Pakistan was being taken for granted began to accumulate support. It may well have been the U-2 incident which stimulated interest in a more independent attitude, since the impression was gaining ground that within the defence installations constructed in West Pakistan, with American assistance, the Americans could do pretty much as they liked. Thus, it was with interest that, six months after the U-2 affair, it become known that Pakistan had accepted, in principle, an offer of Soviet technical assistance in oil prospecting.[14] As if to mark this announcement, anniversary supplements, commemorating Russia's October Revolution, appeared in the Pakistan Press. In January 1961 Pakistan's Minister for Fuel, Power and Natural Resources visited Moscow to finalize negotiations for this measure of technical assistance and, in March, the Pakistan-U.S.S.R. oil agreement was signed.

It should not be assumed that this apparent alacrity in turning towards Russia sprang simply from pique. Pakistan had, for a long time, entertained considerable hopes that, in addition to the oil reserves which have for some time been exploited at Attock in the western province, other resources might be discovered within its boundaries. These hopes had been particularly stimulated after the important discovery of natural gas at Sui, followed by other such discoveries both in East and West Pakistan. Several major British and American companies were given licences to explore and prospect, but without success so far as liquid petroleum was concerned. Meanwhile, the Russians had made some rapid and

---

[14] *D*, 5 and 7 November 1960.

startling contributions towards oil exploitation in India and the people of Pakistan were duly impressed. Two or three months after making an agreement with the Soviet Union for oil prospecting, occurred the affair of Pakistan's Second Five Year Plan and American indifference. In some Pakistani circles, this was interpreted as the reaction to Pakistan's unexpected move in making this agreement with the Soviet Union.

It is, however, extremely difficult and quite probably unprofitable to pursue this ebb and flow of sentiment. Only a few months before Pakistan had made up its mind to entertain the Soviet offer of assistance in oil exploration, the Russian ambassador was asked to explain his remarks on the delicate subject of Pakhtunistan,[15] Again, at a CENTO conference in 1960, exception was taken to the observations of Mr. Khrushchev on the very same topic and it is more than probable that this expression of disapproval owed itself to Pakistan's initiative. In other respects, too, Pakistan had little to thank the Soviet Union for. Since Independence, the Russians had, in general, shown themselves to be better disposed towards India than towards Pakistan. In the various debates held in the Security Council and in the General Assembly of the United Nations, the Soviet Union had consistently thwarted Pakistan, even to the extent of using the right of veto.[16] On the Pakhtunistan question, the Russians had more than once indicated support for Pathan autonomy.

Still, all this notwithstanding, it was felt in Pakistan that the Soviet oil deal had freshened up the rather vitiated atmosphere of Pakistan's Foreign Office. More significantly, two leading British newspapers, *The Times* and the *Guardian*, considered this development presaged a shift in Pakistan's foreign policy in the direction of non-alignment.[17]

The news was received with something less than surprise when, in 1961, it became known that Pakistan was interested in a demarcation of its border with China and that China had agreed in principle. This seemed to indicate a substantial change of the attitude implicit in President Ayub's statement of November 1959

[15] Pakhtunistan signifies an autonomous state for the Pathan tribes. The matter will be more fully considered when we come to the question of Pakistan's relations with Afghanistan.

[16] Soviet arms aid to India, in later years, did nothing to improve Soviet-Pakistan relations.

[17] These views are quoted in *D*, 15 February 1961.

on the subject of a Communist drive towards the warm water ports of the Indian Ocean. It could, of course, be argued that by stabilizing its frontiers and removing causes of dispute, Pakistan was helping to contain any such threat. Such an argument was not, however, entirely consistent with the later statement that Pakistan had no trouble with China.[18]

All this was different, too, from the sentiments likewise implicit in such statements as an address to I.C.A. officials, in February 1960, when he said: '... if we were also to falter... and people were to lose their heads and lose their faith in their leadership and turn Communist, then the pressure against you will increase to that extent'. He went on to add that he hoped Pakistan would make itself 'immune from Communism. And that is precisely what is at stake today.' In July of the same year he uttered a warning that there were communist efforts to make East Pakistan part of a separate state.[19]

I would here stress that the rejection of Communism does not imply a rejection of Communist countries, if by rejection is meant the ignoring of their existence. In passing, it is worth mentioning that the new administration had earlier indicated its support for the principle that the Chinese mainland Government should be admitted to the United Nations. In this there is, of course, nothing exceptional or unprecedented, but the decision to enter upon border talks with China, relative to an area adjacent to Kashmir, with the possibility of consequences upon Sino-Indian relations, which since 1951 had shown signs of deterioration, was something else. It did not take the Indian Prime Minister long to declare that his country would not accept any Sino-Pakistan agreement on border questions although, as we shall shortly see, there has been no great evidence of haste, on the part of the Chinese Government, to complete a boundary agreement with Pakistan.

It was not only India that observed with interest the possibilities of *rapprochement* between Pakistan and China. The Government of the United States was also watching the progress of these moves whose subsequent development belongs, principally, to the period that followed the withdrawal of Martial Law. Although Pakistan initiated the subject in 1961, it was not until June 1962 (a few days before Martial Law was formally withdrawn), that the Chinese Government intimated its agreement with the proposal to delimit

[18] *D*, 19 July 1961.   [19] *D*, 26 July 1960.

and demarcate the border, subject to any revision that might be necessitated when the Kashmir dispute was finally settled. Nine months later, on 2 March 1963, a Treaty was signed in Peking between Pakistan and China implementing the terms of the boundary agreement, but the proviso concerning any later effect of the Kashmir dispute was retained.

Since the negotiation and signing of this important Treaty scarcely belong to the Martial Law period, it is not within the scope of the present survey to consider the details of some later controversy on the question of whether Pakistan gained or lost by the deal. In Pakistan, it was claimed that the Government had ceded no territory under its *actual control*[20] and had gained from China an area of 750 square miles lying beyond the main watershed of the Karakoram Range. India asserted that Pakistan was the loser by 13,000 square miles.

Obviously, the important words here are *actual control* since they give rise to the suggestion that there might have been other territory concerned which was not in *actual* control. As with most boundary agreements and disputes, there is a lengthy historical background which need not be considered here. In this particular case, involving views (the word is used advisedly) of the former British-Indian Government, the correctness of the Pakistani or Indian interpretation could be debated endlessly, but the better opinion seems to be that, taking all factors into account, including the practicability of asserting claims that existed on paper rather than on the ground, the terms of the Treaty were not unsatisfactory to Pakistan.

More significant, perhaps, was the measure of friendly warmth generated during the two years that elapsed between the time that Pakistan initiated the subject and the actual signing. This, on one occasion, was high-lighted by a Chinese declaration to the effect that 'Kashmir does not belong to India.'[21] This statement, vague but satisfying, was very welcome to Pakistan whose relations with other countries, including older friends, seemed to having an uneasy passage at that time. This contact with China undoubtedly helped, among other things, to restore *amour propre*, but whether,

---

[20] See *Pakistan-China Boundary Agreement*, Department of Films and Publications, Government of Pakistan, August 1963, p. 3.

[21] *D*, 5 June 1962. This statement appeared only three days before Martial Law was withdrawn in Pakistan.

in the long run, out of this association the greater benefit will accrue to Pakistan, or to the Chinese, whose far-sighted intelligence is matched only by their capacity for unremitting toil, is perhaps a finer point.

During this period of negotiations, armed hostilities broke out between China and India and the Chinese, having underlined their position in Asia by an easy, almost unhindered advance on Tezpur[22] in Assam, proceeded to announce—unilaterally and, it seemed, with a touch of contempt—a cease-fire followed by a withdrawal to their original positions. These happenings led to a profusion of help to India, by the United States and the United Kingdom, in terms of weapons and munitions of war. Pakistan watched these developments with dismay and some bitterness.[23] To this can be attributed, in part, the openings of air-routes between Pakistan and China which, apart from anything else, have certainly given the Peking Government another window upon the world.

It is against this background that we must now consider Pakistan's relations with Iran, Turkey, and the United Kingdom—countries which fit into the general pattern of the western alliance. The forging of closer friendship with Iran and Turkey was no new development in Pakistan's relations with foreign countries, but the process certainly underwent marked stimulation during the Martial Law period. President Ayub Khan's visits to Teheran and Ankara, in November 1959, coincided with a joint approach by the three countries to the United States, requesting assistance in the form of weapons and warlike stores. In the same month appeared the statement that Pakistan's ties with Turkey were considered to be a corner-stone of policy.[24] The Shah of Iran and President Bayar of Turkey paid a return visit to Pakistan, in February 1960, only three months before General Gursel toppled the Bayar administration and installed a military régime. This *coup* altered nothing so far as foreign policy was concerned and, in Pakistan, the feeling was then expressed that it should be easier for the two Governments to understand one another, speaking as they did the language of the camp rather than of the legislative

[22] Tezpur is 190 miles from the nearest Pakistan border, measured as the crow flies.

[23] President Ayub Khan later commented that the United States and the United Kingdom had let Pakistan down. *D*, 31 October 1963.

[24] *D*, 9, 10, 18 and 20 November 1959.

chamber. In July 1960 Pakistan ratified its border agreement with Iran by which certain areas became transferable from Pakistan.

So with the United Kingdom. Since the world no longer looks to the *pax Britannica* for refuge, but shelters instead beneath the nuclear umbrella provided by the two super-powers, the United Kingdom has ceased to dominate the course of global events as once it did and, within the SEATO and CENTO Pacts, the greater wealth and resources of the United States exercise their inevitable effect. Nevertheless, it was important to Pakistan to notice, at the outset, that the October *coup* evoked no disapproval in Whitehall,[25] but rather a sense of satisfaction that corrupt and effete elements were to be swept out of Pakistan's public life.[26] Discussions, in train at that time, for £9,000,000 credit to be furnished by the British Government, continued notwithstanding the change of government, and it was generally felt that only with a firmer hand would the country cease to be 'the victim of the second-rate and the prey of the corrupt'.[26]

The special relationship that subsists by reason of membership of the Commonwealth found ample expression when Queen Elizabeth II and the Duke of Edinburgh paid a visit to Pakistan in February 1961, and in both wings of the country they received a generous and cordial welcome. The occasion was historically significant, being the first visit to the Indo-Pakistan sub-continent by the British sovereign since 1947, when the titles and prerogatives of the House of Windsor, with respect to the sub-continent, were placed at the disposal of Parliament. In her speeches the Queen spoke in complimentary terms of President Ayub Khan's leadership, gave especial mention to the Basic Democracies scheme, and said that with this leadership Pakistan had a bright future.[27]

All this was, of course, appropriate to the occasion and pleasing to the ear, but it is probable that the Royal visit was more meaningful in the memories that it evoked. It recalled the days when British and Pakistani had fought, worked, and played together. It conjured up recollections of a life shared in school and college, whether as teacher or as pupil; on the field of sport; in office and workshop; in the courts of law, and the offices of public adminis-

[25] *D*, 11 October 1958.
[26] *The Daily Telegraph*, London, 13 October 1958.
[27] *D*, 2 and 16 February 1961.

tration. When the Queen and the Duke departed, they left behind them sentiments of considerable warmth and good understanding.

All the more distasteful, therefore, was the episode of the following year when cases of smallpox in the United Kingdom were traced to Pakistanis who arrived carrying infection. The affair developed acrimoniously and never, perhaps, in the whole course of relations between the two countries, have the feelings of Pakistanis been so much injured. It may well have been that some Pakistanis, reaching the United Kingdom by air, were carrying infection for the simple reason that the health certificates in their possession were false. Though an important consideration, this did not justify the vehemence with which it was reported in the British Press. It was soon recognized in Pakistan that the ulterior purpose was to utilize the affair in whipping up support for the Immigration Bill, then before Parliament, and not enjoying a very smooth passage. This piece of legislation was not agreeable to Pakistan, but the principal offence lay in the ruthlessness with which the whole lamentable episode was exploited in British newspapers which created no good impression in Pakistan and one leading Karachi daily summarized Pakistani feeling in an editorial entitled *The British at their Worst*.[28]

But in the broader context of world affairs, relations between Pakistan and the United Kingdom continued, during the Martial Law period, to follow the pattern which corresponds substantially with those between Pakistan and the United States, with the difference that there is still, no doubt, a greater sense of mutual understanding. This, and a certain identity of outlook, spring from historical associations that require no elucidation here.

The SEATO and CENTO Pacts and, in particular, the close relations with Turkey, must be considered responsible for Pakistan's uneasy relations with the Arab countries. So long as the Baghdad Pact subsisted there was a greater measure of joint interest, later much diminished by Kassem's *coup* in Iraq. This was certainly contrary to Pakistan's ideological wishes and when President Ayub Khan included, in his foreign policy statement of December 1958, an expression of friendship towards countries in the Near and Middle East, no doubt he had the Arab republics in mind. But

[28] *D*, 24 February 1962. The only occasion of comparably bitter feeling occurred during a serious crisis over cricket umpiring at the time of the M.C.C. tour of 1955–56.

it became noticeable later that, whereas at one time he spoke of Islamic unity and an Islamic Commonwealth, he subsequently referred principally to Islamic nationalism as being a guideline for the growth of Pakistan.[29]

It is questionable whether any country in close alliance with Turkey, Muslim or other, can expect to enjoy intimate diplomatic ties with the Arab States, particularly those which aspire to leadership in the Arab world. To be sure, President Nasser paid a visit (his second) to Pakistan during the Martial Law period,[30] which was returned in the November following when President Ayub Khan visited both Egypt and Saudi Arabia. During this visit, he tried to explain the attitude of Pakistan during the Suez crisis and suggested that Egypt had probably misunderstood the purpose of the moves made by Pakistan at that time, a misunderstanding which he attributed to the clumsiness of Pakistan's representatives. Whatever it was, that attitude had certainly provoked from President Nasser the observation that Pakistan had committed an act of betrayal and he refused to allow Pakistani troops to enter Egyptian territory.[31]

The difficulty does, however, go deeper. In the time of the monarchy, Egypt showed no great cordiality towards Pakistan and during President Nasser's administration this indifference continued, even to the point of voting for India during one of the United Nations' debates on Kashmir. It is not clear that the Martial Law administration was able to mitigate significantly this coolness of attitude but then, as I have already suggested, nothing else was to be expected; nor, perhaps, should it be a ground of criticism. If the principles of foreign policy are properly pursued (and any non-pursuance is scarcely thinkable) then the resulting pattern is ignored only at peril.

In one of his Pakistan Day broadcasts,[32] President Ayub Khan said: 'Looked at from a rational angle, our relations with Afghanistan are so easy to improve and yet they have become very intractable because of our inability to get the authorities of Afghanistan to view these problems wisely and in terms of realism.' Pursuing the same idea, he said, on another occasion, that the problem was an artificial one.[33] No doubt, he was thinking of the common

---

[29] D, 6 June 1960, 5 April 1961, 27 August 1964.   [30] April 1960.
[31] The Times, London, 3 September 1956.   [32] 23 March 1960.
[33] At the National Press Club, Washington, D.C., 13 July 1961.

heritage in religious, cultural, and ethnic terms and of a common interest in security and in the prosperity of the people who live on both sides of a common border. On the face of it, also, it must seem that Afghanistan has much to look for from Pakistan for Karachi is one of the nearest ports to which that land-locked country has access. The fact is that since Pakistan's emergence as an independent country, relations between the two have never been markedly warm and, on occasion, have deteriorated to the point of actual violence.

In the independence and partition of the sub-continent, Afghanistan saw an opportunity to raise afresh the question of boundaries which had been settled by the demarcation of the Durand Line in 1893. Even if there had been no partition, but only independence, it is probable that the opportunity would have been seized with equal alacrity, but the fact of partition enabled India to view, with some complacence, this Afghan irredentism and the concern in Pakistan to which it gave rise.

The Afghans claim that the Durand Line was forced upon them by a powerful and imperialist Britain, hungry for colonial expansion, although this does not seem to state the matter accurately. Towards the close of the nineteenth century the British were indeed anxious for a demarcation of the border, but that wish was inspired more by Russian penetration into Central Asia rather than by any anxiety to extend territorial possessions on the North West Frontier. The Afghan Government went on to claim that the British abdication of power in the sub-continent automatically reopened the boundary question. Pakistan's reply was that the question was settled once and for all in 1893, and that Pakistan is the legitimate heir to all the territories falling to it by reason of the Independence Act and the partition settlement.

With some subtlety, the Afghans went further and claimed that the Pathans, being an ethnic group with a distinct language and culture, needed and desired an autonomy of their own to which the name Pakhtunistan was given.[34] It is customary in Pakistan to describe the claim as a stunt, but this glib dismissal ignores the facts of history, since only 150 years ago the Durranis of Afghanistan were ruling in Peshawar. Nor does it dispose of the fact that

---

[34] The ethnic, linguistic, and political complexities in this part of the world are fully discussed by Sir Olaf Caroe in his book, *The Pathans*, Macmillan, London, 1958. See, particularly, Chapter XIX.

the Pathans of Pakistan share an ethnic background with a substantial part of the people of present Afghanistan.

The impact of the idea is clear and constitutes an irritant to Pakistan which the Afghan Government has not failed to pursue. The subversive implications of this manoeuvre are only too obvious—particularly in territories where tribal rivalries still flourish, where nomads move freely and where it is still possible, by the distribution of arms and money, to sow seeds of turbulence. This explains why the old freedom-fighter, Abdul Ghaffar Khan, was for so many years kept under restraint in Pakistan[35] and why the remarks of Mr. Khrushchev and of the Soviet Ambassador caused so much resentment among Pakistanis.[36]

Notwithstanding this belief in the artificiality in the Afghan claims, the wish to see Afghanistan ally itself with Pakistan, Iran and Turkey,[37] as well as the continuance of the conciliatory policy permitting the passage of goods through Karachi to Afghanistan, the Martial Law administration was unable to induce any moderation in its neighbour's attitude. In what appeared to be a moment of exasperation, President Ayub Khan declared that the Pakhtunistan claims were intolerable[38] and that there was considerable Soviet infiltration into Afghanistan,[39] a theme which he elaborated afterwards at the National Press Club in Washington.[40]

In 1955 relations between the two countries had deteriorated to the point at which, on 30 March, the Pakistan Embassy in Kabul was sacked and the following day saw an attack on the Afghan consulate in Peshawar. There were the usual official *démentis* as to responsibility for these outrages, which need not concern us, but the result was a breaking of diplomatic relations which were not resumed until September 1957. In 1959 the deterioration renewed itself and, in September 1960 and May 1961, hostilities broke out in the Bajaur region,[41] a tract 900 square miles in extent, north of Peshawar and the Khyber Pass. The Pakistan Government claimed that an Afghan *lashkar*[42] had penetrated into the Bajaur territory and had been beaten off. The Afghan Government claimed that Pakistan was using its Air Force and ground troops to quell an uprising of discontented tribesmen. During this

[35] Giving partition as a reason, he also sought a measure of Pathan autonomy.
[36] See p. 174.   [37] President's statement, 21 November 1959.
[38] D, 25 March 1960.   [39] D, 6 May 1960.   [40] D, 13 July 1961.
[41] Well-known to readers of Sir Winston Churchill's *Story of the Malakand Field Force*.   [42] A tribal levy.

period, *Pravda* published an article[43] claiming that the Pakistan Government had no less than eight divisions in the area and, supported by tanks and aircraft, were endeavouring to subdue disaffected villages. The article went on to say that the Soviet Union would support all reasonable claims to self-determination. Whatever the merits of these rival assertions, the fact of trouble in the Bajaur region was significant. It is in these parts that the Durand Line presents certain anomalies and Caroe, writing in 1957, expressed the view that if ever there were to be boundary disputes between Afghanistan and Pakistan, it was there that they could be expected.[44] This prevision, coupled with the later fact of disturbance in the Bajaur region, supports the view that the trouble was provoked from the outside and discounts the theory of simple discontent.

In August 1961 Pakistan closed two of its consulates and asked the Afghan Government to wind up its consular and trade missions.[45] This response to the Bajaur situation was more significant than might appear. Notwithstanding the note of acrimony that had prevailed for so long, neither Government had interfered with the movement of trade, either through the age-old caravan routes or through Karachi Port and the Pakistan Railways up to the frontier. The seasonal migration of *powindahs*[46] into Pakistan was an ancient tradition—interference with which would cause considerable hardship—and up to this time Pakistan had raised no objection. Now, however, this freedom to cross the border was withdrawn in the absence of passports and health documents.

This threat to trade relations provoked, from Afghanistan, a threat to sever relations altogether, but the Pakistan Government replied that whatever the consequences the Afghan missions must close. It was then suggested that, at the instance of the Afghan Government which had indicated it might veer more closely to the Soviet Union, the American Government sought a moderation of Pakistan's attitude,[47] but this endeavour, for whatever it was

[43] According to *Keesings Contemporary Archives* this article is understood to have been written by a high Soviet official. It is dated 3 April 1961.

[44] Caroe, op. cit., pp. 382–3. The author was Governor of the North-West Frontier Province 1946–47.

[45] *D*, 24 August 1961.

[46] These are Afghan nomads, owning cattle, whose long custom it has been to cross into Pakistan, during the cold weather, to find seasonal employment and purchase fodder for their herds and flocks.

[47] *D*, 2 September, 1961.

worth, was likewise ineffectual. On 5 September 1961, Afghanistan sealed the border to goods traffic and, two days later, diplomatic ties were severed. Even this did not put an end to hostilities. In October there was further fighting in the Bajaur area and this time it was alleged that Afghan regular troops had accompanied the tribal levies which entered Pakistan territory.

Diplomatic relations were not resumed until 1963, after the Martial Law period had come to an end. Through the good offices of the Shah of Iran the border was reopened in July and later the two countries exchanged Ambassadors.

With the rest of the world, the Martial Law administration continued the policy of finding friends in the interests of trade and of winning support for Pakistan's views on the Kashmir problem. There was, in addition, the necessity for explaining the *raison d'être* of the military government, the circumstances which had led to a seizure of power, and the reforms that the new Government sought to introduce. It could not be concealed that the Martial Law administration was thought of as militaristic and in the nature of a dictatorship, ideas which were encouraged by interests adverse to Pakistan. Hence, some *apologia* was desirable. It was important, also, to convince wealthier countries that they were dealing with a stable administration with which agreements could safely be made. In all of this, President Ayub Khan was successful, and during the Martial Law period valuable trade pacts were negotiated with Japan and Germany.

In his first Press Conference following the declaration of Martial Law, General Ayub Khan, as he then was, stated that he was opposed to any change in foreign policy[48] and this statement summarizes, with fair accuracy, the course that his administration subsequently pursued. In doing so, however, the new administration did succeed in conveying a fresh sense of stability and purpose, and in giving the nation a new confidence and dignity in its relations with foreign countries. But, it should be added, although established policy continued, there was an unmistakable modulation in the latter part of 1960. This does not refer to the threat of a basic shift, which came after Martial Law had been withdrawn, but simply to a distinct orientation. Since the question of Indo-Pakistan relations is also involved, the nature of this change will be considered in the next chapter.

[48] *D*, 11 October 1958.

XIII

Relations with India

THE subject of Indo-Pakistan relations is a notoriously prickly one. Much has been written, and will doubtless continue to be written, on the reasons and circumstances which led to the determinations of the Muslim League—which found ultimate expression in the Lahore Resolution of 1940—to find a Muslim homeland within the sub-continent. Praise and blame for this achievement will continue to be distributed, as they have been distributed so often in the past, yet, *au fond*, it seems that if the Hindu community had not failed to win Muslim confidence, the insistence upon a partition would have been improbable.

If this is so—and bearing in mind that wiser counsel in both countries has never ceased to advocate mutual understanding between them—it is difficult to escape the conclusion that persisting controversy, descending sometimes into actual victimization of minorities, has all the appearance of carrying on the old communal struggle, at another level and uncomplicated by the presence of the British. In one sense, this suggestion of a continuance of the same antagonism must seem lamentable for it implies that the partition has not solved, or has not adequately solved, the problems expressed by the two-nation theory. On the other hand, it also suggests that a simple act of reconciliation must suffice to put an end to all subsisting ill-will. It is fair to say, in this context, that during the Martial Law period it was often said that but for Kashmir there were no differences with India.[1] Further, it has always been distinctly observable that hostility between the two countries, and the outward symptoms of that hostility, were prominent less for their fundamental character than for their convenience as a political football to be kicked around as *domestic* necessity might dictate. In short, promising endeavours

---

[1] President Ayub Khan made several statements to this effect. See, for example, *D*, 11 August 1959, 23 and 24 September 1960.

to normalize Indo-Pakistan relations were cynically thwarted by those who, in either country, had a vested interest in trouble.

When in October 1958 Martial Law was declared, relations between Pakistan and India were remarkable neither for their ease nor for their tension. In his declaration of 7 October 1958, President Iskander Mirza referred to those 'screaming for war with India', which I interpret as a reference to the fulminating diatribes of Mr. Mohammad Ali Choudhury, though his oratory seems to have been for internal consumption rather than a sober appreciation of policy. Indeed, in those days Pakistan, with its unending political crises and party differences, was really in no position to contemplate hostilities against anybody, unless it were that Mr. Mohammad Ali Choudhury, and others of like mind, considered that war with India would exercise a powerfully unifying influence within the country.

At all events, the substance of the situation was that the Kashmir question remained unsettled, and the problem of the division of the waters of the Indus and its tributaries appeared to be as intractable as ever, exacerbated, no doubt, by India's construction of the Bhakra Dam. So far as relations with India were concerned, these two matters dominated the Press conferences on 10 and 30 October when General Ayub Khan said: 'Once there is a solution of the canal waters and the Kashmir disputes, we have no other grouse against Bharat.'[2]

The onset of Martial Law was received in India without criticism and without reserve, although later there was some disparagement of the new administration on the ground that it was undemocratic and alien to the spirit that prevailed in the Commonwealth. On the whole, this attitude was not officially encouraged in India. In any case, an actual test of Indo-Pakistan relations under the new régime could not come immediately, for, as we have seen, the Martial Law Government concerned itself almost exclusively with domestic concerns during its first year.

However, some six months after the Martial Law declaration there occurred an incident which not only provided Pakistan with a sense of triumph and India with a sense of chagrin, but also an opportunity for both countries to display basic good sense. On

[2] Bharat is the ancient name of India and is mentioned in the Indian Constitution. In Pakistan, use is sometimes made of it to emphasise the fact of Hindu dominance in India.

10 April 1959, two Indian Canberra bomber aircraft intruded into West Pakistan territory and, being detected, were promptly challenged by fighters of the Pakistan Air Force. One of the Canberras escaped, but the other, ignoring warnings and orders to land, was shot down, its crew of two reaching safety by parachute. The aircraft was found to be unarmed, but equipped with reconnaissance instruments.

In that year, 10 April was *'Id* day, the day on which Muslims celebrate the end of the holy month of Ramzan, and it seems possible that Indian Intelligence conceived the idea that on this day of rejoicing the Pakistan early warning system might be less alert. If this was so, it is evident that that organization miscalculated. The incident was followed by an exchange of protests and some rather moralizing talk on both sides which, of course, deceived no one, since it is obvious that each country takes a good deal of surreptitious interest in what goes on in the other. Pakistan, well-entrenched behind a good case, treated the whole thing with calm satisfaction. India, for its part, had recourse to the customary prevarication to which governments usually have resort when they have been caught out.[3] Thereafter, both wisely permitted the *contretemps* to expire naturally.

Certainly, this affair did no apparent injury to sentiment on either side, because five months afterwards President Ayub Khan paused, on a return journey from Dacca, to meet Pandit Jawaharlal Nehru in Delhi. The conversation was both cordial and friendly. Both countries, they said, had resolved to forgive and forget, and President Ayub Khan added his opinion that if they did not stick together, they would be defeated separately, an opinion which, it seemed, could only have reference to the view he was then holding that there was a threat from the north to both countries.

Without in any way seeking to impugn the sincerity of the Indian Prime Minister, this fresh and welcome expression of mutual goodwill seems to owe much to President Ayub Khan's belief in his ability, and the ability of his administration, to let some sunshine and fresh air into the darker corners of Pakistan's affairs. It is consistent with his then expressed disbelief in political parties, and with his attachment to the moral force exerted by

[3] A comparison with the manner and tone of the United States Government's statements on Power's detected U-2 flight over Soviet territory is most instructive.

unselfish people imbued with a sense of public duty. Later these Utopian aspirations underwent a change, but they reflected favourably at that time upon the spirit in which the four generals made their decision to seize power and implement it.

The meeting with Nehru seemed to have prepared the way for an all-round improvement in Indo-Pakistan relations, but three weeks later *Dawn* was reporting evidence of an anti-Pakistan drive in India.[4] Coming on the heels of the Ayub-Nehru meeting, it formed a perfect instance of the subtle way in which prospective ameliorations in Indo-Pakistan affairs had so often been pre-judiced. In such cases, it is impossible to apportion the blame, but the example was classic. There can be no doubt that when the time comes to study the course of Indo-Pakistan relations minutely and dispassionately a distinct pattern will reveal itself, showing how statesmanlike moves on either side have been wilfully frustrated or, at any rate, how attempts at frustration made their automatic appearance.

Nevertheless, useful work continued to be done. In October 1959, Lieutenant-General K. M. Sheikh visited Delhi to settle the 'ground rules' for the solution of border disputes, and three months later, in January, President Ayub Khan repeated his belief in the necessity for joint defence with India.[5] More than once, he gave expression to India's interest in Pakistan's security, and if the north-west frontier passes[6] still mean anything, there is no doubt about the substance in what he said. In July 1960,[7] he again expressed a wish for friendship with India, and, in September, a desire to see old bonds revived, but this time some cautionary words were added, for he said it was Kashmir that was keeping them apart.[8]

In one specific sense, this had become very true because, since March, it had been known that negotiations for a solution of the Indus Basin problem were well in train, and in that same month of September Jawaharlal Nehru visited Pakistan and the Indus Basin Treaty was signed. That, certainly, was an occasion impor-tant enough to justify a broadcast to the nation,[9] when President

---

[4] *D*, 26 September 1959.   [5] *D*, 26 September 1959.
[6] On, or adjacent to, the Durand Line, there are three principal passes—the Nawa Sar Pass, the Khyber Pass and the Kohat Pass. Within Pakistan's north-west territory, there are others, including the Malakand Pass through which lies the route to China.
[7] *D*, 27 July 1960.   [8] *D*, 23 September 1960.   [9] 4 September 1960.

Ayub Khan said that the terms of the Treaty were 'the best we could get under the circumstances, many of which, irrespective of merits and legality of the case, are against us.' There is in this address an undertone of apology, as if to imply a sense of sacrifice which the Martial Law administration would have avoided if it could; but what exactly had been sacrificed it is difficult to say. Unfortunately, in both countries, the Indus waters problem has always been wrapped in an incomprehensible veil of mystery, although essentially it is simply a matter of riparian rights, geography, money, and engineering skill. Considering that the problem was, with all its desperate implications,[10] allowed to remain unsolved for thirteen years, and considering that the Treaty eventually signed was based upon proposals framed in 1954, the suspicion is provoked that previous administrations had, on both sides, been content to allow this hazardous source of controversy to remain, each in its own political interests. It may be—since, in the absence of other and better particulars, no precise judgement is possible—that Pakistan did not get all to which it considered itself entitled, but that involves no discredit to the Martial Law administration, which, in disposing of the problem once and for all, did a real service to the nation.

In the preceding chapter it was suggested that, as far as foreign policy was concerned, 1960 seems to have been crucial for Pakistan. As late as June of that year, President Ayub Khan was continuing to hold to his opinion concerning the northern threat. In an article published under his name in *Foreign Affairs*[11] he wrote: 'As a student of war and strategy, I can see quite clearly the inexorable push of the north in the direction of the warm waters of the Indian ocean. This push is bound to increase if India and Pakistan go on squabbling with each other.' The article concludes with the warning that when the sub-continent was divided 'someone or other invited an outsider to step in.'

At the risk of appearing repetitious, it must be recalled that 1960

[10] It is difficult to forbear from repeating the oft-quoted words of Mr. David E. Lilienthal, a former Chairman of the Tennessee Valley Authority, which appeared in *Collier's* of 4 August 1951: 'No army, with bombs and shellfire, could devastate a land so thoroughly as Pakistan could be devastated by the simple expedient of India's permanently shutting off the sources of water that keep the fields and people of Pakistan alive.'

[11] July 1960. *Foreign Affairs* is published by the Council on Foreign Relations, Inc. New York, U.S.A.

was the year both of the U-2 incident and of the decision to make an agreement with the Soviet Union for assistance in oil prospecting. It was, furthermore, in January of 1961 that there occurred the *démarche* in the direction of China, and Nehru's declaration that boundary decisions made by China and Pakistan would not be acceptable to India. By this time, the signs and portents could not be overlooked and, as we have already seen, in February 1961 influential sections of the British Press were speaking of a move in Pakistan towards non-alignment. In short, at the beginning of that year, a re-orientation was distinctly visible, although it was not until July that President Ayub Khan said that Pakistan was disturbed by American policy and that the Pacts to which Pakistan was signatory were under re-examination.[12] Nor was it until May 1962 that a shift in foreign policy was actually being talked of,[13] and not until November of the same year (by which time Martial Law had been withdrawn) do we find newspapers in Pakistan speaking of the American attitude towards Pakistan's reaction to arms aid for India as 'childish and puerile', and of a 'basic policy change' as being 'in the offing'.[14]

Much of all this belongs, of course, to post-Martial Law policy and a good deal of it was, in all probability, officially inspired kite-flying. Nevertheless, putting everything together, it is evident that sometime during the latter half of 1960 a move was started towards a measure of disengagement which, without involving a departure from treaty obligations, disclosed the intention to act with a freer hand in international affairs. That no drastic change of heart was ever intended seems evident from the zeal with which Pakistan continued to pursue its association with Iran and Turkey,[15] but the sedulous cultivation of Chinese goodwill tells a story of its own.

Some of the reasons which impelled the Martial Law administration to take up a more independent attitude towards the western powers I have already glanced at, but it is also certain that a deterioration in relations with India contributed to these. In February 1961 there occurred the disgraceful riots in Jabalpur

---

[12] *D*, 7 July 1961.   [13] *D*, 27 May 1962.   [14] *D*, 21 November 1962.
[15] In 1964 Pakistan joined Iran and Turkey in a scheme of Regional Co-operation for Development. See, however, President Ayub Khan's address at Lahore to the Thinkers' Forum, 4 October 1964, which indicated that the association with Iran and Turkey was now esteemed less for its relation to the western alliance than as an alliance of Muslim nations *vis-à-vis* the Christian west.

concerning which Jawaharlal Nehru and Mr. Jayprakash Narayan spoke with shame and horror. These murderous attacks on Muslims were described as a spontaneous outburst of anger aroused by the rape, and subsequent suicide, of a Hindu girl, said to have been assaulted by two Muslim youths. The truth of this story has never been substantiated and, as for the spontaneity, the official Indian report on the outbreak stated that the attacks were pre-planned. In October, further violence was inflicted on Muslims in Meerut. Agra was declared a troubled area. In December 1961, India invaded Goa and President Ayub Khan made the comment that India's militarism was a threat to all her neighbours. He took care to add that Pakistan's strength was a great deterrent.[16] Two or three months after this, there was more communal trouble in India and, in May 1962, a month before Martial Law was withdrawn, serious rioting occurred in Malda and Murshidabad when many Muslim lives were lost in circumstances of repulsive brutality.

These lamentable episodes did not merely evoke angry protest in Pakistan, but led to a deterioration in feeling between the two countries which the Martial Law administration now made no particular effort to assuage. Various pronouncements made in January 1962 could only be intended as comment on India's invasion and annexation of Goa, for, in that month, President Ayub Khan said that Pakistan was strong enough to repel any aggressor[17] and that the strength of Pakistan's armed forces sufficed to deter any enemy.[18] He also said that, if attacked, Pakistan would use all the arms at its disposal,[19] recalling a statement to similar effect made by Lieutenant-General Sheikh at the time of hostilities in Bajaur. The reference here is to the suggestion that arms supplied to India and Pakistan by western allies were only to be used for purposes of the alliance, but experience has shown that such conditions, even where they are categorically imposed, can rarely, if ever, be enforced.

When Martial Law was withdrawn, therefore, Indo-Pakistan relations were in no very promising state and it was not until 1964 that fresh developments, marked by the visit of Sheikh Abdulla to Pakistan and the grievous loss of Pandit Jawaharlal Nehru, offered renewed prospects of some settlement. With all of this

[16] D, 6 January 1962. [17] D, 4 January 1962.
[18] D, 14 January 1962. [19] D, 21 January 1962

was linked the Kashmir problem, on which President Ayub Khan's military administration had been unable to make any tangible impression.

It is not relevant to present purposes to attempt any summary of that complex matter, or any assessment of its merits, but it is always well to remember that the question of Kashmir is not a two-dimensional problem between India and Pakistan, but a three-dimensional problem involving India, Pakistan, and Kashmir. It is wise to recall Sheikh Abdulla's speech, made during his trial, in which he said that he had never asked for Kashmir to be part of Pakistan, but simply for self-determination, irrespective of caste, creed, religion or region.[20]

All the same, President Ayub Khan was fair when he observed that the signing of the Indus Basin Treaty added further urgency to the need for a solution of the Kashmir problem, since the upper reaches of the three western rivers, whose waters fell to Pakistan's share, flow through Kashmir territory.[21] The validity of this point and of the necessity for a Kashmir settlement can scarcely be disputed. But, apart from this, and apart from Pakistan's long-familiar animadversions concerning India's conduct and the plight of the Kashmir people, the Martial Law administration had nothing new to say and no fresh move to make. It was not until the beginning of January 1962 that other evidence appeared of American interest in the Kashmir problem and moves made by the late President Kennedy were received in Pakistan as constructive. During the Martial Law period, India remained as intractable as ever, and in the middle of 1961[22] Nehru specifically ruled out any possibility of fresh talks on the subject. It is not to be doubted that only the Sino-Indian hostilities of late 1962 and the consequent flow of arms to India from the United States and the United Kingdom created a situation by which India was persuaded to be more amenable, even to terminating the prosecution of Sheikh Abdulla, a proceeding as absurd as it was unending, and agreeing to his visit to Pakistan.[23]

[20] D, 27, 28, and 29 July 1961.   [21] Broadcast on 4 September 1960.
[22] D, 1 July 1961.

[23] Without derogating from the main thesis, events that have taken place since this was written have cast new light on Kashmir problems and prospects. None of these events seems likely to bring greater harmony of sentiment between Kashmiris led by Sheikh Abdulla and the Indian Government. In D, 11 April 1965, it was reported that Sheikh Abdulla had made a statement in London to

On the subject of Indo-Pakistan relations, therefore, the principal achievement of the Martial Law administration was the Indus Basin Treaty, in itself a notable contribution. Apart from this, the best that can be said is that nothing was done that would either exacerbate ugly situations or prejudice the position and the claims of Pakistan in any future negotiation with India. In this there was, to be sure, nothing that constituted material advance, although these are problems which neither contending party, acting alone, could solve.

the effect that as Kashmir had a Muslim majority it must accede to Pakistan in the event of an exercise of self-determination. Sheikh Abdulla's statements and activities during this period of travel abroad caused great disquiet in India and, on return to that country in May 1965, he was not permitted to proceed to Kashmir but was sent to South India under some form of house arrest. In September 1965 there ensued the hostilities between India and Pakistan, followed by further debates in the United Nations Security Council and, later, the Tashkent Declaration. The reception given to the Tashkent Declaration, and subsequent commentary, do not encourage hopes of enduring tranquillity in the sub-continent.

XIV

The Constitution of 1962

THE final achievement—although some in Pakistan might be inclined to question the use of the word in this context—of the Martial Law administration, was the preparation and promulgation of a new Constitution which became completely effectual upon the withdrawal of military government at 8.30 on the morning of 8 June 1962. For a period of forty-four months, almost to the day, Pakistan had been governed without representative institutions, except at the local government level, all policy and the ultimate sanction reposing in military hands.

To be sure, the administrative machinery had, in the main, been that of the 1956 Constitution, into which fact too much need not be read. The situation could be paralleled by the earlier use of the Government of India Act of 1935, by whose provisions Pakistan was substantially administered during the first nine years of its existence. It was a convenience, not an act of homage.

It appears that the 1962 Constitution was very much the work of President Ayub Khan. Announcing it, he said: 'I believe in every word of this Constitution and have complete faith in it.'[1] His principal collaborator in its drafting was, so we are led to understand, his Cabinet colleague Mr. Manzur Qadir, and it seems improbable that the President's military colleagues had much to do with that task. However, these points need not be anticipated, since the substance of this chapter is a description of the events which, during the Martial Law period, preceded the evolution of the new constitutional structure.

We have already seen something of President Ayub Khan's own constitutional ideas in examining the reasons which led him and his group of generals, to sweep away the 1956 Constitution, and in considering the Basic Democracies scheme. It does not appear necessary, therefore, to recapitulate those ideas, to which he gave so much expression during the Martial Law period, about the

[1] Broadcast to the nation, 1 March 1962.

unsuitability of party organizations; the desirability of a presidential system; the introduction of institutions conformable to Islamic teaching and Islamic values, and the absolute necessity for a form of democracy which the people of Pakistan could work and understand and which would ensure stability of government. As we have seen, the first year of Martial Law administration was almost exclusively devoted to the institution of a widely ranging series of reforms, together with some assurance of a constitution designed to meet the circumstances in which representative government has to operate in Pakistan and to give a reasonable prospect of stability. There was the further promise that this would be delayed no longer than circumstance rendered inevitable. Thus, in July 1959 we find General Burki saying that in two years there would be an elected régime, whereupon the four generals would probably go back to their duties:[2] this was prior to President Ayub Khan's promotion to the rank of Field-Marshal. I have already suggested that General Burki's pronouncements were not always conspicuous for their wisdom,[3] and undue significance need not be placed upon that statement except as indicating a frame of mind, particularly among the military members of the Cabinet when Martial Law was not yet a year old. Some months later, in January 1960, President Ayub Khan himself said that he might possibly retire in three or four years.[4] He had served, he said, in one capacity or another for thirty-two years, and was exhausted.[5] Of course, this periodic note of wearied resignation crops up in the utterance of most public figures, and a touch of modest self-deprecation is a recognized convention of political life.

Much more important, at that time, so far as concerned the prospective constitution, was the possibility that no particular effort would be made to incorporate measures whose appeal was simply to Islamic sentiment. In the 1956 Constitution, Article 1 stated that Pakistan would be a Federal Republic to be known as the 'Islamic Republic of Pakistan'. When Martial Law was declared, this was changed by Presidential Order[6] which stated,

[2] D, 3 July 1959.   [3] See Foreword.
[4] See also President Ayub Khan's address to the Karachi High Court Bar Association, 15 January 1959.
[5] D, 16 January 1960.
[6] D, 11 October 1958. The Order was signed by the then President, Major-General Iskander Mirza.

among other things, that the Republic would henceforward be known as 'Pakistan'. This apparent giving up of the Islamic thread did not go unnoticed and questions were soon being asked. Thus, some months afterwards, we find Mr. Manzur Qadir observing: 'I did not say at any time whether the future constitution of Pakistan will be Islamic or not.'[7] In those days, of course, Mr. Manzur Qadir was in charge of external affairs and was not, so far as was then understood, particularly concerned with constitutional questions, and, for that matter, such questions seemed premature so soon after the Martial Law declaration. At the same time, having been a leading practitioner at the Lahore Bar, his views on such matters could not pass unrespected.

In his address, at a reception given by the Karachi High Court Bar Association on 15 January 1959, President Ayub Khan, in specifying matters to be insisted upon in the new constitution, made no mention of Islamic provisions. It seems not to have been until the end of the same year that we come upon his declarations that the new Constitution would reflect Islamic principles. From this time onwards, assurances concerning the introduction of an Islamic bias and the application of Islamic thought find constant reiteration.[8]

The promised Constitution Commission was set up on 17 February 1960, and the terms of reference required it among other things to advise, in the form of a report, on how to secure a democracy adapted to changing circumstances and based upon the Islamic principles of justice, equality, and tolerance.[9] However, two months before the Commission was appointed, President Ayub Khan had something to say about its work. He made it clear that if the Constitution Commission made impractical proposals, they would not be accepted. The Commission, he explained, was 'not being appointed to tell us what we should do. We know what we should do. We are clear in our mind that we cannot adopt the Parliamentary system.'[10] It was at this same interview that he said, touching upon a statement reported to have been made by Mr. Manzur Qadir, on a constitutional point, 'vakils[11] make a straight thing look involved'. All of this came to be remembered

---

[7] D, 15 March 1959.
[8] D, 18 December 1959, 16 and 26 January, 1960, 16 February, 1960, etc.
[9] The terms of reference are set out in full as Appendix VIII.
[10] D, 18 December 1959.   [11] The word means 'lawyer'.

later on, when the Constitution Report was withheld from publication for a period of approximately ten months.[12]

The Commission prepared a list of forty questions, of which 9,000 copies in English and 19,000 copies in Urdu and Bengali were distributed to suitable organizations and to prominent men and women. Anyone who desired it could obtain a copy of the questionnaire and submit his views. In all, 6,269 replies reached the Commission, some emanating from men who had held high office before the Martial Law declaration, and in one or two instances these quickly found their way into the columns of the Press. This Press publication was quickly noticed by the administration, since obviously it was a semi-concealed form of political activity which, under Martial Law, was prohibited. This 'misuse of the questionnaire', as it was termed, met with a prompt response from the authorities, and the Chief Martial Law Administrator[13] issued a warning that the full force of Martial Law would be used against persons 'playing politics'.[14]

The distribution of the questionnaire had revived much of the pre-Martial Law interest in politics, for, in the month of August following this warning, Basic Democrat members of Union Councils and Union Committees were instructed that they had no right to remark upon constitutional matters and any attempt to do so would amount to a violation of the law.[15] All this seems to have been reasonable enough, in view of the fact that Martial Law had been accepted and in view of the assurance—given in the preceding June—that the Constitution Commission was an autonomous body and would execute its task without interruption or interference.[16]

The Report, placed before the President in May 1961, is a sound survey, comparable in thoroughness with those other Reports I have mentioned in earlier chapters. Like them, it possesses occasional overtones which smack of special pleading. This may have been unavoidable. It is difficult to assess these things and, in any case, there does not seem to be any specific inaccuracy or unfair-

---

[12] The Report was submitted to the President in May 1961 and was made available to the public at about the same time as the 1962 Constitution was announced.

[13] Field-Marshal Ayub Khan.

[14] D, 2 and 3 July 1960. The lengthy replies of Mr. Mohammad Ali Choudhury were reproduced verbatim in D, 17 June 1960. They formed a vigorous defence of the 1956 Constitution and an implied criticism of the military *coup*.

[15] D, 9 August 1960.   [16] D, 16 June 1960.

ness. The most serious deficiency, from the general reader's point of view, lay in the anonymous mode of expressing certain historical references, a method which dissipated their weight.[17] Of course, these references touched upon matters so essentially scandalous that possibly no other course was felt to be open, since mention of names may have appeared unfairly invidious. This is one of the minor problems that arise when public life is too deeply tainted with malpractice and hunger for office.

The Report was promptly passed to a five-man sub-committee of the Cabinet, sitting under the chairmanship of Mr. Manzur Qadir. Some five months later, it became understood that the new Constitution would be promulgated early in 1962,[18] information that did not help much because, as already indicated, the Commission's Report was not available to the public and did not become available until after the new Constitution had been announced.[19] This delay in accessibility of the Report led to some dissatisfied murmurings which, in view of the warnings issued in the previous year about unauthorized political comment, was restrained in most quarters. In East Pakistan, as we have seen, other forms of pressure were exerted.

At any rate, the Constitution itself was announced on 1 March 1962, and copies were immediately made available to the public. Its reception was marked by a distinct undertone of reservation, accurately disclosed in the words of an editorial which appeared in *Dawn* the following day. 'Let all patriots give this new scheme a trial in all honesty and sincerity and let us all support and work it.'[20] This note of criticism became sufficiently audible to reach the presidential ear and President Ayub Khan uttered a caution against 'textbook maxims'.[21] When this did not suffice to allay certain forebodings, he fell back on the old spectre of the likelihood of 'bloody revolution'[22] taking place if Pakistan were to revert to a Parliamentary system. Nothing convincing had yet been said, however, about the total acceptability of the constitutional structure and, two years later, the essential reaction continued to

[17] See, for example, the reference on page 10 of the Report to the late Mohamed Ali (of Bogra) and his dealings with the late A. K. M. Fazlul Haq.

[18] 23 September 1961.

[19] The 1962 Constitution was actually printed for publication some four weeks before the Constitution Commission's Report came from the printing press.

[20] *D*, 2 March 1962.   [21] *D*, 6 March 1962.   [22] *D*, 8 April 1962.

find expression in such words as the following: 'True, the Constitution is not as liberal as the unwritten constitution of Britain or the written constitution of the United States, but these countries, we must not forget, have a long history of constitutional evolution. The picture of political orderliness that these countries represent was not made by one hand or in one period . . .'[23]

However, the constitutional affairs of the nation, as defined in the new document, proceeded under the auspices of the Martial Law administration. An election of members to the national and provincial legislatures was held in April 1962, the electors comprising the 80,000 Basic Democrats who had been chosen by vote in 1960. President Ayub Khan did not himself require to seek fresh election because Article 226 of the new Constitution stated that in accordance with the result of the referendum conducted during February 1960, Field-Marshal Ayub Khan should become the first President of Pakistan under the new Constitution.

It is evident that any adequate analysis of the new structure would suffice to fill at least one substantial volume, and would take us far beyond the purposes of the present work. Nevertheless, as perhaps the principal product of the Martial Law period as well as the most tangible expression of those ideas which led to the *coup* of 1958, something about the Constitution of 1962 needs to be included here.

Briefly, the 1962 document provided for a government that comprises a President and a central legislature called the 'National Assembly'. The President must be a Muslim; he must have attained the age of thirty-five and, in addition, be qualified for election to the National Assembly. Upon election, he shall hold office for a term of five years. The National Assembly comprises 156 members, divided equally between the two Provinces, and in each case a minimum of three seats must be held by women members. Like the President, the National Assembly sits for a period of five years, unless it suffers dissolution during that period. Both President and members of the Assembly are selected by an electoral college made up of those persons representing the electoral units into which the country is divided.

There are the usual arrangements for a Supreme Court, High Courts, and the principal officers of State. These, in the main,

---

[23] *Pakistan Annual, 1964*, 'A New Epoch in the Making', p. 5.

follow a well-recognized pattern, and it is not necessary to dwell upon them here.

The powers exercised by the President are considerable and he is the key figure in the constitutional structure. All legislation passed by the National Assembly requires his assent, which he may give or withhold, or he may return the proposed legislation to the Assembly for fresh consideration. If there is a persisting difference of opinion between himself and the National Assembly, he can refer the matter, in the form of a question calling for an answer 'yes' or 'no', to the verdict of the electoral college. The National Assembly has no such right of reference. The President is, however, liable to be impeached if one-third of the members of the National Assembly sign a written notice, addressed to the Speaker, stating their intention to move a resolution calling for the removal of the President on a charge of either wilful violation of the Constitution or gross misconduct.

On his side the President can, within certain limits, prematurely dissolve the Assembly, but in that case he, too, ceases to hold office upon the expiration of 120 days after the date of dissolution. Moreover, he can, also within certain limits, promulgate legislation when the National Assembly is dissolved or not in session. Further, if he is satisfied that a grave emergency exists in which Pakistan is threatened by war or external aggression, or in which the security or economic life of the country is threatened by internal circumstances beyond the power of a Provincial Government to control, he can issue a Proclamation of Emergency. So long as the Proclamation is in force, he has power to legislate in order to meet the emergency by means of ordinances which the National Assembly has no power to disapprove.

All executive authority is vested in the President, who is advised by a Council of Ministers appointed by himself. These Ministers can participate in the proceedings of the National Assembly and any of its Committees, but are not entitled to vote. By a special provision (Article 238), the Defence Minister must, for a period of twenty years at least from the date of commencement of the new Constitution, be a person who has held the rank of Lieutenant-General (or the Navy or Air Force equivalent) unless the President has himself held such rank. The President can also appoint members of the National Assembly to act as Parliamentary Secretaries in relation to the divisions of the Central Government, as he may direct.

In matters of finance the President enjoys considerable freedom and, so far as concerns expenditure already approved, the National Assembly has no power to interfere up to the levels of expenditure approved and the period over which the expenditure is sanctioned. It is only with respect to new expenditure and new taxation that the Assembly exercises any power. The necessity for this restraint about the powers of the National Assembly, in relation to the Budget has been explained as inherent in the Presidential system, without which a deadlock might ensue and the government of the country be brought to a standstill.[24]

There is provision that no law should be repugnant to Islam and the Constitution, in Articles 199 to 206, makes specific arrangement for an Advisory Council of Islamic Ideology. This organization may make recommendations to the Central and Provincial Governments as to the means by which the Muslims of Pakistan are enabled and encouraged to order their lives in accordance with the principles and concepts of Islam. Secondly, it can advise the President, or a Provincial Governor, or the National Assembly, or a Provincial Assembly, whether any proposed law disregards or violates, or is otherwise not in accordance with, the Principles of Law-making as defined in the Constitution. However, according to Article 6, a reference to the Advisory Council is not mandatory.

Articles 5, 6, 7, and 8 contain what are described as the Principles of Law-making and the Principles of Policy, intended to guide the executive and the legislatures and the officers of the administration in the preparation of legislation and in the performance of their duties. These Principles are set out in hortatory language and it is specifically stated in the Constitution that no law and no act of the executive can be called into question on the ground that any of these things were not in accordance with the Principles. The necessity for loading the Constitution with pious aspirations which have no legally binding effect is not at all clear, but it seems that the draftsmen of the 1962 Constitution were copying, with improvements of their own, similar provisions in the Constitution of 1956.

It should be mentioned at this point that the Provincial Legislatures, each of which comprises 155 members of whom five at least must be women, are selected by a similar method of election and their law-making powers are set up on lines which follow those of the National Assembly. The Governor of each Province is

[24] See *The Constitution—A Study*. op. cit.

appointed by the President and each Governor has a similar right, within his provincial duties, of assenting to bills passed by the provincial legislature, withholding assent, or reference back. However, in the case of provincial administration, where there is a conflict of opinion between the Governor and the Legislature, there is no recourse to a referendum but to the President who then places the matter in difference before the National Assembly for resolution.

Considering that the Governors are the President's appointees, the power concentrated in the hands of the three principal executives of the nation is considerable. It is particularly in this sense, coupled with the overriding powers as to emergency and the powers conferred by Article 131, that the Centre can be described as strong, notwithstanding the devolution of so much to the Provinces. Not only does the President exercise a substantial measure of independence, but he can act, in concert with his two Governors, in such a manner as to ensure that his policies shall be effectively implemented. This, by itself, seems to be no bad thing. Policy is either implemented or it is not. The important question is the policy itself and that, in turn, raises the question of the contribution that can usefully be made by a legislature comprising 156 members, representing the interests of more than 90,000,000 people, with no powers of financial control, from whose body the President's advisers are not chosen and which meets only when it is summoned by the President or by the Speaker upon a requisition of at least one-third of the members.

All this, it may well be argued, is of the essence of that form of democracy—a word whose meanings seem to proliferate with the passage of time[25]—which, in the opinion of the author[26] of the 1962 Constitution, is the type that the people of Pakistan can work and understand. But it is equally evident that the true 'strength' of the structure depends, in the last analysis, on two inescapable factors, and these we shall now consider.

The history of Pakistan, from its inception, including the Martial

[25] It was even claimed that Martial Law, as practised in Pakistan, and before the advent of the Basic Democracies scheme, was a form of democracy. See General Ayub Khan's press interview, *D*, 31 October 1958.

[26] In *D*, April 1965, it was clearly stated the Mr. Manzur Qadir was the author of the Constitution. It seems possible that *draftsman* was intended. Whatever the case, it seems probable that Mr. Manzur Qadir's participation in the work of devising and preparing the Constitution of 1962 was considerable.

Law period, shows that the Central Government of the country can never be stronger than either of the two Provinces intends it shall be. The Report of the Constitution Commission indicates the majority of witnesses as favouring a strong Centre,[27] but on the question of what constitutes a strong centre, and how strong, it is the provincial will that prevails in the end, as it has always prevailed in the past.

Secondly, the 'strength' of a strong Centre depends, in the present structure, entirely upon the ability and personality of the President. Given a person who unites in himself, or herself, the necessary integrity, wisdom, and energy, the new structure can serve, as adequately as any other, as the efficient instrument for carrying on the nation's business. The same can, of course, be said of any benevolent dictatorship. In the present case, the further merit is that the people, in some measure, are kept fairly close to the conduct of the administration. At least, whatever may be thought of the electoral system, there need be no sense of total exclusion,[28] although the doubt felt in some quarters on this point has been recognized and the possibility that 'some method can undoubtedly be worked out in due course' has been suggested.[29]

The inherent dangers of a structure too greatly dependent upon the force of character and the ability of a single individual, are only too well-known. If the President is personally weak—the tool of others—or lacking in scruple, the extensive powers that he wields then change their character. Instead of being instruments for effective administration, they become weapons of destruction, pointed towards the people they were designed to serve. The National Assembly is then confronted with the alternative of being an impotent witness to national injury or of being provoked into acts leading to that very instability and internal havoc which the Constitution was designed to prevent.

While the success or failure of the 1962 Constitution is no part of the Martial Law story, that Constitution represents the most important outcome of the Martial Law period and is, therefore, the principal touchstone by which its usefulness can be put to proof. It is, moreover, the principal test of those ideas which impelled President Ayub Khan and his military colleagues to act

[27] op. cit., p. 33.
[28] The election campaign of 1964 is fair evidence of this.
[29] *The Constitution—A Study.* op. cit., p. 22.

in October 1958. It is obvious, from all pronouncements made, even at the outset of Martial Law, that they had for some time been observing the course of the country's decline and had been meditating upon the reasons for it. From much that I have already quoted it will be clear they were convinced of the failure of the earlier system although the more forceful criticism was directed towards the men rather than the measures.

It is equally evident that they held, just as sincerely, that they had isolated the causes of the failure and had discovered methods of solving the constitutional problem. It is important to mention this if only because, after Martial Law was withdrawn and President Ayub Khan carried on the government of the country under the new constitutional arrangements, he was accused of utilizing those arrangements to ensure his continuance as Head of the State.

It is true that within two years of the promulgation of the Constitution, two substantial amendments were made to it and the second of these, passed during 1964, proved to be a highly controversial change, productive of much bitter feeling. Notwithstanding all this, there need be no doubt about the sincerity of the Martial Law administration and the next chapter will tell us why, but sincerity is no assurance of correct evaluation, and still less does it guarantee success. To reach any dependable assessment of what Martial Law meant to Pakistan, it is necessary to see the facts—as I have tried to do in earlier pages—and to identify the pattern, which I shall consider in the final chapter of this book.

XV

The Shape of a Revolution

ALTHOUGH the initial declarations made only minor use of the word, not much time elapsed before the changes of October 1958 acquired the aspect of a revolution.[1] As we have seen, even before the end of that very month, the Supreme Court of Pakistan had applied this description to the military seizure of power, finding in this victorious *coup d'état* all the legal sanction it required.[2] This was, of course, important and even comforting to the new administration, but we are not much concerned with it. After all, it is a time-hallowed maxim that law by power subsists and, where the power goes, the law must follow.

The broad appeal in the revolutionary idea went very much further than that of answering to legal necessities. The notion was, in itself, stimulating, evocative and altogether congenial. It signified a clear break with a past of which no one felt unduly proud; a past all too definitely associated with political gerrymandering, purposeless intrigue, corruption, internal unrest, incompetence and loss of face abroad. Revolution implied salutary change; an irrevocable sloughing off; a process of disinfection which, however astringent, was revitalizing. Thus, in his broadcast of 8 October, General Ayub Khan spoke of the 'hour of trial' from which all might emerge as 'a sound, solid and strong nation'. Hearing these words, Pakistanis might well feel they were about to enter upon their own brave new world.

The potentialities in the idea of standing on the threshold of an era which was arising from the ashes of a corrupt and degrading past, were swiftly recognized. Here, obviously, was the source of inspiration towards a new zeal and a fresh enthusiasm of which the country stood sorely in need. Official literature began to emphasize the fact of revolution and to play down the concept of an imposed Martial Law which, after all, is a neutral, uncreative

---

[1] See Appendices I and II and General Ayub Khan's broadcast on 8 October 1958. [2] *TK*, 28 October 1958.

act and, for that matter, incompatible with the idea of an advancing democracy. By contrast, the concept of revolution seemed to carry with it the notion of popular change and liberation. We have had ample opportunity of observing that at no time in the history of the Martial Law administration was sight ever lost of the democratic idea. In claiming to have instituted a revolutionary government, therefore, the military leaders could well have asserted that they came not to destroy the law, but to fulfil it.

Nevertheless, it is this suggestion of revolution that needs now to be examined. We shall see in due course just how important it is to trace the exact configuration of this claim.

To begin with, much emphasis has justifiably been placed upon the bloodless character of the October *coup*. How different this healthy decontamination of certain Augean stables from the repulsive butchery perpetrated in Iraq or even the hangings that followed General Gursel's overthrow of the Bayar régime in Turkey! Some people might say that so far as that went, the entire circumstances were different and that to have ordered executions in Pakistan would have required a downright and vicious perversity. That may be so, but considering the accusations mutually bandied about during the years preceding, it could have been answered that the politicians had quite successfully convicted each other of capital offences long before Martial Law was declared. Still, the irresponsible use of slanderous charges is another subject. The point now is that those who seek to diminish the merit, fairly claimed by the military administration in this respect, had better go further and declare the reasons which made necessary the merciless slaughter of little children in a palace in Baghdad.

The difficulty arises somewhere else. The abstention from bloodshed was wholly commendable, but what is harder to understand is the paradoxical lenience shown in those other instances I described earlier. For no reason that has yet been made apparent, prison sentences were abruptly terminated; convicted persons were released, and heavy fines not recovered. The relevance of this to certain political offences has already been discussed. There, the remission of punishment could have been interpreted as an act of contempt, as a measure of the insignificance of the guilty persons. In the case, however, of those found guilty of serious crime involving moral turpitude, this policy of severity tempered by prompt and inexplicable acts of mercy must—in the absence of adequate explanation—continue to confuse.

It is unquestionably clear that President Ayub Khan and his military colleagues were right in deciding that Pakistan did not require the letting of blood, but whether the cancers were sufficiently cauterized, is a very different matter. On the assumption that the body politic stood in need of some drastic surgery—and without this assumption all justification for the events of October 1958 must at once evaporate—it is difficult to understand on what ground the military administration resolved, at so early a stage, to mitigate the severity of its treatment. The new Government was making a mockery of its own pretensions when, in circumstances of sensational publicity, offenders were arrested and, upon military trial, condemned to heavy punishment for serious crime, only to enjoy a quiet reprieve not long afterwards.

This, to be sure, is all of a piece with the note of moderation that characterized the acts and deeds of the Martial Law administration. Any examination of reforms instituted during that period, notwithstanding the hyperbolic language sometimes used to describe their excellence, must disclose their nature. And since all this has been studied in preceding chapters, it is unnecessary to inquire a second time into the ultimate effect of land reforms; of the attempt made to reduce corruption and incompetence in the public services; of law and educational reforms; of the efforts made towards bracing up the economic situation of the country and, in particular, towards strengthening its agriculture.

It may well be that President Ayub Khan and his collaborators deemed it wise to follow a policy that, while penetrating in its scope, was conciliatory in its application. It may well be the administration was carefully and deliberately measuring out as much revolution as it thought the country could take, but it is open to question whether adequate economic and social reform could be wrought effectively through a system of painless dosage. If, as we willingly assume, the four generals combined to control the nation's fortunes simply in order to make the changes they by conviction held essential, then it was their business to complete the task and not divest themselves of power until they had done so or, at any rate, until the country was set irreversibly on its path.

It is for these reasons that I consider the institution of a measure of local self-government—within a year of the Martial Law declaration—to have been premature. Of course, the overriding power of the military administration remained, its sanction could still be invoked, but the cutting edge was blunted and the outline of its intention blurred. This measure of abdication fettered the administration with no corresponding advantage, at that stage, to the country. From all that has been written in chapter VIII about Basic Democracies it should be clear that President Ayub Khan, whether he knew it or not, gave hostages to political fortune when he introduced the scheme, and it is doubtful whether he served the nation well in so doing at that early hour.

All this became apparent in many ways and fairly quickly, nowhere more so than over the difficult question of the constitutional application of Islamic values and belief. I have the impression that the earlier intentions of the Martial Law administration favoured a constitutional structure in which the aspirations of the preponderating Muslim majority could be nourished in the simplest and most progressive manner possible. Yet the *Ruet-i-Hilal* controversy[3] indicated not only a resiling from this approach (on which point no comment, here, seems justified) but also a sensitiveness, combined with a lack of confidence, never visible in the earlier days of Martial Law. This encroachment of weakness can only be attributed to undue haste in implementing certain promises for which no voice was urgently clamouring at that time.

How then to describe a revolution in which no blood was shed; in which offenders were punished with apparent reluctance; and whose authors affected to be apologetic for wielding power at all? What is the Martial Law that claims to be democratic and what those reforms whose most distinctive character is their moderation and which could not, even then, always be enforced?

As the events of those forty-four months recede and their outlines acquire further definition, it becomes easier to recognize the declaration of Martial Law for what it really was: a simple reversion to paternalism, that method of government by which the British administered the sub-continent during the period which followed the conflict of 1857 until the changes made in Lord Ripon's time. The two situations are not identical, but the parallels are too many, too exact, and too useful to be ignored.

Both instances were preceded by a mounting confusion that sprang from the inadequacies of the previously existing situation.

[3] See Appendix IX.

About the circumstances that prevailed before the Martial Law declaration, we have already seen something. About the situation in 1858 (it is interesting, but perhaps of no significance, that it preceded by exactly a century the appearance of Martial Law in Pakistan), it was obvious that the sub-continent could not continue to be governed by an organization whose primary interest was, to all original intents and purposes, a trading one, subject to a Board of Control in London. Thus, upon the creation of the Indian Empire, the civil administration carried on the government of the sub-continent, without the assistance of representative institutions and backed by the authority of the Armed Forces. The parallel with the declaration of Martial Law is clear.

In the case of President Ayub Khan's administration, this declaration was accompanied by an unequivocal promise to restore all power to the people. It would not be fair to say that, in 1858, such assurances had been given by the British Government, but it is undoubtedly true that since the beginning of the nineteenth century, various Britons prominently associated with the extension and administration of British rule had spoken and written about the day when power must be restored. Those instances are too clearly inscribed in history to call for repetition here, and, what is more to the point, it is a matter of history that this was done, through a series of reforms that suffered only by their delay. That President Ayub Khan's military administration voluntarily withdrew is likewise a matter of record, the merit in this case being, in my view, an imprudent measure of haste. Even in this we note the odd similarity of an error in timing. As to the correspondence between the old district boards and the *taluka* and *tehsil* councils, on the one hand, and the institutions primarily set up under the Basic Democracies Order, on the other, this is too obvious to be overlooked. The derivation may have been conscious or it may have been unconscious. It may be said there was no derivation at all—as far as historical patterns are concerned it is unimportant—but the configuration is beyond all doubt.

It is true there are distinctions to be drawn and they are important. The administration of the British was foreign and destined sooner or later to depart. The government instituted by President Ayub Khan belonged to the soil and could neither abdicate nor be expelled in the same sense. The liberalizing reforms, which began during Lord Ripon's viceroyalty, were received by the

British administrators with a sense of misgiving and with no marked zeal. The changes of 1960, which began with the Basic Democracies Order, could not but receive the active and total support of the civil services. Even if some members of the Pakistan administration felt doubt about the validity of the scheme and the speed at which the new government was proceeding (and there are no grounds for making any distinct assertion on the point), it was still in their own interest to ensure effective working. The scheme was, after all, the contrivance of their own people and not something which, whatever its merits, was always exposed to the destructive charge of being imported and forcibly imposed.

An accurately identified historical pattern supplies an exact prognosis and I have no doubt as to the path along which Pakistan's political future will proceed. Comparable with the widening effect of the old Indian Councils Acts and the reforms that came after them, there will be a step-by-step reversion to universal adult suffrage exercising the vote without the aid of electoral intermediaries; the basis of the national and provincial assemblies will be broadened; ministers will be responsible to the legislatures which will, in due course, exercise full and completed financial powers. These things may not come easily or without convulsion, but they will come.

It is, furthermore, evident that during the Martial Law administration, some lamps were lit which will not easily be extinguished. Their beams, if still somewhat feeble, nevertheless illumine the way to a better life. The Martial Law experience has taught many useful lessons, not the least of which is that democratic government is not simply a matter of advantages but also of qualifications and a sense of responsibility. It may be true that that experience was sometimes the object of derision, principally (which is, or should be, strange) from other countries faced with problems comparable with those of Pakistan. But those sneers were extremely ill-advised as time and circumstance may very well disclose. Pakistan's constitutional evolution has not been easy or without anxiety, and if the Martial Law declaration was, as I suggest, an instance of *reculer pour mieux sauter*, it follows that the evolutionary process was far from stopping and will not stop.

From all that has been written here—and, for that matter, elsewhere—it is only too evident that the problems confronting Pakistan are numerous, profound, and not easily solved. The same is true of other nations in like case. Taken together, they represent a group of peoples, poor and under-developed, forming a significant proportion of the world's population occupying a significant proportion of the world's land surface. To me it is a self-evident proposition that they, their peoples, and their troubles, need to be understood and that it will be bad for the future of this planet if they are not.

The time is approaching when a generation will have passed since the last shots were fired in World War II and there was heard the first fine oratory about the end of colonialism and the helping hand for the newly emerging nations. Colonialism is clearly on its last legs and, as for the helping-hand, that certainly has been extended. Whether anybody finds adequate satisfaction in the results, is a lot less clear, for it stands out like Mars at perihelion, that the kind of understanding necessary to make that help as effective as it needs to be, has not yet been achieved. It was in the hope of making a contribution to it that this book was written.

Appendix I

PROCLAMATION

[*Dated 7th October, 1958 made by the President of Pakistan*]

No. F. 81/Pres/58, 25th. October, 1958, Gazette, 31st. October, 1958—
The following PROCLAMATION made by the President at 10.30
p.m. on the 7th. day of October, 1958, is published for general information:

'For the last two years, I have been watching, with the deepest
anxiety, the ruthless struggle for power, corruption, the shameful
exploitation of our simple, honest, patriotic and industrious masses, the
lack of decorum, and the prostitution of Islam for political ends. There
have been a few honourable exceptions. But being in a minority they
have not been able to assert their influence in the affairs of the country.

'These despicable activities have led to a dictatorship of the lowest
order. Adventurers and exploiters have flourished to the detriment of
the masses and are getting richer by their nefarious practices.

'Despite my repeated endeavours, no serious attempt has been made
to tackle the food crises. Food has been a problem of life and death for
us in a country which should be really surplus. Agriculture and land
administration have been made a handmaiden of politics so that in our
present system of government, no political party will be able to take
any positive action to increase production. In East Pakistan, on the other
hand, there is a well organized smuggling of food, medicines and other
necessities of life. The masses there suffer due to the shortages so
caused in, and the consequent high prices of, these commodities. Import
of food has been a constant and serious drain on our foreign exchange
earnings in the last few years, with the result that the Government is
constrained to curtail the much needed internal development projects.

'Some of our politicians have lately been talking of bloody revolution.
Another type of adventurer among them think it fit to go to foreign
countries and attempt direct alignment with them which can only be
described as high treason.

'The disgraceful scene enacted recently in the East Pakistan Assembly
is known to all. I am told that such episodes were common occurrences
in pre-partition Bengal. Whether they were or not, it is certainly not a
civilized mode of procedure. You do not raise the prestige of your
country by beating the Speaker, killing the Deputy Speaker and dese-
crating the National Flag.

'The mentality of the political parties has sunk so low that I am unable any longer to believe that elections will improve the present chaotic internal situation and enable us to form a strong and stable Government capable of dealing with the innumerable and complex problems facing us today. We cannot get men from the Moon. The same group of people who have brought Pakistan on the verge of ruination will rig the elections for their own ends. They will come back more revengeful, because I am sure the elections will be contested, mainly, on personal, regional and sectarian basis. When they return, they will use the same methods which have made a tragic farce of democracy and are the main cause of the present widespread frustration in the country. However much the administration may try, I am convinced, judging by shifting loyalties and the ceaseless and unscrupulous scramble for office, that elections will be neither free nor fair. They will not solve our difficulties. On the contrary, they are likely to create greater unhappiness and disappointment leading ultimately to a really bloody revolution. Recently, we had elections for the Karachi Municipal Corporation. Twenty per cent of the electorate exercised their votes, and out of these, about fifty per cent were bogus votes.

'We hear threats and cries of civil disobedience in order to retain private volunteer organizations and to break up the One Unit. These disruptive tendencies are a good indication of their patriotism and the length to which politicians and adventurers are prepared to go to achieve their parochial aims.

'Our foreign policy is subjected to unintelligent and irresponsible criticism, not for patriotic motives, but from selfish view points often by the very people who were responsible for it. We desire to have friendly relations with all nations, but political adventurers try their best to create bad blood and misunderstandings between us and countries like the U.S.S.R., the U.A.R. and the People's Republic of China. Against India, of course, they scream for war, knowing full well that they will be nowhere near the firing line. In no country in the world, do political parties treat foreign policy in the manner it has been done in Pakistan. To dispel the confusion so caused, I categorically reiterate that we shall continue to follow a policy which our interests and geography demand and that we shall honour all our international commitments which, as is well known, we have undertaken to safeguard the security of Pakistan and, as a peace loving nation, to play our part in averting the danger of war from this troubled world.

'For the last three years, I have been doing my utmost to work the Constitution in a democratic way. I have laboured to bring about coalition after coalition, hoping that it would stabilize the administration and that the affairs of the country would be run in the interests of the masses. My detractors, in their dishonest ways, have on every opportunity, called these attempts Palace intrigues. It has become fashionable to put all the blame on the President. A wit said the other day, "If it rains too much it is the fault of the President and if it does not rain it is the fault of the President." If only I alone were concerned, I would go on taking these fulminations with the contempt they deserve. But the intention of these traitors and unpatriotic elements is to destroy the prestige of Pakistan and the Government by attacking the Head of the State. They have succeeded to a great extent, and, if this state of affairs is allowed to go on, they will achieve their ultimate purpose.

'My appraisal of the internal situation has led me to believe that a vast majority of the people no longer have any confidence in the present system of Government and are getting more and more disillusioned and disappointed and are becoming dangerously resentful of the manner in which they have been exploited. Their resentment and bitterness are justifiable. The leaders have not been able to render them the service they deserve and have failed to prove themselves worthy of the confidence the masses had reposed in them.

'The Constitution which was brought into being on 23rd. March, 1956, after so many tribulations, is unworkable. It is full of dangerous compromises so that Pakistan will disintegrate internally if the inherent malaise is not removed. To rectify them, the country must first be taken to sanity by a peaceful revolution. Then, it is my intention to collect a number of patriotic persons to examine our problems in the political field and devise a Constitution more suitable to the genius of the Muslim people. When it is ready, and at the appropriate time, it will be submitted to the referendum of the people.

'It is said that the Constitution is sacred. But more sacred than the Constitution or anything else is the country and the welfare and happiness of its people. As Head of the State, my foremost duty before my God and the people is the integrity of Pakistan. It is seriously threatened by the ruthlessness of traitors and political adventurers whose selfishness, thirst for power and unpatriotic conduct cannot be restrained by a government set up under the present system. Nor can I any longer remain a spectator of activities designed to destroy the country. After deep and anxious thought, I have come to the regrettable conclusion that I would be failing in my duty if I did not take steps, which in my opinion, are inescapable in present conditions, to save Pakistan from complete disruption. I have, therefore, decided that:—

(a) The Constitution of the 23rd. March, 1956 will be abrogated.
(b) The Central and Provincial Governments will be dismissed with immediate effect.
(c) The National Parliament and Provincial Assemblies will be dissolved.
(d) All political parties will be abolished.

(e) Until alternative arrangements are made, Pakistan will come under Martial Law. I hereby appoint General Muhammad Ayub Khan, Commander-in-Chief, Pakistan Army, as the Chief Martial Law Administrator and place all the Armed Forces of Pakistan under his command.

'To the valiant Armed Forces of Pakistan, I have to say that "having been closely associated with them since the very inception of Pakistan, I have learned to admire their patriotism and loyalty. I am putting a great strain on them. I fully realize this, but I ask you, Officers and men of the Armed Forces, on your service depends the future existence of Pakistan as an independent nation and a bastion in these parts of the Free World. Do your job without fear or favour and may God help you."

'To the people of Pakistan I talk as a brother and a fellow compatriot. Present action has been taken with the utmost regret but I have had to do it in the interests of the country and the masses, finer men than whom it is difficult to imagine. To the patriots and the law abiding, I promise you will be happier and freer. The political adventurers, the smugglers, the black-marketeers, the hoarders, will be unhappy and their activities will be severely restricted. As for the traitors, they had better flee the country if they can and while the going is good.'

Appendix II

PROCLAMATION OF MARTIAL LAW

[Government of Pakistan Notification No. 977/58 dated 7th. October, 1958. Gazette Extraordinary, 15th. October, 1958]

1. Whereas I adjudge it essential for national requirements to exercise jurisdiction within the international boundaries of PAKISTAN, I, the Supreme Commander of the Armed Forces of PAKISTAN, do hereby give notice as follows.
2. Martial Law Regulations and Orders will be published in such manner as is conveniently possible. Any person contravening the said Regulations and Orders shall be liable under Martial Law to the penalties stated in the Regulations.
3. The said Regulations may prescribe special penalties for offences under the ordinary law.
4. The said Regulations may appoint special Courts for the trial and punishment of contravention of the said Regulations and Orders and of offences under the ordinary law.

Mohammed Ayub Khan, HP, HJ,
General,
*Supreme Commander and Chief Martial Law
Administrator in PAKISTAN.*

Appendix III

MARTIAL LAW REGULATIONS

[*Reprinted from the* Gazette of Pakistan, Extraordinary, *dated 15 October 1958*.]

Whereas Martial Law has been proclaimed and is in force in the area within the boundaries of PAKISTAN, I, General MOHAMMAD AYUB KHAN, Supreme Commander of the Armed Forces of PAKISTAN and Chief Martial Law Administrator hereby direct that the following regulations shall be observed in PAKISTAN:—

MARTIAL LAW REGULATIONS
PART I

No. 1

The whole of PAKISTAN will be considered as the Martial Law Area.

(a) The Martial Law Area will be divided into the following Zones:—
   (i) Zone A—KARACHI Federal Area including MALIR.
   (ii) Zone B—Whole of West PAKISTAN less Zone A.
   (iii) Zone C—Whole of East PAKISTAN.

(b) The following Commanders of the Pak Military Forces are hereby appointed as Administrators of Martial Law in their respective Zones:—
   (i) Zone A—Major General MALIK SHER BAHADUR.
   (ii) Zone B—Lieut General MOHAMMAD AZAM KHAN.
   (iii) Zone C—Major General MOHD. UMRAO KHAN.

(c) Orders under these Regulations and additional Regulations hereinafter known as Martial Law Orders and Martial Law Regulations may be issued by me or by any Administrator or by any other officer authorised by me.

No. 1A

(a) *Special Courts.*—Special Courts of criminal jurisdiction shall be of the following classes:—
   (i) Special Military Courts.
   (ii) Summary Military Courts.

Special Military and Summary Military Courts shall have the power to try and punish any person for contravention of Martial Law Regulations or Orders or for offences under the ordinary law.

The criminal courts as by law established shall have power to try and punish any person for offences under the ordinary law and for contraventions of Martial Law Regulations or Orders.

(b) *Special Military Courts.*—An Administrator of Martial Law may convene Special Military Courts in his area of administration for the trial of any offence committed in any area to which these Regulations extend; provided that the term ordinary law as above mentioned shall in each case be held to include the provisions of any special law for the time being in force in that area.

Subject to the provisions of these regulations a Special Military Court shall be constituted in the same manner, and shall exercise the same powers and follow the same procedure as a Field General Court Martial convened under the Pakistan Army Act, 1952 and the provisions of that act and of the rules made thereunder shall apply to, and govern all such proceedings; provided that:—

(i) Any person exercising the powers of a Magistrate of the first class or of a sessions judge may be appointed a member of the court;

(ii) The court may pass any sentence authorised by law or by these Regulations;

(iii) All sentences of death shall be reserved for confirmation by an appointed Administrator of Martial Law, irrespective of his rank.

(c) *Summary Military Courts.*—An Administrator of Martial Law may, by general or special order, empower any magistrate of the first class or any military or naval or air force officer provided that he has been specially selected for this particular duty to hold a Summary Military Court in his area of administration for the trial of any offence committed in that area.

Subject to the provisions of these Regulations a Summary Military Court shall exercise the same powers and follow the same procedure as a Summary Court Martial held under the Pakistan Army Act, 1952 and the provisions of that act and the rules made thereunder shall apply to, and govern, all such proceedings, provided that;

(i) No other officer shall be required to attend such proceedings;

(ii) The court shall not be required to record more than a memorandum of the evidence or to frame formal charges;

(iii) The court may try any offence without reference to superior authority;

(iv) The court may pass any sentence authorised by law or by these Regulations except death, transportation, or imprisonment exceeding one year or whipping exceeding 15 stripes;

(v) The proceedings of every Summary Court shall without delay be forwarded for review to the Administrator of Martial Law in the area in which the trial was held.

An Administrator of Martial Law may by general or special order, give directions as to the distribution among the Summary Military Courts of cases to be tried by them.

No. 2

Notwithstanding anything contained in these Regulations, the criminal courts as by law established shall continue to exercise jurisdiction over persons accused of all offences committed under the ordinary law and also under these regulations.

No. 3

PUNISHMENTS

(a) Punishments shall be awarded according to the following scales:—
    (i) Death.
    (ii) Transportation for life or for not less than 7 years.
    (iii) Rigorous imprisonment for not more than 14 years.
    (iv) Whipping, not more than 30 stripes. Whipping shall not be inflicted on females or persons over 45 years of age.
    (v) Fine. Unless a maximum is mentioned, the amount is unlimited.
    (vi) Forfeiture of property, either completely or in part or destruction of property either completely or in part. Where any person is sentenced to have his property forfeited or destroyed, that sentence shall apply to any property in which he has any interest whatever.

The sentence of death shall be inflicted by hanging.

(b) The following combinations of the above punishments are permissible:—
    (i) with (v) and/or (vi)
    (ii) or (iii) with one or more of (iv), (v) and (vi)
    (iv) with (v) and/or (vi)

(c) At the end of each Regulation dealing with an offence, a penalty is mentioned for its infringement. This is the maximum penalty. Unless otherwise stated, any punishment or permissible combination of punishments no part of which is higher in the scale of punishments than the maximum penalty may be awarded for that offence.

(d) In these Regulations (a) the word recalcitrant includes any external enemy of PAKISTAN and mutineers or rebels or rioters and any enemy agent, (b) the expression "PAKISTAN Forces" includes the military, naval and air forces, the Police Force and the Civil Armed Forces of PAKISTAN.

No. 4

Any matter touching Martial Law which is intended to be announced, published and telegraphed through radio stations, printing presses and telegraph offices in PAKISTAN respectively, by any person other than by an officer of Armed Forces authorised by me, will be subject to pre-censorship by the respective Martial Law Administrators. Omission to comply with this regulation is punishable. Maximum sentence 7 years R. I.

No. 5

Any person who attempts to contravene or abets the contravention of any of these Regulations shall be punished as if he had contravened that Regulation.

No. 6

If with intent to help the recalcitrants any person does any act which is designed or is likely to give assistance to the operations of the recalcitrants, or to impede operations of PAKISTAN Forces, or to endanger life, he shall suffer death and no less punishment.

No. 7

If any person joins or attempts to join the recalcitrants he shall suffer death and no less punishment.

No. 8

No person shall wilfully damage public property or property which is employed for the maintenance of public services or of supplies to PAKISTAN Forces or to the civil population. Maximum penalty death.

No. 9

No person shall loot. Maximum penalty death.

Explanation.—To loot means to commit theft (a) when public order is disturbed by actual or apprehended recalcitrant attack, or by panic or rioting, or (b) during a black out or a period during which lighting has been reduced or controlled or (c) in respect of any property left, exposed or unprotected in consequence of war conditions or (d) in any premises damaged by war operations or destroyed or vacated for military reasons.

No. 10

No person shall commit decoity as defined in the PAKISTAN Penal Code. Maximum punishment death.

No. 11

No person shall assist or harbour any recalcitrant by giving him information or by supplying him with shelter, food, drink, money, clothes, weapons, ammunition, stores, forage or means of conveyance, or by assisting him in any way to evade apprehension. Maximum punishment death.

No. 12

No person shall be in actual or constructive possession of any firearm, ammunition, explosive or sword without a bonafide license. The Administrators may however ban the carrying or possession of any weapon (including those with license) except by special permits issued by him. All such articles not covered by such permit shall be handed over as directed by Administrators. Maximum punishment 14 years R. I.

No. 13

Any person who attacks, resists or injures, or causes to be attacked, resisted, or injured any member of the forces, whether civil or military under my command or any civil official, shall be punishable. Maximum punishment death.

No. 14

Every person who sees or comes in contact with the recalcitrants or has knowledge of the movements or whereabouts of the recalcitrants shall without any delay give full information thereof to the nearest military or civil authority. Wilful failure to do so shall be punishable. Maximum punishment Transportation for life.

No. 15

No person shall damage, tamper with or interfere with the working of roads, railways, canals, aerodromes, telegraph, telephone, wireless installations or with any other government property. Maximum punishment death.

No. 16

No person shall:—
  (a) Disobey or neglect to obey any Martial Law order duly made in accordance with these regulations; or
  (b) Obstruct, impede or interfere in any manner with any person who is acting in the execution of his duty under Martial Law; or
  (c) Make any false statement which he knows or believes to be false in order to obtain a pass or permit issued under Martial Law.

Maximum punishment 14 years R. I.

No. 17

No person shall destroy, deface, remove, or in any way tamper with any notice exhibited under Martial Law. Maximum punishment 10 years R. I.

No. 18

Every person shall when required to do so give his correct name and address and produce his permit or pass to any military or civil officer or any soldier or policeman. Failure to comply shall be punishable. Maximum punishment death.

No. 19

No person shall wilfully give false evidence or refuse to give evidence in any investigation or trial held under these regulations. Maximum punishment death.

No. 20

No person shall commit any act or be guilty of an omission or make a speech:

    (a) which is to the prejudice of good order or the public safety; or

    (b) which is calculated to mislead or hamper movements of or imperil the success of or tamper with the loyalty of forces under my command.

Maximum punishment 10 years R. I.

No. 21

No person or syndicate or firm shall hoard foodgrain in violation of existing orders and any orders issued under these Regulations. Maximum punishment death.

No. 22

Wilful adulteration of all kinds of food shall be punishable. Maximum punishment 14 years R. I.

No. 23

No one shall hoard, wilfully indulge in unwarranted dilution or mixing or unauthorised manufacture of medicines of all types. Maximum punishment 14 years R. I.

No. 24

No one by word of mouth, or in writing or by signals, or otherwise will spread reports, calculated to create alarm or despondency amongst the public, or calculated to create dissatisfaction towards the Armed Forces and Police, or any member thereof. Maximum punishment 14 years R. I.

No. 25

No one shall hoard any article of public necessity or refuse to declare his stock of commercial commodities when required to do so by any military or civil authority or fail to put on sale goods meant for public purchase. Failure to comply shall be punishable. Maximum punishment 14 years R. I.

No. 26

No one shall indulge in 'Black Marketing' of any commodity or goods. Maximum punishment 14 years R. I.

No. 27

Smuggling of all kinds is prohibited. Any one caught in the act of smuggling or found helping a smuggler with money, goods, shelter, food, drink, transportation or with any other type of assistance or who withholds any information about the smugglers or fails to pass on such information without delay to military and civil authorities shall be punishable. Maximum punishment death.

No. 28

Child lifting and abduction of women is an offence. Maximum punishment death.

No. 29

Strikes and agitations in educational institutions and public utility works and installations are prohibited. Any one who strikes or helps to bring about a strike or propagates a strike shall be punishable. Maximum punishment 10 years R. I.

MOHAMMED AYUB KHAN, HP, HJ,
GENERAL,
Supreme Commander of the Armed Forces
of PAKISTAN and Chief Martial Law
Administrator in PAKISTAN.

Place: KARACHI.
Date: 7th October 1958.

Appendix IV

CENTRAL GOVERNMENT OFFICIALS REMOVED FROM SERVICE OR OTHERWISE PUNISHED BY SCREENING COMMITTEES

Details are given in *D*, 28 June and 3 July 1959. The break-down appears to be as follows: 138 Class I officials (top-ranking grades); 221 Class I officials, both gazetted and non-gazetted classes (intermediary grades) and 1,303 Class III officials (clerical grades). These figures do not include officials of the Provincial Governments who were scrutinized by committees appointed by those Governments. To keep the record straight, it should be said that of the Central Class II officials, fourteen were removed from service as distinct from being compulsorily retired and, among the Class III officials, 110 were likewise removed from service. Including Provincial Government servants, it is understood that in one way or another, 6,600 officials, of varying rank and grade were adversely affected in some measure by these screening operations.

Appendix V

CHARGES AGAINST CERTAIN PUBLIC MEN UNDER EBDO

For anyone who is interested in the type of charge brought under EBDO, *D*, 26 February, 16 and 23 March 1960, are instructive. Instances will there be found which achieved newspaper prominence because of the high office held by the men concerned as, for example, the late H. S. Suhrawardy (a former Prime Minister of Pakistan), C. E. Gibbon (a former Deputy Speaker of the National Assembly of Pakistan), Mian Mumtaz Khan Daultana (a former Chief Minister of the Punjab), and Hasan Mahmood (a former Chief Minister of Bahawalpur).

Appendix VI

THE PRESS IN PAKISTAN

The historical background and principal formative influences are well stated in Mr. S. Natrajan's book, *History of the Press in India*.[1] The position that has developed, after partition, is very usefully contained in the *Press Commission Report*. What follows here has principally to do with the position that emerged during and after Martial Law.

Generally speaking, the Press in Pakistan has always enjoyed a fair measure of freedom and, when it chose, exhibited a considerable independence of attitude. If this liberty has on occasion degenerated into unwelcome and unreasonable licence, such a tendency was never markedly worse than that which prevails elsewhere from time to time, and is inherited, in part, from methods of agitation utilized in the days of British rule. No doubt the Press in Pakistan has been influenced on occasion by official patronage of various kinds or, on the other hand, by threat of prosecution and even actual prosecution. In a more extreme sense, it could be threatened with, or actually subjected to, serious loss by prohibition on publication for a time, or by forfeiture of financial security where this had been demanded as earnest of good conduct. Recourse to these methods was infrequent and tempered with discretion, because it involved the Government of the day in criticism and led to a 'bad Press': for obvious reasons newspapers tend to stand shoulder to shoulder on such occasions.

At no time could any Government claim to have the undivided and total support of all sections of the Press unless it were on some national issue such as Kashmir. On domestic affairs, the only time on which it could have been said that the Press was unanimous in its support and approval was during the earlier days of Martial Law when, in any case, criticism was virtually not permitted.[2] I have already commented on the sycophantic tendency of that time and, perhaps because of it, there was a reaction as soon as Martial Law was lifted, almost as if some journalists wanted to compensate for that period of unrestrained adulation.

Because the Martial Law administration enjoyed the undivided

[1] Asia Publishing House, London, 1962.
[2] See MLR No. 4 (requiring censorship). The operation of this MLR was soon withdrawn, but see also MLR 24, 34, and 51, which prohibited the publication of material causing dissension, ill-will towards the Armed Forces, ill-will among sub-sections of the nation, etc.

sympathy and support of the Press, and in view of Martial Law Regulations relating to what might safely be published and what not, the question of undue influence or pressure on the Press scarcely arose, and the instances of proceedings against newspapers and similar institutions under Martial Law Regulations were neither numerous nor oppressive.

In September 1959 the Editor of *Ittefaq*, an East Pakistan newspaper, was detained under Martial Law Regulations (No. 24) which prohibited publication of material likely to cause dissension. In June 1961 the Government issued an Ordinance taking over the management of the Associated Press of Pakistan, a privately owned organization which distributed news, but in this there seem to have been no political or similar implications whatsoever. It appears that the organization was heavily in debt, not only to the Posts and Telegraphs Department, but also to Reuters and to the Associated Press of America. The organization was, apparently, confronted with an impossible situation and was on the verge of financial collapse.[3]

By far the most notable single act, *vis-à-vis* the Press, for which the Martial Law administration was responsible, took place in the earlier part of 1959, when the controlling share interest in Progressive Papers Ltd., was expropriated, but even this enforced expropriation was effected under the provisions of the Security Act of 1952, legislation passed during the Prime Ministership of the late Khwaja Nazimuddin.

Progressive Papers Ltd. owned and published the *Pakistan Times*, one of West Pakistan's leading dailies (published in Lahore), as well as a prominent Urdu daily, *Imroz*, and a weekly, *Lailo Nihar*. The controlling share interest belonged to the late Mian Iftikharuddin and his son, Mr. Arif Iftikhar. In consequence of the procedure under the Security Act, the then existing direction and management were superseded by an Administrator, appointed by the Government and the controlling interest was disposed of by auction.[4] These shares were acquired ultimately by Choudhury Zahur Illahi, a politician and businessman (but see also below).

The statutory notice, compelling dissolution of the Board of Directors and vesting control and management in the Administrator, was accompanied by a further notice stating the newspapers in question were being printed and published with the aid of funds from foreign sources and, at the same time it was stated in an official Press Note that certain undertakings were actively engaged in printing and publishing material heavily subsidized by foreign agencies. The late Mian Iftikharuddin had been active in politics for many years and was known to have left-wing sympathies. He was a wealthy man and the prospectus of Pro-

---

[3] *D*, 16 June 1961.
[4] See *D*, 19 April, 2 May, 1 and 7 August 1959.

gressive Papers Ltd., issued at the time of offering the shares for auction, disclosed that no less a sum than £362,183 14s. 4d. had stood to his credit with Lloyds Bank Ltd., London. This disclosure appears to owe itself to Martial Law Regulation No. 45 requiring declaration and surrender of all balances held abroad.

Having in mind the necessity for a re-codification of the law relating to newspapers and printing-presses, the new administration turned its attention to this problem and, in 1960, the Central Government (Ministry of National Reconstruction and Information) produced the Press and Publications Ordinance. The important changes made by this Ordinance have been discussed in the earlier chapters of this book. However, after the withdrawal of Martial Law in 1962, and with the disappearance of restraints, the tone of the Press showed in some respects a marked deterioration, coupled with a developing tendency towards criticism of the new Constitution and President Ayub Khan's new Government. In the result, a distinct note of antagonism became perceptible with merits on both sides which call for an examination substantially longer than is possible here.

That there were grounds for criticising the methods of the new administration could hardly be disputed. The manner, for instance, in which the Report of the Franchise Commission was withheld from the public and then produced to the National Assembly, on the eve of prorogation could not satisfy a Press nurtured on democratic ideals. But if the Government was sensitive to Press criticism, it had reason for objecting to the manner in which that criticism was, all too often, stated. It was, it may be said in passing, regrettably noticeable that with the formation of a National Assembly under the new Constitution, the level of debate very rapidly descended to something close to the disheartening standards that had prevailed before Martial Law. Much of this senseless bickering in the Chamber found its way into eagerly awaiting newspaper columns. Furthermore, the Government could legitimately complain of unfair reporting, the peculiarly unpleasant habit of utilizing misleading headlines and the copious use of quotation from Assembly members' speeches, obviously intended for consumption outside the House.

Thus, in August 1963, it became known that the Government had under contemplation the possibility of introducing measures that would restrict these wilder excesses and many rumours circulated, including the possibility that the Press as a whole would be nationalized, that journalists would be 'screened', and so on. The matter took fire very quickly and, in order to avert legislative action, it was proposed that journalists should themselves devise a code of professional ethics that would put an end to undesirable practices.

It should be explained here that because of the revision of responsibilities, as between the Central Government and the Provincial

Governments, the responsibility for legislative action relating to the Press had in 1962 devolved upon the Provinces. Thus, when the new Press Ordinances appeared early in September 1963, they were promulgated by the East and West Pakistan Governments respectively. The restrictive sections in this new legislation aroused a storm of protest. There were joint meetings of editors and journalists and a one-day, nation-wide newspaper strike was organized. A month later, President Ayub Khan agreed to hold the objectionable sections in abeyance, until such time as amending action was complete, it being understood that the profession would also settle down to the task of producing its own professional code. There, at the time of writing, the matter rests, with the profession still dissatisfied with the legislative position and the professional code still undrafted.

It is clear that the revising Ordinances of 1963 were injudiciously conceived and were put out in a high-handed way without adequate consultation. The result was a reverse for the administration, but it could not be said that a true solution of the problem had been achieved and the profession continued to complain of the illiberal state of the law. The Government, on its own side, pointed to the need for an improved state of responsibility in some sections of the Press.

The measure of strength that the profession enjoys was further demonstrated, in 1964, when two journalists, employed by the *Pakistan Times*, were summarily dismissed at the instance, it appears, of the West Pakistan Provincial Government. It was the old and familiar problem of refusing to disclose a source of information. The matter was firmly taken up by their Union and the two men were reinstated. Thus, any impression that the Press in Pakistan is tied to the Government's chariot is not, and never has been, true except when no alternative was possible during Martial Law.

The fact that no Government has ever been quite sure of the Press has had its own consequences. As far back as 1954 the ruling party of that time, the Muslim League, feeling the need for a newspaper whose loyalty and support could be relied upon, established an English daily of its own, *The Pakistan Standard*. This journal constituted the first attempt at pure party control, and was not markedly successful in any sense. The paper survived for about a year and then quietly closed down. With the coming of Martial Law, the dissolution of political parties and the freezing of their assets, *The Pakistan Standard* had no hope of revival.

In March 1964 a National Press Trust was set up, evidently with the knowledge and approval of President Ayub Khan's Government.[5] The terms of the Trust Deed do not appear to have been made public and, so far as can be understood, this is a private trust on which a number of businessmen have settled sums of money amounting, possibly, to Rs.1

[5] *O*, 25 January 1964.

lakh each.[6] These contributors, referred to by the ambiguous title of 'settlers', do not, it seems, participate in the management of the Trust and what return they get on their money, and what is to happen to the money if the trusts fail, is not known.

It has been stated that the Trust was set up for the establishment and publication of newspapers with 'truly objective outlook and devoted to the cause of national progress and solidarity and to acquire, promote, and develop all other forms of mass information'.[7] In pursuance of this aim, the Trust acquired on 1 August 1964 the controlling interest in the *Morning News*, an English daily newspaper, published simultaneously in Karachi and Dacca. The trend of policy, under the new proprietorship, was indicated, five days later, by a front-page article, stringently criticising Khwaja Nazimuddin, then President of the 'Council' Muslim League and a prominent opposition leader. Later in the same month the Trust acquired the controlling interest in Progressive Papers Ltd. (the company mentioned earlier in this Appendix) and in Mashriq Ltd., an East Pakistan newspaper-owning company.

[6] £7,500 or US$21,000.
[7] *MN*, 6 August 1964.

Appendix VII

LIST OF INQUIRY COMMISSIONS SET UP BY THE MARTIAL LAW ADMINISTRATION AND OF THE REPORTS RECEIVED DURING THAT PERIOD

Company Law Commission
Constitution Commission
Credit Inquiry Commission
Educational Reform Commission
Federal Capital Commission
Finance Commission
Food and Agriculture Commission
Franchise Commission
Jute Inquiry Commission
Land Reforms Commission
Land Revenue Commission
Law Reform Commission
Manpower Commission[1]
Maritime Commission
Medical Reforms Commission
Pay and Services Commission[1]
Police Commission[1]
Press Commission[2]
Price Commission
Scientific Commission
Social Evils Commission[1]
Sports, Culture, Art and Literature Committee
Sugar Commission
Taxation Inquiry Commission[2]
Textile Inquiry Commission

[1] Report not yet made available to the public.
[2] Commission instituted before Martial Law.

Appendix VIII

TERMS OF REFERENCE OF THE CONSTITUTION COMMISSION

[Set up on 17 February 1960]

To examine the progressive failure of parliamentary government in Pakistan leading to the abrogation of the Constitution of 1956 and to determine the causes and the nature of the failure.

To consider how best the said or like causes may be identified and their recurrence prevented;

And, having further taken account of the genius of the people, the general standard of education and political judgement in the country, the present state of a sense of nationhood, the prime need for sustained development and the effect of the constitutional and administrative changes brought into being in recent months, to submit constitutional proposals in the form of a report advising how best the following ends may be secured:—

A democracy adapted to changing circumstances and based on the Islamic principles of justice, equality and tolerance; the consolidation of national unity and a firm and stable system of government.

After the inquiry had started, the Commission received the following additional term of reference:

In the light of the social, economic, administrative and political reforms which are being carried out by the present régime, particularly the introduction of the Basic Democracies, what would be the most appropriate time-table for the implementation of the proposals to be made by the Constitution Commission?

Appendix IX

THE *RUET-I-HILAL* CONTROVERSY

The phrase *Ruet-i-Hilal* signifies the appearance of the crescent moon, and its importance relates to certain religious observances which in Islam follow the lunar calendar. In this respect, they are movable in the same sense that certain Christian religious observances are movable. In the latter case, however, these fasts and feasts are regulated by the movement of the earth round the sun and are determined by the days on which they happen to fall in each year. However, in the case of Islamic observance, the occasion is initiated by the actual appearance of the new moon, i.e. *the Ruet-i-Hilal*. For any particular locality, this is usually determined by a committee of venerable and learned men usually known as the *Ruet-i-Hilal* Committee. Membership of such a Committee implies piety and respect and is usually a tribute to the position which such a man occupies in the religious life of the community. Nevertheless, none of this is guarantee against dispute and occasions arise when there is argument whether the crescent moon has been sighted or not and, as with other forms of religious disputation, heated emotions are sometimes generated.

During the Martial Law administration, it was proposed that for the convenience of everyone, and in order to ensure uniformity, the simplest and best course would be for the Meteorological Department of the Government to say whether the new moon had appeared or not. It could, after all, be safely assumed that the staff of the Department had the same religious interest as any other Muslim to which could be added their astronomical knowledge and instruments for precise observation. These proposals did not, however, commend themselves to the *Ruet-i-Hilal* committeemen.

In March 1961, upon the occasion of *'Id-ul-Fitr*, the great festival that marks the end of Ramzan, the *Ruet-i-Hilal* Committee of Karachi disputed the accuracy of the observations of the Meteorological Department. In the result, those people who accepted the appearance of what was irreverently described as 'the Government's moon', observed *'Id* on one day, whereas those who followed the views of the unofficial committee, celebrated on another day. This was hardly satisfactory and, in effect, spoiled the solemnity and the pleasure of what is the most important religious festival of the Muslim year. Not only so, but tempers ran high and, as so often happens, public tranquillity was threatened.

An editorial appeared in *Dawn* under the title *This Confusion Must*

Cease and, after discussing the merits of all sides of the case, the editorial suggested that when all opinions have been placed before him, the Head of the State should decide whether the new moon had been seen or not. For his part, President Ayub Khan insisted that not only could the meteorological experts say whether the crescent moon had been sighted, but that scientists could even predict when the moon must appear. He later pointed out, for the edification of the *'ulema*, that religion had come to serve man and that science had come in the service of both.[1]

The upshot of the controversy appeared to have been that, thereafter, the services of the Meteorological Department were dispensed with, in this connexion.

The complexities referred to in this Appendix are, of course, quite distinct from those with historic origins. The Bohra community, for instance, follows the Egyptian observance with regard to dates. In Pakistan, this means that the Bohra community observes the Muslim festivals with about three days' difference from the rest of the country.

[1] *D*, 18, 19, 21 and 23 March 1961.

INDEX